WICKED SUCCESS IS INSIDE EVERY WOMAN

WICKED SUCCESS
IS INSIDE
EVERY
WOMAN

·

VICKIE L.
MILAZZO

WILEY

John Wiley & Sons, Inc.

Published by John Wiley & Sons, Inc., Hoboken, New Jersey.
Published simultaneously in Canada.

NACLNC is a registered service mark and collective membership mark of Vickie Milazzo Institute.
Female Fusion is a registered service mark of Vickie Milazzo Institute.

For general information on our other products and services or for technical support, please contact our
Customer Care Department within the United States at (800) 762-2974, outside the United States at
(317) 572-3993 or fax (317) 572-4002.

Wiley also publishes its books in a variety of electronic formats. Some content that appears in print may
not be available in electronic books. For more information about Wiley products, visit our web site at
www.wiley.com.

Library of Congress Cataloging-in-Publication Data:

Milazzo, Vickie L.
  Wicked success is inside every woman / Vickie L. Milazzo.
    p. cm.

  Includes index.
  ISBN 978-1-118-10052-3 (cloth); ISBN 978-1-118-16271-2 (ebk);
ISBN 978-1-118-16270-5 (ebk); ISBN 978-1-118-16269-9 (ebk)

  1. Success in business. 2. Businesswomen. 3. Women executives.
  4. Successful people. 5. Women—Psychology. 6. Self-actualization (Psychology)
  7. Success. I. Title.

  HF5386.M5784 2011
  650.1082—dc23

                      2011028240

Printed in the United States of America

10 9 8 7 6 5 4 3 2 1

*To my mom for setting me on my voyage of discovery,
to all the women exploring their extraordinary potential
and to my husband Tom for loving the woman
inside and outside me.*

CONTENTS

Preface   xv

5 PROMISES
*Make These Promises to Unleash the 10 Forces
Within You*   1

5 Promises Provide the Fuel   1

Promise 1: I Will Live and Work a Passionate Life   4

Promise 2: I Will Go for It or Reject It Outright   7

Promise 3: I Will Take One Action Step a Day Toward
My Passionate Vision   10

Promise 4: I Commit to Being a Success Student
for Life   12

Promise 5: I Believe as a Woman I Really Can
Do Anything   14

Harness Your 10 Feminine Forces with the 5 Promises   17

1   FIRE
Ignite Your Inner Fire to Live Passionately   19

Passion Fans the Flame of Wicked Success   21

Let Your Passions Move You   22

Discover Your Fire to Live Passionately   24

The Passionate Path Isn't Quick and Easy   29

The Passionate Path Isn't Balanced   31

Passion Doesn't Burn the Same for All Women   31

10 Strategies for Living Passionately   32

Ignite Your Fire with the 5 Promises   39

Evie's Fire   41

2 INTUITIVE VISION
Imagine Unlimited Possibilities to Capture Your Vision

Your Vision   43

Intuition Is Cognition on Steroids   45

Imagination Trumps Knowledge   45

Order Off the Right Menu   47

Show Up with No Guarantee   49

Use Silence to Arouse Imagination   51

Get Out of Your Head   54

Trust Your Way Through the Chaos   56

Relax Your Way into Wicked Success   58

Practice Mentally Everything You Want
to Accomplish   61

Get Down with Beethoven   62

Accelerate Achievement with Hypnagogic Imagery   63

Speed Up to Be Mindful   64

Link Your Vision to Your Passion   65

Be Ready with Your Next Vision   66

Capture Your Intuitive Vision with the 5 Promises   68

Maggie's Vision   70

3 ENGAGEMENT
Engage Commitment to Achieve Big Things

Engage Commitment to Achieve Big Things   73

Engage Your Fears to Conquer Them   75

Ditch Perfectionism   80

Break the Feel-Good Addiction   82

Engage One Big Thing at a Time   84

Get Whacked Like a Buddhist   91

Engage in What's Right, Not What's Easy   96

Engage the Details   98

Shrug Off Restrictions   99

Don't Be a Commitment Queen   100

Engage to Achieve Big Things with the 5 Promises   103

Leigh's Engagement   105

4 AGILITY
Flex Your Agility to Grab New Opportunities   107

Shake It Up   109

Flex Your Curiosity   111

Challenge a Fixed Viewpoint   113

Stretch to Intensify Agility   116

Dive Deeper Every Day   116

Schedule an Agility Break   118

Add the Right Tools to Your Agility Arsenal   120

Agility Is a Two-Minute Investment   122

Don't Be a Relic of Past Splendor   123

Get in Sync with Agility, Not Insane
with Diverseness   124

Leave Your Old Comforts at Home   128

Flex Your Agility with the 5 Promises   130

Blanche's Agility   132

5 GENIUS
Intensify Your Intelligence for Accelerated Success   135

Collaboration Is Collective Genius   136

Leverage People Who Are Already
Wickedly Successful   138

Now That You've Got the Advice,
Be Genius and Heed It   140

Genius Hears Other Voices   142

Challenge the Experts   144

Remove Your Own Burrs   146

Trust Your Own Voice 147

Stop Hanging with the Biggest Losers 148

Genius Combines IQ and Hard Work 150

Employ the Genius of Einstein 154

Intensify Your Genius with the 5 Promises 163

Chris's Genius 165

6 **INTEGRITY**
Practice Uncompromising Integrity for
Authentic Success **167**

Breaching Integrity Betrays Opportunity 168

Every Act Counts 169

Stand Up for Your Integrity 170

Consensus on Integrity Is Elusive 172

Every Promise Counts 176

Be Accountable to Your Integrity 177

Do the Right Thing When No One Is Looking 177

Don't Bring an Elephant into the Room 179

Refuse to Be an Integrity Victim 180

Avoid the Lure of Manipulation 181

Put Your Integrity Where Your Mouth Is 182

Kiss Off Complainers 183

Keep Your Integrity Public and Your Dirty
Laundry Private 186

Practice Uncompromising Integrity with the
5 Promises 187

Jan's Integrity 189

7 **ENDURANCE**
Fuel Your Endurance to Energize Your Performance **191**

Keep Dancing Your Passionate Vision 193

Fuel Your Endurance with Persistence 195

Stop Running on Empty   197

Fuel Endurance with Incremental Payoffs   198

Fuel Endurance with the Right Focus   199

Endure for the Fun of It   203

Take to the Air Like a Butterfly   205

Fuel Your Endurance with Fire   206

Harvest Energy to Increase Your Endurance   208

10 Strategies for Building Your
Endurance Muscles   209

Fuel Your Endurance with the 5 Promises   212

Susan's Endurance   214

8 ENTERPRISE
Become the CEO of Your Career and Life   217

Be First at the River to Get a Drink   218

Satisfy Your Thirst at the River of Choice   220

Venture Out from a Solid Foundation   223

Command Financial Control in
Your Enterprise   228

Assemble an Extraordinary Framework   230

Everything Is Marketing   233

Don't Just Create an Experience—Create an
Unforgettable Memory   239

Be Your Own Number One Fan   244

Don't Be a Commodity   245

Negotiate Like You Mean It   246

Retie the Connection Over Fried Oysters   249

Networking Is Not Working   250

Keep the Wind in Your Sails   252

Become the CEO of Your Career and Life
with the 5 Promises   255

Martha's Enterprise   257

9   **RENEWAL**
Reclaim Your Life Energy Through
Frequent Renewal   259

Renew Your Relationship with Yourself   260

Renew Your Physical Energy Daily   263

Replenish Your Emotional Energy   267

Nurture and Renew Your Spirit   275

Recharge Your Mental Energy   276

Celebrate to Intensify Renewal   278

Renew Your Energy with the
People You Love   279

Renew by Giving Back   281

6 Strategies for Total Renewal   282

Renew Your Life Energy with the 5 Promises   284

Lindsay's Renewal   286

10   **FEMALE FUSION**
Fuse with Incredible Women to Attain
the Impossible   289

The Story of the First Female Fusion   290

3 Stories of Women Forever Changed   293

Female Fusion Is a Protective Caprock   297

Fusion Is More Than a Women's Group   298

Fusion Needs Heat   298

Female Fusion Requires Purpose   301

The Basic Fusion Format Is Simple   301

Activate Your First Fusion   302

Spark Fusion Throughout the Entire Group   306

Unleash Boundless Fusion Energy   307

Fuse with Professional Colleagues   309

Have Fun with Fusion as You Attain
the Impossible   309

Activate Female Fusion with the 5 Promises   311

Vickie's Fusion   313

Savor Your Wicked Success   315

Acknowledgments   317

Book Club Guide   319

About the Author   321

Index   323

PREFACE

WHEN MY PUBLISHER at John Wiley & Sons, Inc. emailed me asking if I was interested in writing a new book, I immediately responded "No, I am deep in projects and way too busy."

You see, I don't write how-to books or give motivational speeches for a living. The last book I wrote was my 2006 *Wall Street Journal* bestseller *Inside Every Woman*. I'm a business owner, a working CEO actively involved in managing a multimillion-dollar company with 23 employees. I live and thrive in the business trenches every day and love most of those moments.

The day after I said no to Wiley, I woke up knowing I had to say yes to this book. I couldn't stop thinking, "What a difference five years makes and what a difference five years doesn't make." When I wrote my book in 2006, the first questions I asked you, my readers, were: "What would your life look like if every moment of it was absolutely enriched, fulfilled and swelling with joy? Think about it—your health, relationships, career, spirituality and finances are the best they can be and you greet each day with energy and enthusiasm for whatever comes your way. What would accomplish that?"

These questions were suddenly feeling too "Pollyanna-ish" and I was forced to ask myself whether these aspirations were even relevant to women today, much less possible. In the five short years since *Inside Every Woman* debuted, women are facing more challenges than ever and increasingly scrambling to keep up and survive in a world that is getting smaller, faster and flatter every second of every day.

Most women are still climbing out of a hole created by the worst economic recession since the Great Depression. Middle-aged women are supporting not just themselves, but their parents and their "returned-to-the-nest" children. Young women, financially challenged to break out from under mom and dad, are struggling in jobs (if they can find one) that don't cover life's necessities.

With the world in such flux and so insecure, it's no wonder that "hooking up" and "sexting" are becoming the new relationship models. Yet another challenge for women who yearn for meaningful relationships that fulfill more than a momentary urge.

As if that's not enough angst, there's also an onslaught of time-sucking distractions, game apps, the Internet everywhere, Facebook, Twitter, texting, virtual relationships and reality TV shows (that are anything but). All this buzz constantly competes with our ability to accomplish Big Things in our lives. Add to that our smartphones, which none of us would live without, but which keep us tethered to the noise. No wonder undertaking new goals and getting to the heart of your womanly desires seems like just another impossible dream.

No question these are unprecedented times, but these are also exciting times that offer unlimited opportunities. Women have more of a voice today. We are outpacing men not just in bachelor's degrees but also advanced college degrees, increasingly becoming leaders and the primary family breadwinners.

At the same time, what a difference five years *doesn't* make. Here's a zinger of a reality check: Women earn a mere 75 percent of what men earn. Women with the same level of education as men, executing the same job description as men, get paid less than men.

Doesn't that fact piss you off? Most women can describe ad infinitum how they work a lot harder (some women breadwinners hold two to three jobs at one time) for a lot less. And they're not happy about it. Here's what some of my friends say:

Women have to work twice as hard as men to be thought half as competent. Of course, thankfully, that's not hard.
—RACHEL

Wow! It has taken several generations to get this far? We have run rings around the men in the workforce and still do not get the same pay!
—JUDY

We do 175 percent between job and home. Welcome to womanhood.
—DIANA

Don't even get me started . . .
—ELAINE

Unless you're Demi Moore, you will outlive the man you love. And unlike your male counterparts, you are more likely to spend your last years in poverty. Statistics show that, like it or not, you will probably have to work well beyond age 65.

Choices for women are abundant, but at what cost? Women tell me they're more exhausted than excited by all the opportunities. Just one more "to do," as if we don't have enough of those already. Who needs more work, more stress, more responsibilities? Why should we accept having less time for fun and the simple satisfactions of life?

Success should include *living* the life we make for ourselves, not merely existing in it. If you haven't been reduced to your breaking point one or more times in your life, you're either very young indeed or probably not a woman.

I wrote this book so that you can be one of those women who are free to glide gracefully through the demanding chaos and exciting uncertainties and ask such provocative questions as:

"How do I begin to create a life and career more on my own terms when I'm too busy simply existing?"

"How do I even find the time to imagine a goal that stimulates my purpose and fulfills my dreams when I can't get five minutes to myself?"

"How do I embrace fear as a growth opportunity to accomplish those goals?"

That's why I titled this book *Wicked Success Is Inside Every Woman*. These exaggerated times call for a wicked mind-set. To get out of survival mode and into success mode you have to embrace a new, wickedly resourceful mind.

I mean wicked in an exaggerated, uncommon way, a way that has nothing to do with green witches or evil thoughts but instead has everything to do with an outrageous viewpoint and perspective.

I'm a "buck-up" style woman who has little interest in people who expect something for nothing, or who think success will come through mental osmosis via their iPads stuffed full of self-help MP3s, podcasts or "easy-ways-to" eBooks.

I've spent 29 years giving real women concrete, no excuses, take-no-prisoners advice on how to make wicked career changes and start real businesses.

I've been privileged to work with, mentor and socialize with successful businesswomen all over the world. I interact with thousands of women on Facebook, through my blog and through other forms of social media. Some of these women I haven't personally met, but all of them feel free to "tell it like it is" and express in no uncertain terms the challenges and concerns facing women in every part of today's world.

I have huge respect for women. That's why this book is not a self-help book. It isn't a magic formula, a quick fix for success. I won't promise you a 4-hour workweek, a corner office, 10 pounds off in 10 days or that Mars will ever begin to understand (much less listen to) Venus. I won't disrespect you with pat answers. This is a buck-up book with a buck-up plan for women who are ready to buck up. I want you to use me and my life plan to help you find your way to the wicked success that is inside every woman.

When I announced to my executive team at Vickie Milazzo Institute the decision to write *Wicked Success Is Inside Every Woman*, I could see some disappointment on their faces, especially that of my financial director. After all, I generate significant income for the company and am very active in its day-to-day activities. Frankly, it wasn't a good economic decision. They knew it and I knew it. But like most women, I'm not completely motivated by economics, I'm motivated by passions.

I'm passionate about how the world is changing and what that means to women (not just American women, but also the women in China, Korea, Vietnam, Indonesia, Poland and others, who are reading translations of my first book in their own languages). What women need to do is step out in front of the coming change.

I don't need your money (my financial well-being doesn't depend on whether or not you buy, steal, borrow or share this book). I only want your success—the success you fully deserve as a woman. If you're ready to liberate yourself from day-to-day drudgery, if you're no longer willing to scrape out an existence, I'll show you how to use 5 Promises that will unleash 10 extraordinary strengths inherent to all women. You can summon them as often as you choose, to achieve anything you want.

How do I know there aren't just a handful of women graced with such awesome forces? For 29 years I've trained thousands of real women to combine their 10 Feminine Forces (strengths) with their professional expertise to start their own businesses, real women who are achieving unreal success. Ordinary women creating consulting businesses generating six- and seven-figure incomes, kissing 10-plus hour workdays goodbye, taking control of their careers, lives and finances and beating back the exhaustion that was crushing their fire.

I guarantee that none of these women has anything you don't have. My company employs more women than men, so I've been on both the mentoring side and the receiving side of the extraordinary Feminine Forces you'll explore throughout this book. Women's strengths continue to help grow my company and have been a big reason for its success.

This book is not about what's wrong with women. It's about what's right with us. After all there are more than enough messages, from fashion magazines to your boss, telling you everything that is wrong with you.

I love women. I love men too—especially my husband Tom, my dad Sal and my twin brother Vince—but I find so many more unexplored possibilities in working with the feminine energy.

You don't have to give up your life, your time or your relationships to be successful. Make the 5 Promises and harness the 10 Strengths I've used for 29 years to have more life, more time and more satisfying relationships.

As you read this book, I hope you'll feel like you're sitting down for a cup of healthy green tea or a glass of healthy red wine with a good woman friend . . . a friend who inspires, encourages and pushes you to think in a more exaggerated, uncommon and wicked way.

Wicked Success Is Inside!

A woman is the full circle. Within her is the power to create, nurture and transform.
DIANE MARIECHILD

The bolder your promises, the richer your bounty.
VICKIE L. MILAZZO

5 PROMISES

Make These Promises to Unleash the 10 Forces Within You

5 PROMISES PROVIDE THE FUEL

I discovered the 5 Promises in 1982 when I faced the reality that I was unhappy with the direction my life was taking. It wasn't easy after putting hard work into becoming a registered nurse (RN), earning my bachelor's and master's degrees and working 6 years in the hospital, to find I was extremely disappointed by my career choice.

I'd gone in wide-eyed, thinking I'd have fun and make a real difference, cure people, help people to be healthier and, in my grandest ambition, even improve the state of healthcare, only to bump up against the reality that no matter how hard I worked, my efforts would never make a dent, much less an impact.

I was too mouthy and opinionated for an institutionalized system that only rewarded me when I kept my opinions to myself. I was also moving far too slowly toward financial success, having to work overtime just to pay the mortgage on my 1,100-square-foot condo and I was forgetting what it was like to have fun on the job.

Forget waking up early, raring to get to work. I was waking up 10 minutes before it was time to get out the door and rolling into work

1

a little disheveled, no makeup and, if I didn't chug down at least one cup of coffee, a little crazed.

Looking in the mirror at a woman I didn't recognize, I asked her, "What's happened to me?"

Growing up in New Orleans, I was raised believing life was meant to be fun and work should be fun, too. Yet I was living more of a T.G.I.F. (Thank God It's Friday) life, when what I wanted was a T.G.I.T. (Thank God It's Today) life. Not only was my passion waning, I wondered if I might be wasting my potential.

A quick look at my colleagues who'd been in this career for 20 years or more showed me a future without excitement and passion. Burned out, unhappy and, worst of all, apathetic, these nurses had no interest in resurrecting their careers. I imagined myself 5 years, 10 years, 20 years into the future, and the vision was not pretty. All I could see ahead was more exhaustion, fewer highs and eventually a bitter, burned-out nurse, old before my time. Not even close to the New Orleans spirit I grew up with.

Dissatisfaction is the perfect antidote to complacency. I seized my dissatisfaction, stared hard at that woman in the mirror and demanded a different career destiny. I wanted a big, vivid, spicy, succulent life. I wanted to experience passion, fun and wicked success.

I still wanted to be a nurse, but on my own terms. My only option: Start my own business, be my own boss, make my own rules. With $100 in my savings account, I did just that.

First I had to get to work on me—to transform the Vickie who got me into this unsatisfying role at the hospital into a new, more radical version of me. The former Vickie had to go. I stripped bare and started fresh with 5 Promises.

Believing these 5 Promises would open me up to the woman I wanted to be and needed to be, I vowed to live them and they performed beyond my expectations. They became the 5 Promises I have continued to renew daily for more than two decades. The 5 Promises transformed not only my career but also what could have been a ho-hum life into an audacious life of fun, hard but rewarding work, joy, excitement, romance, love and exhilarating experiences at every turn.

The 5 Promises opened me up to the extraordinary strengths, or 10 Feminine Forces, that are inside every woman. The 5 Promises and 10 Feminine Forces have worked for me through all the passages of my development as a woman. They've bolstered me and goaded me for 29 years, propelling me from underpaid hospital nurse to business owner to inventor of a new industry to owner and CEO of a multimillion-dollar business to an *Inc.* Top 10 Entrepreneur and *Wall Street Journal* bestselling author.

In the 5 years since this book first came out, I've had the fortune to take these 5 Promises on an electrifying new test drive, over stubborn obstacles, through murky, unfamiliar waters and again they worked in a huge way. Guiding me through the harshest economic period since the 1920s and 1930s, they served as my board of directors in business and personal challenges.

Although it may sound unlikely (and you can ask my husband Tom if you don't believe me), I rise each morning overflowing with excitement and with the physical, mental and emotional energy I need to accomplish a remarkably busy schedule, even managing to find time for myself every day (yes, every day) for exercise and moments of quiet. And I take off 12 weeks each year.

That's how powerful these 5 Promises have been for me. Fully recession-tested, they continue working for me daily, and they can do the same for you.

I'm not going to pigeonhole you. I love that women come in all shapes and sizes (despite what we see in our fashion magazines), not just physically but emotionally and mentally. No two women are alike in lifestyle, social upbringing or earthly desires, yet all women share certain strengths. Inside every woman, and inside you, is an amazing fire that, when fueled, can release volcanic potential.

Meet Suzanne:

My grueling job included being on call 24/7. I was also going through a nasty divorce and had primary custody of my three children, ages 4, 6 and 8, with no child support. To top it off, I found I needed a hysterectomy for a precancerous condition. I was depressed, sleep-deprived, stressed, short-tempered, financially upside down and in debt. A financial advisor told me there was no way I could retire, even with Social Security. I felt I was on a sinking ship.

I'm a categorical example of one of those careers Vickie revolutionized. Today I love my life, I love my career and I spend time with my children. I consistently bring in a comfortable six-figure income—and it just keeps getting better.

In my years of stirring the fire for uncounted women, I know that summoning the phenomenal power of your 10 Feminine Forces through the 5 Promises will enable you to attain any future you envision and desire. The courage to commit is easily within the grasp of every woman on this planet, including you.

Begin unleashing the interconnected strengths within you by making my 5 Promises *your* 5 Promises. When you do, these 5 Promises will remind you to dream again and guide you in directing your vision to achieve truly wicked success.

PROMISE 1: I Will Live and Work a Passionate Life

My first promise took me back to my childhood and my Italian family in New Orleans. Life without passion and fun was considered no life at all. My family was passionate about everything, from the food we ate (after years of marriage Tom still can't believe my family will talk about what's for dinner while eating lunch), the ball games we played on the street, the card games we played with pennies from our allowances, to just sitting around on the front porch having conversations about who knows what. Passion and fun became inexorably intertwined for me.

I grew up in a hardworking blue-collar household—actually, a "no-collar" household, because in New Orleans, with no air conditioning, we wore T-shirts. We lived in a modest shotgun house, with limited material things, and that was okay because passion and fun were free. I grew up believing life was fun, and looking back, I know the expectation made it so.

My first job at age 15, I'm knocking on doors selling Avon to total strangers. Fun. Next job, selling burgers at Burger King. Fun. When I decided to become an RN, I believed this would be the ultimate thrill, and at first everything was fun. Starting an IV. Fun. Cleaning up a patient's crap. Fun. Saving a life, the most fun of all.

Then one day I woke up, and on that day, starting IVs and cleaning up crap? Not fun.

I wanted more passion, more joy in the part of my life that sucked up 10 hours every day. To ensure that I would succeed in leaving my unsatisfying job behind and would successfully start my own business, the first promise I made to myself was to live and work with that same passion I experienced as a child.

I couldn't help thinking back to when I was 8 years old, to one of the passions that ignited in me at that early age. For hours each day I taught an imaginary class. Every time my dad saw me absorbed in teaching he would come in and send the class to recess, encouraging me to play outside with my real friends. I would quickly call the class back to order and get back to the lesson of the day. No one in the family has any idea what I was teaching, nor do I, but I was darned passionate about it, and not even Dad could stop me.

We all know when we discover something we feel passionate about. We feel amazingly engaged and energetic. Desire becomes energy.

Have you ever experienced a time when desire overcame all physical, emotional and intellectual barriers? Remember your first crush, first boyfriend or when you discovered sex?

Why can't we experience that passion—that vitality and energy—not only in love or desire but every day? Believe me, you can. When you wake up every day to a life and career that are your heart and soul, a life and career you're passionate about, you will experience maximum joy.

So much of our life is spent working. Some women separate work and life, and the separation can only lead to dissatisfaction. We don't have two-compartment lives—a career life and a personal life. We only have one life. You can't turn off one and turn on the other. It doesn't work that way. Work is life, and for most of us life includes work. What a waste if we don't feel the fire in our careers.

Financially, my ambitions in starting my own business were modest. I merely set out to match my $28,000 annual nursing salary (pitiful, even 29 years ago, for people who save lives). My personal ambitions, however, were grand. I demanded a life of passion, freedom, flexibility and control over my existence and my destiny as a woman. After all, what is success without passion?

Within three years I'd tripled my income. Today, I own a highly respected and often emulated multimillion-dollar business.

As the *New York Times* reported, I "crossed nursing with the law and created a new profession" when I started teaching other nurses how to become legal nurse consultants. Creating a career, a product, a job or in my case, a profession that enables you or others to pursue and capture their own dreams, that's the kind of Big Thing that can happen when you commit to Promise 1.

My company grew every year, peaking at $16 million before the unexpected happened in September 2008, the worst economic crash experienced by any individual in this country younger than 70. I didn't see it coming, and when it did, I wasn't at all worried. By nature I'm an optimist and, after all, my company wasn't selling mortgages. We had glided through other serious downturns in the market, including the dot-com bubble and 9/11.

I couldn't have been more wrong. Like every other small business in the United States, we were jolted. Suddenly I was working harder than ever just to meet payroll for 23 employees who were in fear of becoming another unemployment statistic.

The essence of Promise 1, "I will work a passionate life," saved my company from being just another statistic. I'll talk more about the strategies I employed, but the crux of our success started with passion—passion for our company and its mission, passion for our products, passion for each other and passion for our clients.

No matter what you hear, business is personal. I had to make personal sacrifices during this time to do what's right, not what would be easy. Passion kept me going. My passion rubs off on my staff, creating a powerful dynamic that kept us slugging away daily.

Promise 1 reminds me to never confuse success and passion, and for me there is no success without passion. At 8 years old teaching was passionate play. At 28, I returned to my passion by turning teaching into a business, and I've been playing ever since.

When you're successful, opportunities present themselves, but here's how powerful Promise 1 is: Throughout my ventures, I've been tempted by many flattering and interesting offers, the most tempting of which was to join a powerful law firm as a partner my first year out of law school. I turned it down.

Why? Because of Promise 1. When we live and work our passions, we take an uncompromising approach to being honest with ourselves and others about what we value and possibly redefining success in a way that others don't comprehend.

The more successful we become, the more likely we can find ourselves working 24/7, yet never finishing the work. That's why Promise 1 says "I will live and work a passionate life." This promise reminds us to define success on our terms, not everyone else's, and to take time for living passionately, not merely becoming such an automaton that our only passion derives from work. Living a passionate life means carving out time for all the passions in our life, including those that renew body, mind and soul, as well as our bank accounts. That's why I take time each day, plus those 12 weeks of vacation every year, to enjoy my hard-earned success.

Commit to this first promise right now and use the ideas in this book to make it happen. Don't worry if you have no clue what your passions are, exactly. As you read and work this book, you'll discover the passions that will propel you to a totally fulfilled and wickedly successful future.

PROMISE 2: I Will Go for It or Reject It Outright

With a full-time job and the necessity to work overtime just to pay my mortgage, I wanted my dream of starting my own business to be more than an idea. How could I possibly make this dream a reality and not just a hallucination? Dreams, like angels, can lift us high above the world, taking us away from the daily grind. And oh how those dreams do lift and encourage us, until we let them fade into fantasy.

I've met women who admit, "I gave up my dreams years ago." When we give up on our dreams, as those women have, the same dreams that once lifted us out of our daily drudgery now show up as failures and make us so miserable that we'd welcome a monstrous New Year's Day hangover as a relief.

I'm not much into hangovers. What I am into is making promises to my dreams. So the second promise I made to myself was to go for what I wanted all the way or to decisively reject it outright.

A dream or a goal you have may not be right for you, but whatever you decide, you owe it to yourself to buck up to the decision. Don't leave the dream dangling with "one day, some day, I might get around to living my dream" and the reminder of what you don't have the time, courage or enthusiasm to grab. Do it or forget it. Go for it or reject it outright.

Don't wait for the conditions to be perfect or for a guarantee you'll get the outcome you want. That will never happen. People who wait or dabble usually end up at their retirement parties rewarded with a glass of watery punch and a piece of plain white cake. Own up to your passions, then step out and grab hold of them with both hands.

After creating a new industry, I had no guarantee of outcome. I just grabbed my dream, putting into it everything I had and more.

Skydiving is a great metaphor for going all the way. When you skydive you can't be partially in, especially once you're out. Despite a fear of cliff-hanging heights, I stepped out of an airplane at 14,000 feet to skydive. I was terrified. Once out of the plane's cabin, I couldn't step back in. I was truly committed, even if not by choice, and the exhilaration I felt later at overcoming that lifelong fear proved to be a catalyst for future accomplishments.

Most of us stay in the safe cabin of everyday life because of our fears. Fears are simply growth opportunities, the opportunity to step out again and again. Yet so often we never step out into the audacious dreams that smolder and spark inside us. What would your life look like if you didn't have the choice of that safe cabin? If your only option was to grab that dream and dive into it? To go all the way once you made the jump?

Don't allow fear to freeze you in place, or one day, some day, you'll be sipping retirement punch regretting all the things you didn't do. Success is not about the achievement. It's not the pay raise, the thinner body, the better-looking husband. The achievement is stepping out. When you define success as stepping out, you can succeed every day because you can step out every day.

I had no certainty that my company would survive the recession, especially when it persisted, leaching the blood, sweat and marrow out of us for months and then years. It was like being tossed out of an airplane without a parachute. Talk about a breathtaking growth opportunity. To survive this crisis, we had to step out and go all the way. Defining success not as more revenue or more profits but as bucking up and stepping out helped me to keep my eye on the ball, make tough decisions and do the things I needed to do for our success.

When the credit markets shut down, students could no longer get educational loans from Sallie Mae to fund their education for our program. Overnight our business model had to change. So what did we do? If Sallie Mae wasn't going to loan our students the $13,000, then we would. We had to decide right then and there. We didn't have months to research and deliberate the decision. We barely had time to even think about it, and absolutely no guarantee of success. We had to go for the idea or reject it outright. Overnight we became our own "finance company."

When you're putting out the cash, instead of cashing the cash, the bottom line is not pretty. It would have been easy to second-guess ourselves. Had we just rushed into the worst decision of all time?

As it turned out, this single bold decision is one essential reason we survived the recession. I've had no business training, but I can tell you no business school trained anyone to successfully handle what all entrepreneurs confronted during these dismal recession years. We dove in all the way and did what was needed.

One thing that always helps me go for what I want is perspective. My mom Marise gave me that. She had a dream of traveling far beyond New Orleans, where I grew up. She read books that took her to the Eiffel Tower, Big Ben and the Sistine Chapel, and she planned on visiting all of them. Then she met my dad. She often said, "When we have enough money, we'll travel." But then she had children, and she said, "When the kids are grown and out of the house, we'll travel." Then the kids were out of the house and my mom died—at age 48—from breast cancer. Her travel dreams never came true.

Is it possible you're waiting to live your dreams? If so, what are you waiting for? When you get enough money? When you lose enough weight? When your job is perfect? When your spouse is perfect? Don't wait.

My mom's death taught me that the time is now. When I'm afraid to take a risk, which is often, and not just during a recession, I honor my mom by asking myself, "What's the worst thing that can happen?" The perspective of knowing it's not cancer or death helps me to do the thing I fear.

It's perfectly okay to admit that a commitment is not right for you and to reject it outright. This is your life, your wicked success.

What's not okay is to hold back and put less than everything into a commitment that is your passion. If you want something, go for it all the way and go for it now. When you do, you won't always succeed but you will wake up every day to a life and career you love.

PROMISE 3: I Will Take One Action Step a Day Toward
My Passionate Vision

How was I going to pull off my business idea? Not only did I have a
full-time job, I was creating a new business model—consulting with
attorneys on medical-related cases.

I envisioned beyond the horizon to an alternate world where the
nursing and legal professions merged, a world as a legal nurse consultant.
My new world did not yet exist, but I believed I could make it so. And
while belief in my vision was crucial, belief was just the beginning.

To achieve the reality, I coupled belief with action. I vowed to do
something every day to move my vision forward. My TV found a new
home in the closet. I cut back on socializing with friends and knuckled
down to doing at least one thing daily for my business, no matter how
exhausted I was at the end of the day.

When a national news anchor from CNN asked me how I got to
where I am today, in light of my humble beginnings, I was hoping to
say something profound. But the truth was, I did it one step at a time.
Dreams and visions are great, but without action they are nothing
more than hallucinations. Without daily action, my visions might have
scudded away and dissolved like clouds. I've met many smart people
who had dreams and ideas but never did anything to make them real.
They didn't take action.

Like anyone striving to accomplish any whopping big goal, I had to
take a lot of steps—talk to that first attorney, get my first project, build
my first client relationship. Most important, I had to take action every
single day. And it worked.

I lacked business savvy, yet with each small step I gained both
knowledge and momentum. Sometimes I glided through and other
times I strained to inch forward, but the accumulated effect of all those
steps brought me to where I am today. What I learned in the process
and what still applies now is that it's less important *what* I do and more
important that I *do something*. I was developing the habits and discipline
necessary to make my vision a reality.

Yes, I acted on a breakthrough idea in my profession, but others
could have done the same. What separated me from another nurse who
may have had similar ideas was that I took action steps to realize my
dream. The idea comes first, but success is in the motion.

We're never measured by how we show up in the good times. We're measured by how we show up for challenges and crises.

When the recession hit hard, I was passionately invested in not downsizing. I did not want to put this company on a course of spiraling deterioration, although I confess my hit list was ready—I knew exactly who would go first if I had to pull the trigger.

I could feel the fear. My staff was used to 20 to 30 percent bonuses and fat pay raises. Not just the executive team, but everyone, down to the guys in shipping. I wanted them to know this wasn't only my challenge to deal with, nor just management's problem to solve. It was theirs too. If they were to share in the good times, they had to share in the not-so-good times. They'd have to buck up and invest their energy and passion in keeping our company viable without fat raises and bonuses.

Fear and worry are useless emotions. Yet we're human. So how do we focus energy on our vision and purpose when fear rips at us? Through action. For me action pushes the fear out.

I challenged the team at Vickie Milazzo Institute to formulate a recession strategy. We started with an all-day brainstorming session, assessing our budget and where we could cut without compromising the integrity of our product and the service to our customer. My company is an open book. Everyone knows exactly how much we take in down to the penny. We'd always been fat, never worrying about budget. We had one, but if we went over—hey, no problem. The coffer was always full.

But overnight the world had changed, and we had to merge with the change or get run over and flattened by it. Somebody was going to feel the pain, and if we didn't want it to be the customer, it had to be us.

To their credit, my staff busted their butts going after this project as though their jobs depended on it. And their jobs did. They effectively reduced our budget 50 percent.

They didn't accomplish this amazing feat in one brainstorming session—it took five—but the result led to a profitable year in one of the worst down economies of our time, and we did not have to downsize a single employee. And not a single person took a pay cut, which was most companies' second reaction to the recession after downsizing.

Success is not about what you do when the road ahead is golden and every dip and turn smoothes your way. Success is about how you respond when you hit the biggest, nastiest roadblock of all time.

Successful women love the action as much as the dream. By taking action every day you develop the habit and discipline to make your vision a reality. When you focus not just on the idea but on making it happen, you stay in motion, not merely dreaming your passions but living them.

Make this third promise now, that you will take at least one action step every day for the next 30 days on the Big Thing that will bring you closer to your passionate visions in a big way. Once you're hooked on the natural high of action, focusing on more impactful actions and taking giant leaps comes easy. Start with the first 30 days. Turn that into 60 days, then 90 days...

Success is in the motion. The more action you take, the easier it is to step out and do your next Big Thing. Anything you're going for: advancing your career, starting a business, improving a relationship . . . Do something!

PROMISE 4: I Commit to Being a Success Student for Life

I pioneered the industry of legal nurse consulting, so there was no one to teach me how to do what I set out to do. Yet I didn't feel alone. I gathered the biggest CEOs and successful business owners in the country—at least those who'd written a book—and devoured everything I could find about launching a business. I became a success student of business strategy—for life.

Some of the best advice I received when I started my business was, "Vickie, you will encounter many challenges you will not know how to handle. But there's always someone out there who has already successfully handled that very challenge."

Luckily, we live in the midst of an information age created by a revolution in communication possibly even more world-changing than any of the past, including the Guttenberg press, radio and television. Our children are growing up with technology we think of as a tool, but which they consider to be a natural extension of their hands and minds. The skills they master before third grade, and take for granted as akin to walking, for some of us still must be learned—or maybe not learned. We must be willing to grow, to learn and to adapt, even if that means having a child teach us how to embrace the next big technology advance.

All great athletes and performers practice every day, with coaches to keep them practicing perfectly. Even after they achieve a level of success, they continue to practice and take instruction from their coaches, learning new ways to reach higher levels. They are lifetime students.

Success breeds success. Becoming a success student for life is about practicing being successful. What's hard today is easy tomorrow—with practice.

There are two ways you can learn:

- The hard way—through trial and error, making lots of mistakes. You're going to do some of that anyway, but this is a slow, expensive path to success.

- The easier way—through the experience of others who've already successfully overcome the problems and discovered the answers. This is the quicker path to success.

So much to learn—so little time. Why choose the hard way when you can choose the quicker, easier path to wicked success? Don't we always say, "I wish I'd known when I was 20 what I know now?" When we're 80, we'll be saying, "I wish I'd known when I was 40 what I know now." Find a 40-year-old and an 80-year-old and collaborate. Leverage for yourself what others have already learned.

I've been in business for nearly three decades, and I still learn every day—from my students, staff, favorite writers, speakers and business experts. When I find myself discarding other people's ideas all too readily without fully listening, I ask myself, "Vickie, would you rather be right or listen and be successful?"

Collect white and gray matter wherever you can find it. I joke that typing a question into the Google search box is one of the most effective ways to search for answers, because it seems there's not a single question that hasn't been asked and answered from a dozen different viewpoints.

Intelligent women know what they don't know and when to seek answers. Smart women appreciate that what works today won't necessarily work tomorrow, and that aggressive learning is a competitive advantage to achieving any desired goal.

Surround yourself with as many successful mentors as possible. And don't limit yourself. When people ask me, "Who's your mentor?" I can't pin it down to one person. I've been mentored by different people in different ways at different times.

One person can mentor you on starting a business, another on balancing family and career. If you model or collaborate with only one person, you'll always be one step behind her; but if you model many, you can one day be the wickedly successful woman mentoring other women.

Choose mentors who have something interesting to say and an interesting way of saying it. Learn from their mistakes as well as their successes. Think of your mentors as a collective genius with whom you can bounce ideas around and perfect your vision. Magnify your wicked success through theirs.

Be smart enough to ask for what you need. You may be surprised at who is willing to help you.

I prefer to listen and learn from mentors who are far more successful than I am. I attribute much of my success to choosing wisely: mentors who elevate me to new levels. I don't want to learn from someone who's not walking the talk (like a relationship expert who's not in a relationship, or a business expert whose business is writing books about business, not running a business).

Commit now to being a lifetime student, to actively seeking out new, challenging experiences and people who will push you to your next level.

PROMISE 5: I Believe as a Woman I Really Can Do Anything
Success is not determined solely by IQ, experience, or good looks. Women who succeed believe in themselves enough to take calculated risks.

Belief is a choice. You can challenge any limitations that are placed on your belief. Belief is not wishful thinking. Belief is the mental acceptance that something is true even though absolute certainty may be absent. Belief is what pushes you to go all out—to put your heart and soul into the effort. Do you really put your all into something you don't believe in? Think about it. After you found out your parents were Santa it didn't really matter whether you were naughty or nice.

During the era of the telegraph, people believed that's all that was needed. Then someone believed there could be so much more and invented the telephone. Surely the telephone was all that was needed, until someone believed there could be so much more and invented the cell phone. Surely the cell phone was all that was needed, until Apple turned the world on its ear with the iPhone.

Faith is a powerful thing, but seeing is believing. When Roger Bannister broke the 4-minute mile, the previous world record had stood for 10 years. Bannister believed he could break it, and he did, at 3 minutes 59.4 seconds. But what's really interesting is that a month and a half later another runner broke Bannister's record. And in the next 40 years, more than 700 more runners cracked that 4-minute barrier. They achieved that milestone because knowing someone else had done it helped them believe they could do it, too.

I had imagined what I wanted—and, yes, that's the essential first step. We imagine, then we must believe if we're going to achieve. Imagine. Believe. Achieve.

I was lucky to go to an all-girls high school. Coed schools have advantages, too, but when I grew up men were expected to be the business geniuses, women to be helpful homemakers. I gained confidence in those formative years from not having teachers telling me the boys were smarter, or calling on them instead of me. As a young woman I honestly believed I could do anything. Believing you can do it is 90 percent of the win.

But six years into nursing, a profession that receives minimal positive feedback, I'd been stripped of my youthful confidence. So when I walked into my first interview with my first attorney-prospect, my legs were literally shaking. I was so nervous I wasn't sure I could make it through that interview, much less secure him as my first client.

What got me through was remembering who I was, an RN whose specialized knowledge this man needed, even if he didn't know it yet. As a critical care nurse, if that same attorney was in a hospital gown with his backside showing, I would have no problem introducing myself with one hand and inserting a Foley catheter with the other.

I managed emergencies as easily as making the bed every morning, making split-second decisions that, for patients, were the difference between life and death and I'd handled these life-threatening situations while the doctors were nowhere to be found. If I can succeed in such complex situations, I decided, I can easily do something as straightforward as talk with an attorney.

Talk I did, and despite that clumsy start I walked out with my first client, one who would eventually pay my mortgage, plus six figures annually in consulting fees, for years to come. Not bad for a woman with no business education or experience.

Many women tell me, "If I could change my career or my relationship, I'd change my life." That's not the way it works. You change yourself, you change your career, you change your relationship. Einstein said, "You can't solve a problem with the same consciousness that created it." These are powerful words challenging us to recreate ourselves when we want something new. To transform anything you must transform yourself, and a huge part of the transformation is believing in your own wicked success.

Expand what you're willing to believe about you. I've met many women who use their children as a crutch for why they don't achieve wicked success. "I've got two children. I don't have time to succeed big." One woman entrepreneur who created a million-dollar company expanded her belief. "I'm solely responsible for my three children. I don't have time *not* to succeed."

Any time I hesitate to go for what I want because I've stopped believing in myself, I invoke Promise 5 and remember, "I'm a woman. I can do anything." I'm so practiced at believing Promise 5 that when the recession first hit us, I wasn't worried. Then it lingered and lingered, and lingered some more. I found myself doubting my decisions.

Was selling a $13,000 education program to RNs who earn $50,000 a year a hallucination? The fear I avoided at the beginning gripped me and wouldn't release. I couldn't deny the fear, and fear opened the door to disbelief. I had to be in the moment, feel the fear, feel the pain and come out on the other end of that fear, believing I could thrive again.

So I looked to my 29 years of experience as an entrepreneur, to the experience of the team at the Institute and to all we'd accomplished. Normally, I spend little time basking in past accomplishments. I focus on the now. But reviewing my past successes helped me to remember the challenges I'd tackled and how I'd survived them.

Along with that belief in myself and my team, I tapped into my belief in the universe. I couldn't deny that my business world was different and frightening, but I believed the universe would not abandon me. I'm not one to go around Barbie-dolling it with a fake smile, so I'm not saying the path through these hard times was easy, but I tried to embrace the good in every setback and every soul-sucking hour.

What was my foremost recession lesson? I couldn't buy into everyone's fear and expect to succeed, so I shut out the naysayers and got deep with Promise 5.

Anytime you're afraid, look to your past successes and find your own examples of personal or career accomplishments that give you pride and encouragement. Acknowledge your successes, let them push you forward and bolster your resolve. Any time you're not grabbing the opportunity, tell yourself, "I am a woman and I can do anything!" If you believe you're strong, that you will achieve your goal no matter what the challenges and no matter what anyone else tells you, you will succeed.

HARNESS YOUR 10 FEMININE FORCES WITH THE 5 PROMISES

The 5 Promises not only helped me to launch and grow my business, they advanced a stronger Vickie. Not in a masculine way, in a more feminine way. In 1982, when I launched myself full speed into my vision, business advisors and mentors were mostly men. I belonged to an entrepreneur group in the 1990s and was the only woman member. They were great men, and I learned from them, but I was determined not to be one of those women who emerge from success as a more masculine form of myself. I'd met a few of those women, and they could easily have turned me off entirely to wicked success. Fortunately, I believed I didn't have to be one of them.

The 5 Promises helped me to realize success on my own terms, as a woman who loved being a strong woman with 10 Feminine Forces—fire, intuitive vision, engagement, agility, genius, integrity, endurance, enterprise, renewal and fusion. These forces are not purely women's domain. Men certainly exhibit many of them. But women synthesize these strengths in a potent energy that is distinctively female, and we should not be afraid to express them.

Most of us see ourselves as having one strength—for example, "I'm persistent." At most we rely on two or three to get through our day. Or we only summon all 10 when we're faced with a crisis.

Dorene shared with me, "I never thought of myself as strong, but I've endured 14 hours of labor, not once but twice. If I can endure that, I can endure anything. Now that I know I have these strengths, I can use them to my benefit to achieve any goal." Like Dorene, you can harness these strengths now. Don't wait for a recession or any other crisis.

You'll hear from other women in this book, women who've applied the 5 Promises and 10 Strengths themselves. I'm not asking you to trust me on this. I want you to honestly explore and test these 5 Promises and how they will guide you in harnessing your 10 Strengths. If you don't commit, you'll never know just how wickedly powerful they can be for you.

The magic of the 5 Promises is that they are not complex; they can work for any goal and will lead to instant success. They will be your board of directors, nudging you, encouraging you, guiding you to be stronger and holding you accountable for living and working in a way that honors you as a woman. This proven life plan works. Commit now and I'll walk you through it step by step. Embrace your amazing new life of wicked success without limits.

Promise Big and Promise Now!

I resolved to take fate by the throat and shake a living out of her.

LOUISA MAY ALCOTT

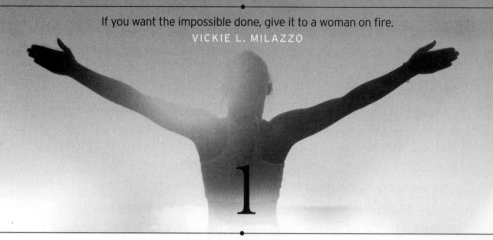

Well-behaved women rarely make history.
ANITA BORG

If you want the impossible done, give it to a woman on fire.
VICKIE L. MILAZZO

1

FIRE

Ignite Your Inner Fire to Live Passionately

Women are born passionate. We love hard. We cry hard. When we care about something passionately we can change the world.

Forget Madonna and Lady Gaga. The real heroines lived in times when strong women were not in vogue. French military leader Joan of Arc, American temperance reformer Carrie Nation, abolitionist Harriett Tubman and women's rights activist Margaret Sanger changed the world because their passions drove them to stand strong for what they believed. All passionately talented women—women like you.

Life is not about having or not having passion. All women have it inside. Either you honor that passion in your life or you don't.

Often we fear passion. We fear it won't stick, so we avoid it altogether. We fear that, like a lover, passion will "betray us"; but it's our passion that drives us to wicked success day after day after day.

Passion is not just one dream job, one perfect relationship, one child. Passion is a way of living every moment to its fullest.

Every woman has the potential to dig deeper, to find the way to her passion and to live with fire. This won't make your life easier, but it will certainly make it richer.

When I was growing up in a modest shotgun house in New Orleans, nothing about my childhood suggested I was destined to travel, but that didn't stop me from becoming a world traveler in any way I possibly could. I travelled through the eyes of beautiful glossy brochures to many countries. I wrote to the consulates of every country I could think of for free information, and when I opened our mailbox, the adventures began. Through the most amazing photos in those glossy publications, I walked the Great Wall of China, trekked the Himalayas and tracked lions, wildebeest and elephants on the Serengeti. Each imaginary trip I took on paper was vivid and exciting.

Years later, when I became a nurse, there was little money or time for travel. But I found ways to indulge that passion. I attended one or two nursing conferences a year, choosing destinations that beckoned. I also traveled during my two-week vacation, no matter how tight my budget. These modest experiences made the passion inside me burn deeper, and when I turned my passion for legal nurse consulting into an education company, I included travel as part of my vision.

Over a period of several years I traveled to 48 states teaching one-day seminars on legal nurse consulting. While enjoying the endless beauty, bounty and diversity of the United States, I probably ate in every Applebee's in the country—twice. Those seminars and the associated travel allowed me to create and cement my brand while seeing places I would have never visited otherwise. In cities large and small Tom and I enjoyed museums, local culture, festivals— garlic, crawfish, Italian and just about every other festival you could imagine.

My passion for travel has since expanded to more remote places. I have sipped yak butter tea with monks in the Himalayas, eaten sheep's brains with Berbers in Morocco, enjoyed the kava ceremony on a private island in Fiji, rice wine with a Hmong tribesman in the highlands of Vietnam and drained a gourd of grassy maté with gauchos on a Patagonian estancia. But I did draw the line at a fresh bowl of cow's blood with my Samburu host in Kenya.

Because I dug deep into my passion for travel I consciously created a life that embraces travel. Life is too short not to spend it on what you're passionate about.

PASSION FANS THE FLAME OF WICKED SUCCESS

Without the fire that only passion arouses, success eludes us. If you're not passionate about an idea, why would you do what it takes to carry it out? Pursuing that idea would be way too hard without passion.

To excel at rock climbing, you have to push through the pain and discomfort of scraped hands and aching muscles, and to do that you must have fervent passion for the sport. Find that same passion in your job and you'll be far more successful than a woman who isn't on fire.

We all know people who exist in passionless and purposeless lives like cardboard cutouts. Is that really living?

I'd rather live a life of passion than one of passivity, even if that passion may not reap extravagant financial reward. Money will not get you out of bed in the morning. While it does help to have money once you're up and moving, you still need an underlying passion for what you do and where you put your energies.

To live passionately is to act. If you're true to yourself, you'll put energy behind your passions and take the necessary actions to bring them to fulfillment. You'll make time for the fire that burns inside you.

I started my first business at the age of 8. There were no revenues and the only profit from teaching my imaginary classes was passion. Today, work for me is still passionate play. But now I teach real classes to real people for real profit.

What if you're not sure what you're passion is? Does that mean you'll never find it? No, because passion is not just one thing, not just a career, a cause or a relationship. Passion is a way of approaching and enjoying life to the fullest. The gain is the passion itself, not a prize of victory, more money or more friends, although such rewards will likely follow.

Passions derive from values and beliefs. If you value excellence, you might be like Carol, the education director who is just as passionate about creating the perfect policy and procedure manual as she is about meticulously planning a conference for hundreds. Valuing a healthy body can fire you up for a daily 5:00 a.m. workout that another woman would consider insanity.

I love Broadway theater, and when I go to a musical or play I'm always amazed at the ability of the actors to perform the same show night after night after night, yet never make you feel that it's just another day at work. On Wednesdays and Saturdays they do two shows. During the matinee, the actors know they have to do it all over again in six hours. They can't go on cruise control to reserve their energy. They have to give it their all, as though this is the only performance they're ever going to give.

They go deep and pull up the passion they have for acting and the passion they have for their audience, to make that performance look like it's a first.

That is what successful women do. Whatever their game, they give it their all and make it look like it's the first time, like each person or project is the first, the one and only. That's the path to wicked success.

Passions change and evolve. At any moment passion is a choice. What you're passionate about is a choice.

A woman can be passionate about anything (although my husband often reminds me that straightening the magazines on the rack and folding a perfect hospital corner on our bed are compulsions, not passions). My friend Yvonne, passionately immersed in her career, had a child she hadn't planned for and now she's equally passionate about raising, teaching and loving that child. She manages both career and child with focused passion.

Passions are lived out in as many expressions as there are women. Yours are inside you, and they will reveal themselves if you listen carefully.

LET YOUR PASSIONS MOVE YOU

We all know there's no one magic formula for prosperity and happiness, but there is one common denominator I've found among wickedly successful women: They have a passionate drive to do what they do. They're on fire.

Some inner spark in the mind, spirit and soul burns intensely, driving them over seemingly insurmountable barriers. Passionate women don't do what they do just because they can—they do it because they're irresistibly compelled. This is wicked success. This is happiness—being on fire. Not how much money you have in your bank account. Not how many school activities you participate in. Not how thin you are. Not being retired at age 55.

Alicia Alonso, the Cuban ballerina, is recognized as one of the finest classical ballerinas of all time. Her achievement is all the more impressive because Alicia is one woman we probably should never have heard of. Her soul was fired up to dance, but her body wasn't cooperating.

At 19, when she was not yet a famous dancer, Alicia was diagnosed with a detached retina. Her condition required three successive operations and left her with partial sight but no peripheral vision. After surgery Alicia was instructed to lie in bed, perfectly still, for a year. But Alicia's flame would not be extinguished by mere physical limitation. During her year of enforced bed rest she danced in her mind and with her toes to keep her feet, memory and passion alive. She taught herself to dance *Giselle,* a difficult ballet that demands the ballerina's full range.

When Alicia returned to the stage, every prop and light was placed exactly the same for every performance, so that she could memorize her moves and dance even with her limited vision. The deadly peril of the orchestra pit awaited her slightest misstep or memory lapse. Still, Alicia Alonso achieved world renown and was honored with the highest designation a ballerina can earn, *Prima Ballerina Assoluta.*

Was it only talent that made her one of the world's most successful ballerinas? Or was it her driving passion to do what she loved despite overwhelming odds?

Jean wanted to start her own business. I realized I couldn't determine what was driving her, so being the direct person I am, I went straight for the jugular and asked, "Why do you want to start a business?" Equally blunt, she said, "I want money to buy nice things, a nice car, nice clothes and a nice house."

Payoff is essential for entrepreneurship, but the missing ingredient I saw in Jean was fire for the business itself, not just the rewards of the business.

Contrast Jean's approach with Lauren's. Her business model is actually more difficult, requiring investors, a large front-end capital outlay and a commercial lease. Knowing how the economic recession tested my own passion and stamina for my business, I predict Lauren is more likely to succeed. Why? Because, unlike Jean who is money-driven, Lauren is driven not just by the passion of wanting to own her business, but also by the passion of the business itself. Her passions will move her during the good times, the bad times and all of the times in between.

Without the inner fire that only passion arouses, success—and I mean long-term, authentic success—will elude you. Money can never be the only long-term driver. Passion and purpose for the work need to be the fuel of your desire and your actions. You succeed not because you want the monetary rewards, but because you need to succeed for your very soul.

Here's an interesting fact: Studies have shown that money does make people happier—but only to a certain point. Once your basic needs and a little bit more are met, your happiness seeks new avenues. Despite what you've seen on television, a Mercedes, a boat or a closet filled with Armani won't make or keep you happy. (Okay, maybe my own private jet would make me happier.) What will make you happy consistently is having experiences full of passion and purpose. In fact, studies also show that experiences produce longer-lasting "highs" than does the act of buying stuff. By experiences, I'm not just talking about vacations and birthday parties; experiences also include the work you do.

Here's to Lauren and all the passion, purpose and success she will enjoy during her lifetime. Here's to all of us living lives and careers filled with passion and purpose. Live and work your passion and you'll never "work" a day in your life.

DISCOVER YOUR FIRE TO LIVE PASSIONATELY

What you're passionate about is a choice, and every choice you make is a choice for or against passion. What's your passion? What really makes you feel alive? What percentage of your life does passion represent? How does your passion fit into your business or career or relationships? If you can answer these questions, you're well on your way to living passionately.

But what if you're not sure? If your passions have not yet got you leaping into action, use the following exercises to coax them to life.

And please, write in this book. This book is not for you to just read. Use it to think and write your way to wicked success.

1. **Connect with your early interests.** Much of what I was passionate about as a child is a big part of my life now. It didn't happen instantly, but I ultimately reconnected with those childhood passions

and incorporated them into my adult life. Can you recall a pleasant childhood memory of playing? What comes to mind first? *Write it down, no matter how absurd.*

_____

_____

_____

_____

_____

Thinking about this play scenario, ask yourself: Did you love it? Were you good at it? Did you engage in it every chance you could, without being pushed? Did your parents have to drag you away from it? *Now, describe it in detail.*

_____

_____

_____

_____

_____

Perhaps your memory comes from your teen years or early adulthood. Or it might be the first time you recognized a special talent, developed a latent skill or derived pure pleasure from an accomplishment. Recall even one time when you felt passionately excited and no one had to push you into action, then you'll know how to ignite your passion for success. Write down *something*, even if you aren't quite certain, or it seems outrageous.

2. **Acknowledge your current interests.** Imagine you have all the money you need and nine months to do anything and everything you want to do—pursue any career or hobby, live in a new state or country, sing with your favorite band or climb Mount Everest. You're free of worry about financial or practical matters during that entire time. What would you do?

   Grab a pen and take three minutes to stretch your imagination. Write down everything that comes to mind. Don't limit your answers to the obvious, such as traveling or spending more time with family and friends. *Write fast, as many things as you can think of. When your three minutes are up, stop.*

_____

_____

_____

_____

_____

Glance quickly over your list. You'll notice that a few items give you a profound feeling of excitement, urgency or possibly, disappointment. *Circle three that ignite a spark.*

Next, considering your everyday world as it exists right now, take two minutes to list everything you might want to accomplish in the next year. After two minutes, stop. Circle three items that spark passion inside you.

_____

_____

_____

_____

_____

3. **Go inside, listen and choose your actions.** Women tend to pile on the responsibilities. We already do more than twice the housework and more than three times the childcare as the men in our lives. Why buy into the myth that we must handle it all—home, children, career, care of an aging parent, social obligations, financial wizardry—and still have energy for great sex? Listen to your inner voice and you know that myth is ridiculous. Yes, we probably can handle it all— we're women, we can do anything—but why should we? Men would never expect to juggle so many responsibilities.

Martha, has been cooking breakfast and dinner her entire married life. When her husband retired, he wanted her to make lunch, too. At first she hopped in and did it. But soon it grated on her that his retirement meant she had more work to do. She's at retirement age too, and preparing another meal was contrary to her passion for enjoying life. She decided it was time to retrain him, and that's exactly what she did when she told him, "Our wedding vows included better or worse but not lunch. You're on your own for lunch."

How many everyday responsibilities in your life can be eliminated? Or delegated? Or hired out? Or automated? Which responsibilities no longer support you? Let them go. Eliminating just one or two items from your busy schedule frees up time to pursue your passionate interests. *Write down two responsibilities you will no longer handle personally.*

_____

_____

_____

_____

4. **Keep listening and quickly reject whatever you're not passionate about.** We all go through stages where our energy comes from a particular source, and once that source no longer provides a driving vitality, it's okay to let it go and ignite a new fire.

There was a time when I loved to entertain. I was passionate about cooking and loved having friends over to eat. Then one day I was just as happy eating out, choosing to relax with my friends without the bother of planning, shopping, cooking and kitchen duty.

At first I felt guilty about not being the entertainer. I was still passionate about cooking; I'd just lost my passion for entertaining. A Saturday morning spent in the kitchen chopping, grinding, blending, cooking, imagining and creating will do almost as much good for my soul as a massage or walk in the woods. The epiphany struck—I don't have to be passionate about entertaining anymore.

While that fire burned inside me, I did it, I loved it. Then other passions took over and I moved on. When a passion burns out, let it go.

If your burning passions are not yet evident, rejecting everything you clearly are not passionate about can help you get closer. Try backing into your passions with the following exercise.

Look at what you absolutely don't want to do. "I don't want to do this, or this. . . ." *Write down five things you absolutely don't want to do.*

_____

_____

_____

_____

Then write down five things you might not mind doing. "Maybe I would like to do this . . . or this."

_____

_____

_____

_____

_____

Eventually you'll hit on something that speaks to you: "Yes, I could really enjoy doing this." Is that a passion? Maybe, maybe not. Only by exploring it will you know. *For now, write it down.*

_____

_____

_____

_____

_____

Be patient. If you don't get a fire in the belly that feels like real passion, keep exploring. Maybe for now it's only a spark. The flame has to start somewhere.

5. **Foresee the reality of your passions.** Frequently we crave a result without foreseeing the full implications of that result. Fame brings intense responsibility and an end to privacy. Breaking a record opens the door to all contenders.

   Alice wanted to be a keynote speaker until she saw the lifestyle that keynoting represented—living out of a suitcase, sleeping in hotels away from home and loved ones. By speaking locally, with only occasional trips out of town, she was able to modify that passion without forsaking it.

   Suzi dreamed of opening a bed-and-breakfast and playing host to new guests every day. Soon after opening, she found that her time was spent cleaning, cooking, washing dishes, invoicing and answering the reservation line. That reality wasn't what she signed up for, so she changed it by hiring a manager and staff. Now she enjoys her dream of entertaining guests, without toilet duty.

Joan was a talented actress but was only marginally successful at it. She appeared on Broadway in the leading role of Belle in *Beauty and the Beast*. She played different roles on TV shows such as *Friends*. But one day she woke up and decided she could no longer accept the reality of living on $700 one week and $30 the next. She still loved acting, but recognized she would never make a significant living at it. She moved on to another profession and embraced it with the same fire as she did acting.

I love to travel. I travel 20 weeks a year for business and pleasure. The benefit—I've seen a small chunk of the world and loved most minutes of it. The realities: Cavity searches at the airport, inedible airline food (when you can get food), 12-hour flights, lost luggage and seats so unfriendly to my body parts that I'm ready to abandon them in the seat pocket in front of me. I miss a few parties and weddings, too. Knowing these realities, I can steel myself in preparation. I always have my smartphone, to stay connected. I always have plenty to read or do. I always take food in my carry-on. Can I live with the realities to live this passion? Yes.

Whether you want children, want to be married to the love of your life, want to start your own business, want to quit your job or do all of these, answer these questions: *What benefit will you gain by living your passions? What are the realities of that lifestyle? Does this passion support your other life goals? If not, how can you modify or merge them?*

_____

_____

_____

_____

_____

THE PASSIONATE PATH ISN'T QUICK AND EASY

After I started my business, I went to law school at night, but decided I preferred the freedom and flexibility of owning my own business. After I graduated, a group of attorneys I consulted with offered me a position as an associate attorney. Saying no was easy. I graciously and easily declined, thinking, "Why would I want to do that? I'm doing what I love, having more freedom and making more money than any new associate attorney."

A year later a partner at the law firm approached me and said, "Okay, if you won't come on as an associate, we're inviting you to be a partner." This attractive offer was unprecedented and raised the stakes considerably. The offer was more financially lucrative than I thought my business could be. Suddenly, saying yes to my passion wasn't so easy. I loved consulting with these attorneys, and if I was to practice law with anyone, these were the guys! Plus, a partnership would guarantee a bigger and brighter future every year, financially and in other respects.

After my ego stopped dancing around the room, pumping its arm and shouting "Yes!," I stopped and listened to the promises I'd made to myself. Promise 1: "I will live and work a passionate life." Practicing law was not my passion, even with such ideal conditions. My passion was teaching.

I needed to trust my passion. Trust I did, and I declined the offer. Eventually, this decision paid off big, both financially and emotionally. My passion was so strong that I surpassed the law firm's offer in every way while maintaining my freedom, creating my own financial security and, most of all, enjoying the career I'm passionate about.

That kind of decision isn't easy. What's easy is to compromise, say yes to a lukewarm interest because we think, or someone else thinks, it's a smarter decision. Live and work your passions and the reward will come, maybe not always financially, but in a way that matters to you.

I had the opportunity both to interview and be interviewed by Daryn Kagan, who at the time was a news anchor for CNN. Daryn knew at age 16 she wanted to be a television reporter. After five years at a local TV station, she asked to move up to anchor. Repeatedly, her boss passed her over to hire blondes. "There's just this 'it,'" he told her, "and some people have it and some don't. Clearly, you don't."

That was harsh, but Daryn refused to let her boss define her direction, her passion or her success. She circumvented his limiting beliefs and forged her own path. She convinced him to put her on as weekend morning sportscaster, a position she invented, and for over a year she worked that job for free. Daryn, who had a passion for sports, saw an opportunity to get noticed at a much higher level in a field where women were not the norm. Later, when a position opened up at CNN, she got it and after only three years became an anchor.

Sometimes the smartest move is to move on, especially when the here-and-now doesn't support your passion. Had Daryn believed her first boss's assessment of her future in television she might never have achieved anchor status. Don't let others define you, your passion or your direction. When Daryn's passion was tested, she paid her dues, then moved on, following her own path and reaching the outcome she desired.

THE PASSIONATE PATH ISN'T BALANCED

The passionate path doesn't always involve a life of balance. Balance is a myth perpetuated by self-proclaimed self-help experts. This myth has women feeling inadequate and lousy about ourselves, because we get exhausted trying to balance it all.

That's why it's important to choose a career or business you're passionate about. When I first started my business while working a full-time job, my life was out of balance, but I was loving every moment of it.

Surround your workday with people and experiences you enjoy, so when you fall in bed after a 16-hour day you still feel fired up from having fun. Don't buy in to the myth of balance. Instead, find balance within a passionate life.

Despite the fact that many of us fantasize about never having to work, it's the women who accomplish something big while under loads of stress who actually live longer. These are women with passion and purpose. I was excited to read that finding, because balance would bore me. Passion is what I live for.

PASSION DOESN'T BURN THE SAME FOR ALL WOMEN

Not everyone feels and expresses passion in the same way. Being Italian, I tend toward the active, fire-in-the-belly, excited way of seeing and doing things. My husband says I'm like a summer storm. I blow in, there's thunder, lightning, wind and rain, then I blow out.

My Vietnamese housekeeper, Thi Thu, is the calmest person in the world. She moves almost silently around my home and appears unflappable no matter the situation. Where her passion sparks is when we're in the kitchen. She's passionate about cooking and especially passionate about telling me how to cook. Whatever the preparation, the dish or the plate we put it on, she has a passionate opinion and expresses it freely.

She arranges shrimp on a plate around a sculptured mound of seasoned rice with all their tails pointing just so. Her salads are mosaic perfections, every vegetable cut precisely and layered in bands of color. When I make a salad, I chop it up any old way I can and toss it all together. It's food. Clean it, chop it, eat it. Her dishes are works of art. Mine are works of sustenance. Anyone can tell by the results that she loves preparing meals, but watching her go about it with such amazing calm you'd never recognize her passion.

It's okay if your passion burns differently. What's important is that the fire burns bright for you.

10 STRATEGIES FOR LIVING PASSIONATELY

In March 1982, when I had the privilege of seeing Alicia Alonso dance, she was 61 years old. I had no doubt that her passionate drive accounted for her long, successful career. That same month I started my business. This woman and her unflagging energy have inspired me ever since.

We are measured not by how we deal with victory and accomplishment, but by how we deal with failure and disappointment. When life gets tough, I remember Alicia and other passionate women like her whose blazing fire wouldn't be stifled.

10 Ways to Live Passionately

1. **Commit to the fire.** We live in an increasingly passive society, where we can sit and watch the news, play video games, text, communicate via Facebook, Tweet, or Skype or play FarmVille and believe we're involved, when all we're doing is idling in place while life passes us by. We're not doing much, yet it seems we're doing a lot.

   Passivity is dangerous to passion, because passion never resides in a passive house. A passionate woman doesn't sit in front of her computer waiting for the world to approach her. She's alert and moving. When a scintillating opportunity appears, she seizes it on the spot.

2. **Practice being fiery.** If you're thinking, "I'm not naturally passionate," don't despair. You can practice passion as easily as you can practice any sport.

I'm not a sports fan, unless I'm playing, but one night Tom dragged me to an ice hockey game "kicking and screaming." Within minutes I was into it. I didn't know the rules, didn't understand what was happening down on that ice, but I was beating on the glass, yelling at the players, the goalies, the referees and having the time of my life. I was practicing passion—at least, that's what I told Tom.

Approach your day and your life with positive energy. Nothing destroys passion quicker than negative energy. "I'm passionate about music, but I hate my day job" is not the energy that will propel you to succeed in that day job until you can quit to pursue your passion for music. It's okay to know you're in a temporary way station, but be happy in your way station. Find at least one aspect of your job to be passionate about. No experience is a waste; it's training for what comes next.

Anytime you feel you're not living passionately, you have two options: You can make the most of the experience, or you can make yourself miserable. Let's face it, we can't skip the parts of life we don't enjoy, and few of us can enjoy every single moment.

Susan runs five miles a day, even in rain or sleet and when I mistakenly mentioned that she loves to run, she quickly corrected me: "I don't love running, I love the benefits of running." Even though I know Susan well, I had no idea she didn't love running.

Practice passion in every situation and make everything you do your passion training ground.

3. **Get fired up about the right stuff.** You have this amazing strength of fire, but how are you using it for your life? Are you fired up about the right things—the things that will advance your life and career? I hear you—all fired up about your favorite TV show, a bad relationship, a rude person in the grocery store. *News flash: CSI* is gonna solve that crime, whether you're watching or not. Ten years from now you're going to have trouble remembering the name of the guy who broke your heart, and the rude person in the grocery store isn't thinking about you. Why not put some of that fire into you and see how your life changes?

4. **Do something, even if it's wrong.** Ninety percent of success is showing up. Whether you're selling an idea, trying to land a new job or learning to paint, the bottom line is that you have to show up.

Many people are afraid to commit to a passion because they expect a firecracker to go off, a light to shine or a voice from the heavens to proclaim, "This is it!" Maybe that firecracker will pop, maybe not.

And what you're passionate about today may arouse no interest tomorrow. New passions emerge and you evolve. Yet, even when you recognize that your passion today might not be your passion tomorrow, that it's okay to move on, committing to one path as opposed to another is often difficult. Do something anyway, even if it's wrong.

5. **Ignite your own fire.** Only you can define your passion. My dad is 87 years old. Sal has had two heart attacks and two bypass surgeries and has outlived two wives. Based on statistical probability he's pretty much "out of warranty," but keeps going and going and going because he has a reason for waking up every morning. My dad's passionate about playing poker at a local casino, to the point that I have to call him at specific times each day or miss him entirely. He's not a big gambler; he rarely wins or loses more than $30, and usually ends the week even. You and I might shake our heads at such a passion, but it keeps him young and feisty.

Wicked success is spelled in many ways. For one woman it's millions in the bank. For another it's the luxury of spending more time with family. It's your success; spell it the way you want. Don't seek or wait for approval, and don't be disappointed if others (even those closest to you) don't get your passion.

Too often we buy into other people's definition of what's right or wrong, how we should or shouldn't proceed. If you're waiting for approval or for someone else to ignite your fire, stop being so well-behaved.

My motto is, "I do it my way—you got a problem with that?" That motto helps me to live my fire, not everyone else's. My way doesn't always work, but at the end of the day, I'm comfortable failing if I know I followed my own passion. This is your life, your passion, no one else's.

Don't just break rules, make your own rules. A woman in my company is practically combustible. She's been setting fires all over our office since her first day, accepting the responsibilities of her job while constantly making new rules and brilliantly gaining acceptance for them. After completely rewriting her job description, she became passionately involved in every aspect of the company. What new rule would you have to make to light your own fire?

6. **Ignite your fire with a spark.** Women often think their passion is not worthy, that it should be bigger, bolder, more important. You don't have to start with a blaze.

My business started with a spark, not a blaze. My goal was modest: to pay the mortgage on my 1,100-square-foot condo without having to work overtime. I didn't envision the multimillion-dollar company I've since created. After fanning that spark for three years, I hit my first $100,000-year and thought I'd won the lottery. If someone had predicted that I'd one day have a $16-million year, I would have said, "That's not possible."

Sparks ignite fires. Only you can decide which spark is worthy of your time and energy, but a small passion that drives you is better than no passion at all. Anita Roddick, who took The Body Shop from a passionate idea to more than 2,500 stores worldwide, says, "If you think you're too small to have an impact, try going to bed with a mosquito."

Small sparks give us confidence to light bolder fires. What spark could you ignite now, today? Fuel one small spark, and soon you will be rewarded with the blazing fire of bold passion.

7. **Translate your passions into written goals.** In the business world it's common knowledge that what gets measured gets done. A Harvard Business School study revealed that only 3 percent of the population has written goals; 14 percent have goals, just not written down; and 83 percent have no clearly defined goals. The study further revealed that the 3 percent with written goals earned 10 times more than the others. If you've written yours down, when was the last time you reviewed them?

As I often remind my husband, having a map or directions isn't helpful if you don't refer to them. Goals are a guide, not an endpoint, but the power of written goals is indisputable. Only after writing a goal down can you sincerely examine it and define the strategies to make it happen.

8. **Create time and opportunity for your passions.** In a busy, demanding schedule, it's easy to believe we have no time for passions, and believing makes it so. Conversely, if we fiercely believe in the promises we make to ourselves, we'll carve out time to pursue our passions.

Many authors rise an hour early to finish writing a book. Many successful career women use their lunch hours to study, place important phone calls or otherwise make progress in pursuing their passions. Entrepreneurial homemakers stay up to pursue their venture long after the family has gone to bed.

If you love to travel but the economy has you down, promise yourself that you'll travel once a year then twice a year after that. Make that goal your priority. Daily lattes and working on your Manolo shoe collection may need to be bridled and controlled.

Are you passionate about what you spend 60 to 80 percent of your time doing? If so, you'll undoubtedly succeed. If not, change that ratio.

9. **Align your relationships with your passions.** It's not uncommon for a woman's passion to conflict with important relationships. This is true whether the relationship is with your supervisor, your best friend or your significant other. Will you change your vision to hold on to the relationship, or change the relationship to hold on to your passion?

An important success trait is the ability to detach from people who aren't on course with you. It doesn't mean that everyone you know and love has to agree totally with your choices. But don't waste time with people who only want to diminish you.

I have a friend who put her career on hold after she married and had children. She stayed at home until the oldest was 4 years old, when she began doing volunteer work to get out of the house. That wasn't enough, so she took a full-time job, which required her to travel. She was making more money than her husband, even after four years off the market. Her in-laws, who believe a woman's only function is homemaker, bombarded her husband with their negative opinions. Emotionally torn, he wanted to support his wife, but was conditioned by loyalty to his parents' ideals. Naturally, his wife also felt conflicted, eager to pursue her vision but emotionally invested in her husband and family.

I encouraged her to go with her vision, because it's her life. Too many women give up career dreams to protect a relationship. That's traditional, but it can drive you into a mental institution. And some dreams, if you don't pursue them timely, will pass you by. When you're finally free, you've missed the window of opportunity. To her husband's credit, he went along because he valued the relationship as much as she did.

Conversely, a former student, whose husband felt threatened by her earning more money than he did, dissolved her successful consulting business and gave up her six-figure income. To avoid conflict in her relationship, she renounced her passion. How crazy is that? Maybe she should have renounced her husband's limited thinking and surrounded herself instead with people who believed in her.

A relationship must be mutually beneficial, and any genuine relationship will adjust to change. When you recognize that someone is extinguishing your fire, ask yourself whether you should gracefully detach and move on. Open a communication path. Share how much your vision means to you, and the people in your life may surprise you.

The game of life is challenging enough when players support one another. Life is more fun when the people on your team are truly aligned with you and your passions.

10. **Keep the passion alive by stoking the fire.** Not everyone can switch passions so easily. For example, you invest years in education, gaining experience and advancing in your profession. Switching to a totally different profession means starting from ground level, reinvesting your resources in an unproven venture and climbing a different ladder to a different future. That's fine if you truly yearn to start over and your passion drives you in that new direction. Many people's passions burn brighter when they make sweeping changes.

I've invested 29 years building my company. I started as a consultant working out of my home. To grow my business I hired one employee, then another and today I have 23. Always passionate about business, I'm not always passionate about employees; and while I love my work and my company, I don't love every aspect of it. Do you ever feel this way about your life, your job, your career or significant other?

Stop and reevaluate. If you're like me, maybe you're not experiencing the dreaded "burnout," but only a need to stoke your fire.

Do what you do, but find a different focus. Or do what you do differently. My best growth ideas come when I toss out the old embers and stir things up.

Writing this book stoked my fire. Is there a spark or ember you can stoke to a blaze? What aspect of your passion have you not fully explored? What new opportunities are available to you today? Passion is precious. Don't let the mundane routines that surface in any pursuit dampen your fire. Look within and find a spark you can fan to full flame again.

IGNITE YOUR FIRE WITH THE
5 PROMISES

PROMISE 1
I Will Live and Work a Passionate Life

Write down at least one passion from the earlier exercises. Do it, even if it's only a spark.

_____

_____

_____

How do your passions relate to what you do now? Calculate the time you spend each day living and working your passions. If it's less than 75 percent, how can you increase that time?

_____

_____

_____

PROMISE 2
I Will Go for It or Reject It Outright

What holds you back from living your passions? Is it physical, mental, emotional or financial? Is it driven by adverse responsibilities or relationships? How can you eliminate or minimize the obstacles?

_____

_____

_____

PROMISE 3
I Will Take One Action Step a Day Toward My Passionate Vision

What one action will you take today toward living your passions?

_____

_____

_____

PROMISE 4
I Commit to Being a Success Student for Life

What do you need to know to pursue your passions? How can you obtain this knowledge? When will you commit to learning it?

_____

_____

_____

PROMISE 5
I Believe as a Woman I Really Can Do Anything

Recall a passion that fired you up, however briefly. List three principles you can take from that to your next, bolder passion.

_____

_____

_____

>> DOWNLOAD THE 5 PROMISES FOR FIRE AT **WickedSuccess.com**.

EVIE'S FIRE

Certain things that I'm on fire about push me forward, especially at work. Ever since I was young, I have always been passionate about making a person feel happy or pleased. In my first job, working as a cashier, this passion transcended into building good relationships with customers. Subsequently I was promoted to supervisor. Then I was promoted again, to a "cash clerk." I'm the last person who needs to be counting money, but my managers translated my passionate behavior to mean that I would probably do anything in that company well. Through passion for being a good employee, and lots of recounting, I got through it.

Today, my passion is still customer service, and I have written and spoken professionally about the subject. Although my education is in marketing, I mentor and work directly with customers. I also train and coordinate customer service for a high-energy company, mentoring customer service representatives to be as passionate about our customers as I am. No matter where you are in life, you have to be on fire about at least one aspect of your job to really make a difference and stand out. Passion is the one thing that gets me ahead. I'm still working on my college degree, but I've had no problem surpassing people who already have a college degree, by making more money and holding higher positions. It doesn't

make me more or less smart. My passion fuels my fire.
I guess that says a lot about passion.

Evie, 35
CUSTOMER RELATIONS COORDINATOR
AND MARKETING CREATIVE

Women are born passionate and have the potential to live life passionately. Dig deep, discover the fire in your soul, then read on to see how intuitive vision can broaden your realm of possibilities.

Before I go out on the stage, I must place a motor in my soul. When that begins to work, my legs and arms and my whole body will move independently of my own will. But if I do not . . . put the motor in my soul, I cannot dance.
ISADORA DUNCAN

See the change you want to be.
VICKIE L. MILAZZO

2

INTUITIVE VISION

Imagine Unlimited Possibilities to Capture Your Vision

W omen and intuition go together like cats and curiosity. The
concept that women are more in touch with instinctive inner
guidance is so intrinsic to our culture that most people (even men)
accept it without expecting any scientific explanation.

On the side of science, the larger splenium of the corpus callosum
accounts for greater interconnectivity between the left and right
hemispheres of women's cognitive brains. Some scientists believe this
broader connection enables women to access both sides faster and easier
than men. Women are not more "right-brained," as is the myth; their brain
functions are actually more holistic and generalized. We fluently engage the
limbic brain, where higher emotions are stored, and the instinctive brain,
which is responsible for self-preservation. This holistic combination of
emotion, instinct and cognition equates to women's intuition.

Does it make sense to have such an extraordinary tool and not use it?
Not in my book.

Regrettably, it's drilled into us to not trust our intuition, especially
in the workplace. Around male CEOs, when I intuitively whip out a
great idea, presumably from thin air, I see them fidget. Uncomfortable

with my rapid response, they want me to gather my facts before I make a move or decision. But here's the reality: If you always wait for facts, you'll rarely make a move. And when the facts fall into place, which facts will carry the most weight in your decision-making process?

I've learned to trust my intuition. I've also learned to pull together the factual and statistical data to give the person I'm trying to persuade a measure of comfort.

Intuitive vision does not mean going to a psychic to find out if that hot new love interest you met on Facebook is Mr. Right. Intuitive vision is about connecting with your imagination, paying attention, trusting, perhaps experimenting a little and seeing where that takes you.

By trusting my intuition I created a new industry where a void formerly existed. My intuition told me lawyers needed nurses, even if they didn't know it yet themselves. A focus group of attorneys might have discouraged me, and if I'd let them, where would I be today?

Think about a situation where you totally trusted your intuition to guide you, and it worked out perfectly. Think about a situation where it didn't. Was that really your intuition or someone else speaking to you—parents, boss, lover? Follow your gut and you'll be right more often than not.

That's not to say that intuition is infallible. We can passionately desire to go in a particular direction, and even have a clear vision of where we're going, only to be rerouted by circumstance.

As an example, when I first realized that my nursing career was not taking me where I wanted to go, I imagined a new path. Since teaching was my lifelong passion, I envisioned a business teaching patients how to improve their health, something hospitals had little interest in. A need for that service clearly existed, and I acted on my idea, but there was no insurance reimbursement for patient education, so my idea was not realistic, at least not as a way to make a living. I imagined a passionate future only to hit a solid wall of disappointing but indisputable facts.

Then I decided to become a legal nurse consultant, and was thrilled to realize I'd be teaching attorneys and their clients about the healthcare issues in their cases. Redirected and rekindled yet again, my passion burned even brighter when I expanded the concept and began teaching other RNs to become legal nurse consultants.

Sometimes your vision doesn't materialize exactly as you imagine it, but trust it anyway. If you feel passionate enough, and continue to refocus your vision as circumstances change, you'll find your true path can lead to more wicked success than you first imagined. It's intuitive.

INTUITION IS COGNITION ON STEROIDS

After I was in business for a number of years, the legal nurse consulting profession I created caught on, and a related industry association sprang up as a result. That association did not, however, align with my vision to create a certification program. Knowing that certification was important for the industry's future, I created it myself.

Fired by my passion, trusting my intuitive vision and unwilling to accept the group's limiting beliefs, I created an entire curriculum, a certification credential and an even larger industry association. The National Alliance of Certified Legal Nurse Consultants (NACLNC) remains the nation's largest legal nurse consulting association (NACLNC.org). My intuition proved to be cognition on steroids. I jumped off the slow train full of mundane thinkers, defined certification standards, and in what seemed to others as lightning-fast, put my own unstoppable train in motion.

Sure, I had facts and experience to back me up, but not enough to convince a group that was afraid of change. Sure, their inability to see what I could see tested my beliefs, but my vision was so strong I had to go for it. After investing enormous amounts of time, money and energy in the certification, I achieved staggering success, not only for myself but for thousands of women who have achieved certification status.

If anyone ever tells you one person can't accomplish anything big, or you shouldn't go against the odds, don't believe it. Intuition worked for me. And it will work for you. It all starts with your intuitive vision.

IMAGINATION TRUMPS KNOWLEDGE

Anything ever invented had to first be imagined. Topping the list of visionary geniuses are Leonardo da Vinci and Albert Einstein.

Da Vinci imagined many inventions that were made possible only after technology caught up with his vision. He was 40 years ahead of Copernicus when he wrote, "The sun does not move." To study the stars, da Vinci imagined "a large magnifying lens." Sixty years later Galileo made it happen. Da Vinci also envisioned parachutes, armored tanks and helicopters, often including detailed drawings in his notes.

This one person's imagination was more advanced than an entire world's knowledge.

Albert Einstein's thoughts took simple form, but with far-reaching possibilities. He imagined what a light beam would look like if he were to race alongside it. "Imagination," he wrote, "is more important than knowledge." Eventually, his mental images led him to form his world-changing theory of relativity. Years later science finally proved what Einstein had theorized based on his studies and intuitive vision.

A female genius you may not know was Margaret Knight. Mattie's talent for invention emerged when, like many children of the 1860s, she worked in a cotton mill. After witnessing a mill accident at age 12, she envisioned and designed a shuttle-restraining device to prevent workers from being injured. Later she envisioned a paper bag to replace the tall envelopes being used to hold groceries and other purchases. At 29, she invented a machine part that would automatically fold and glue the flat-bottom bags we use today. Dubbed "the female Edison," Mattie Knight eventually patented 26 other inventions, including rotary engines and automatic tools.

Despite the "fact" that many important discoveries resulted from intuitive vision, rigidly left-brained, fact-focused thinkers often dismiss intuition as useless. Don't let them intimidate you.

Women need to tap into their intuitive intelligence. Even data-dependent "experts" often disagree about which facts to rely on, as well as the interpretation of so-called facts. Every set of facts is subject to as many interpretations as there are interpreters. If you wait for facts to weigh in with your vision, you might be waiting long after someone else has grabbed the vision and run with it.

J. K. Rowling's imagination defied all the facts. The facts were emphatic: Children today don't read, and even if they did read, Rowling's book was too long, too dark and much too complex. Rowling's passionate vision told her that children would indeed read her book. In any case, her passion compelled her to write it. Despite the rejection of her first book by numerous publishing houses, her Harry Potter series has enraptured children and adults everywhere with its imaginative plots and vivid characters. Harry Potter is also the biggest movie franchise in Hollywood history, and Rowling became the first author to become a billionaire from the sale of her "unreadable" books.

Our intuitive vision is uniquely intelligent, bigger and more powerful than any set of facts. If imagination was good enough for da Vinci, Einstein, Knight and Rowling, it's good enough for me.

If I could successfully imagine a classroom of students that didn't exist, then I could imagine consulting with an attorney. I could imagine teaching a real class of future Certified Legal Nurse Consultants. I could imagine a national association of more than 5,000 members. And I did.

As children, our imaginations are boundless. As adults, we become practical and stop imagining. Let's face it, talking to make-believe friends as a child is called imaginative. Talking to imaginary friends as a grown-up elicits, "The psych ward is right down the hall."

Or we only imagine the worst: Your spouse is late coming home; you don't think traffic, you think multicar collision. Your mother-in-law drops by; you don't think she wants dinner, you think she wants to move in. We all have imaginations; we just don't always use them with productive intention.

Your emotional brain, the limbic region where passions and fears battle each other, cannot distinguish between reality and intuitive vision and your rational, thinking brain, the cortex, cannot feel those emotional battles. Since the limbic brain cannot think, but only feel, it reacts to your dreams as it would to a real experience. Knowing this, you can impassion your mind with any desire you actively envision, and that passion will, in turn, drive your positive actions toward making the vision a reality. In other words, if you vividly envision the desired result, and reinforce that desire by frequently revisiting the vision, your passion will make it happen.

ORDER OFF THE RIGHT MENU

My husband and I were having dinner with my dad at a favorite Italian restaurant. After an animated discussion with the waiter, Dad, always a picky eater, ordered a pasta dish that wasn't on the menu, telling the waiter exactly what he wanted in it.

The food arrived beautifully presented and prepared exactly as requested. Bits of scallion, tomato, garlic and peppered chicken glistened over a bed of fettuccine, all infused with a light tomato-basil sauce and dusted with Parmesan cheese. My father's dish looked so good I wanted his instead of my own.

I expected him to be delighted. Instead, he compared it to a different pasta dish from a different Italian restaurant. Rather than enjoying his dinner, he found fault with the waiter, the restaurant and the chef for not serving this other recipe. The dish was prepared wrong, he said: too many tomatoes, not enough garlic and the sauce wasn't right!

I sat stunned and amused. Gently, I interrupted his litany of complaints, reminding him that he had received exactly what he ordered. In fact, after tasting it, I liked it better than the dish he compared it to.

"I may have gotten what I ordered," Dad replied, "but it wasn't what I wanted."

My father expected the waiter to read his mind and bring him something other than what he ordered. Eventually, Dad's appetite got the best of him and he enjoyed his meal to the last bite. After all, when you're hungry, even the wrong dish fills your stomach.

Are you making your choices off the right menu? I see women every day who are living the wrong life, working the wrong career, because they ordered off the wrong menu. Haven't we all done that at times? We want different conditions in our career or relationships, but as long as we stay where we are, physically or mentally, the changes we want are not even possible.

Do you feel cranky about your situation and environment? If your life isn't where you want it to be, you may, like my father, have expectations about what you're being served. You may have tried your best to order exactly what you wanted. Yet what's on your plate is not what you expected.

As an employer, I love hiring young people, because I enjoy their enthusiasm and energy, but I prefer to get them after they're seasoned by at least one other job experience. Otherwise, their expectations lean toward a naive vision of what being an employee is all about, and they become dissatisfied.

If the dish you want is not on the menu, perhaps you're in the wrong place or space. Be open to ordering off new menus. If you stay at your same job and order off the same old job menu, don't be surprised when you get what you've always gotten, even though it's not what you want. Remain intuitively open and you might find a new, greater career passion.

One reason I and other women battled our way successfully through the recession is our intuitive ability to order off new menus. By being open to new possibilities you'll discover life is an adventurous banquet filled with tasty, satisfying experiences and unexpected passions.

It's your meal—you get to choose. Feast often at a brand-new restaurant.

SHOW UP WITH NO GUARANTEE

Intuitive vision doesn't mean blindly stepping off a cliff or dropping your paycheck on lottery tickets and trusting you'll win. Skydivers carefully pack their own parachutes, scuba divers check their own gear and entrepreneurs write their own business plans. When you start any new venture, you can and should strategize, but you can't guarantee the outcome. Skydivers break bones, scuba divers get the bends and business owners fail. If you want a guarantee, forget it.

You have to trust in your intuitive vision enough to show up and invest the full effort, with no guarantee of the upshot. That might feel scary, but the only certainty is this: If you do nothing, you'll achieve nothing.

Since I was 4 years old I've been playing penny poker with my family. We were serious about our poker, so serious that we'd toss our allowance in the pot. As a poker game heats up, winning players stack up their chips until they think they have a really good hand. Then, cockily or quietly, depending on the player's personality, someone pushes all his or her chips to the center of the table and says, "I'm all in." This heavy bettor is hoping not only to capture a big pot, but also to take some of the others out of the game.

The other players are wondering, "Does she really have a winning hand, or is she bluffing?" Eyeing that big pot in the middle of the table, they're questioning whether to fold or go all in, too.

The excitement builds around the table, and the risk taker inside you comes out, especially if you believe you've got the winning hand. You push your pile of hard-won chips into the middle.

That's what "go all in" is about. To win big, you play big.

Tom, my family and I were playing quarter poker—we've upped the ante since I was 4—and Tom showed me his hand. Having already dropped out, I whispered, "Go all in, Tom." He said, "Vickie, I could lose everything."

If you haven't guessed, Tom's the conservative, penny-pinching member of the family, who probably wouldn't go all in if he had pocket aces (that's two aces in his hand) with two aces on the table. We were playing with quarters here, a pot total of $3.75.

Between his hole cards and what was on the table, Tom had a winning hand but was afraid to take a chance on it. To my dismay, Tom didn't go all in. Even though he eventually won the hand, he won a much smaller jackpot than he could have. Being the risk taker I am, it left me shaking my head at his timidity.

Don't Wait for a Royal Flush

Then recently, I found myself sitting at a dollar poker table in a real casino, playing Texas Hold 'Em. I sat there holding pocket aces. Now, all you need to know about poker is that pocket aces is a "go all in" kind of hand. It's not a guaranteed winner, but it's as close as you can get in the poker world. It's a hand that begs you to take all of those treasured chips in front of you and, win or lose, push them to the betting pile. I sat there, holding back, weighing the odds in my head.

Did I go all in? No. I didn't want to lose my dollars. I was acting as timid with my dollars as Tom had with his quarters. It wasn't just about losing the dollars; it was about being knocked out of the game. Those aces offered no guarantee I would retain my place at the table. Only a royal flush could guarantee a win. Uncertainty froze my hand to my chips.

Isn't that what really holds us back from going all in? Aren't we frozen in fear by the possibility that we'll be knocked out of the game? And there's no guarantee we won't be.

No world champion ever attains such status without going all in. A sure win is an impossibility. Professional athletes are willing to risk everything to become world champions. They're willing to go all in, with no guarantee of success, risking being knocked out of the game; and sometimes they will be. But if they intuitively play the right cards, they'll win big.

That's why I define success as showing up and stepping out. Showing up today, and paying the price today, determines tomorrow's success. If you want a guarantee, forget it. Trust your intuitive vision, make the investment. Eventually the payoff will come, even in a recession.

What happened to me at the dollar poker table? Instead of boldly demonstrating the strength and confidence in my hand, I merely raised and ended up winning a smaller pot than I should have.

What about you? When pocket aces come your way do you show up with no guarantee, or do you hold back waiting for a promise of success?

Don't hold out for a royal flush. Those don't show up often. A world-champion poker player draws a lot of bad hands. Even if dealt pocket aces, a champion might lose. You'll draw some bad hands too, but think intuitively, think like a winner and put your chips out there on the table. You've probably already been dealt the hand you need to win. Women who play big and win show up with no guarantee.

Thankfully, I was a much better player when I launched my legal nurse consulting certification program. I had no guarantee that anyone would show up, but I did it anyway. Starting any new venture, you have no assurance of success, satisfaction or profitability. You possess only passion, whatever facts you've gathered and your intuitive vision.

Promise to play big anyway. Go all in every day, every hour, every minute, every second, and I promise you will achieve wicked success.

USE SILENCE TO AROUSE IMAGINATION

You can't illuminate your vision in the darkness, but without even realizing it we try to do just that. We wake up daily to clutter pouring in—constant television, texts, email, Facebook and the Internet at home, talk radio in the car, TV news programs at the airport and loud music in restaurants. Soon our senses become dulled and our vision lusterless. How can a woman connect with her intuitive vision when she can't even think straight, constantly bombarded as she is with thousands of outside messages?

To conceive any vision you must first get quiet. Create the space and consciousness that allows your intuitive vision to flourish. Push the clutter aside, turn down the volume and purge your space of pervasive noise. Silence arouses imagination.

Make it your goal to eliminate clutter from your mind, your day and your life. I started with my physical environment, which is the easiest to control. My day is so busy that I created a minimalist, quiet home, a sanctuary I return to at the end of the day.

I then uncluttered my office. Walk in, look around and you'd think I have no work to do. There's plenty of work, but the uncluttered office keeps my big, fat to-do list of clutter from blocking my creativity.

Next, and hardest of all, I began to unclutter my mental environment—banishing negative thoughts, worry and the like. I'm still working on that one.

I rarely watch TV or listen to talk radio, and I don't crave an hourly update on current events. I appreciate that these activities are popular ways to relax. But you cannot wake up to clutter and a day of real or virtual bombardment, then go to bed with that same level of intrusion and still have the mental space to find your intuitive vision.

I have my own clutter addiction to battle—movies. We have a home theater system, but nothing beats sitting in a dark theater with a big bag of popcorn. My addiction got so bad for a while that I found myself going to really bad movies, wondering later why I'd wasted that time and money. I still love going to good movies, and I must frequently recommit to not sitting in a movie theater just to get away from it all. No more bad movies for me—starting next Friday.

Choose renewing ways to relax, such as strolling through a park, soaking in the tub, gazing up at the stars or reading a great book.

Jane shared that she wakes up, goes to work, comes home and goes to work again while taking care of two daughters and a husband. She said, "I don't get one minute to myself. I've lost the connection to me." I encouraged her to start with five minutes, and she did. She sat in her closet where no one in the family would think to look for her. Now that's creative!

How much time do you spend daily in silence? What will you give up to get five more minutes? How will these five more minutes help you to connect with your intuitive vision?

As with most ambitious endeavors, eliminating all the clutter in your life can seem overwhelming at first. The trick is to start small and get creative. Try these three easy steps:

1. **Clear your space.** Take 10 minutes daily to unclutter your physical environment, at home and work. File that stack of papers that's been sitting on your desk for months. Devote 15 minutes a day to cleaning out a closet or room that's only slightly less attractive than

the city dump. Don't tackle the whole space. Start with one corner, then move on to another until it's done.

Susan shares what clearing did for her:

I tend to shop without a plan. I buy what I like without thinking about where the item will live once I get it home. So, after living in my home for 11 years, I was out of storage space. There was not an inch to be found anywhere.

I made a conscious decision to purge. My agreement with myself was that I would clean out one bag of stuff every day. After only one month, I was truly amazed with my progress. There was something about purging all those things, many of which I hadn't seen in years, that lifted a weight off me.

2. **Cut the brain clutter.** We're bombarded by brain clutter from the moment we wake up to a jarring alarm. Start small. Eliminate one outside stimulus, one TV show or a half hour on FarmVille or Facebook. Then eliminate another. Instead of reading three newspapers or magazines, read one. While driving, replace talk radio with inspirational music that stimulates ideas and opens a space for success. Meditate as you fall asleep, or read something relaxing that brings you peace, not agitation.

Eliminate one recreation or hobby that no longer satisfies. Tom asked me one day, "Do you want to go to the art festival?" I used to enjoy this event, but that day it didn't appeal. I said, "No," and in that single word eliminated potential recreational clutter, opening that space for a more satisfying type of fun, such as a visit with friends or a walk through the Japanese garden.

Be equally selective about how you spend time with friends and family. You might not think of a relationship as clutter, but it can be. It's easy to get caught up in other people's stuff. Are casual, unsatisfying relationships keeping you from your vision? Would fewer, more meaningful relationships in person and in social media satisfy more? Do you truly value your 300 friends on Facebook?

Consciously assess your relationships, and when you find one that you don't value, eliminate it, or at minimum, reduce the exposure. Don't succumb to guilt—especially where family is concerned.

You do want to love your family, but you don't have to like every family member, and you don't have to spend your annual vacation with them when a weekend will do. Uncluttering is about making choices in all the areas of your mind, space and time.

3. **Put off procrastination.** Procrastination leads to worry and anxiety, which is mind clutter. You're anxious about the upcoming meeting because the report due is still rough, at best. You worry about overdrafting your bank account because you've put off balancing your checkbook. Instead, just put off procrastination.

Tackle one area of procrastination each week and eliminate it. Schedule it in your calendar, as you would any important appointment, and when that time arrives, do what needs to be done. Your mind will feel refreshingly alert and uncluttered.

Yet procrastination is not always bad. I hear people say, "Finish what you start," or "You had that idea, where did you go with it?" Every day I wake up with new ideas, but there is only so much time, and selective procrastination allows the best ideas to rise to the top. Misplaced stubbornness, as in "I started it, I have to finish it," not only exhausts you, it creates clutter.

Use your intuitive vision to weed out idea clutter. In the emergency room all nurses learn the value and skill of triage. When several patients come in at once, nurses treat the sickest ones first. That's triage.

You can triage ideas. All ideas are not equal, so match your ideas to your intuitive vision to determine which to focus on first.

GET OUT OF YOUR HEAD

It's so easy to overthink an issue and talk ourselves out of things we really want, and into things that we don't. Wickedly successful women are quick and decisive.

Many entrepreneurs I mentor share how much time and effort they spend setting up their business, creating the perfect logo, the perfect office and the perfect conditions for getting started. They're convinced that they must be perfectly ready or they won't have that perfect chance, so they accomplish nothing more than moving the tchotchkes around to the perfect positions. The problem? They're overthinking.

Almost every time I've done the opposite of what my intuition's told me to do, I've regretted it later. This includes hiring and firing employees; dealing with clients, subcontractors and vendors; and even in personal relationships. I've often known what was right, but when I sat down and overanalyzed it, I ended up making the wrong rational decision for all the wrong reasons. If I'd stayed with my intuition and acted on that decision, I'd have spared myself the pain.

We rationalize out of fear of change and because we don't trust ourselves to make the right call at the right time. We can justify anything given enough time to think about it—staying in a job we hate, sticking with a toxic relationship, not standing up for ourselves because we don't want to hurt the feelings of a friend or family member, or not getting out and moving forward with our business.

The emerging entrepreneurs I described know they're ready but do everything they can to talk themselves out of their vision. After they finally hit the market and snag their first client, they realize the peril of living inside their heads. One entrepreneur shared that when her first prospect called back, she was mentally rehearsing excuses for not taking on the project.

As Jane says, "Everything positive that happened so far in my life has been because I trusted my gut. You do not have to be a genius if you trust your intuition, but you can be a genius if you do. For sure, if you don't get out of your head, you can get lost."

Joy says, "When I took tap dancing 20 years ago I tried to break down the elements of the steps, and I couldn't dance a step—but when I just let go and stopped thinking about it my feet would fly!"

What about you? Are you spending too much time overthinking a situation in your career or life instead of simply acting on what your intuition tells you? Our intuition is usually much smarter than we realize or allow it to be. Look back at your past decisions—those made by your gut versus those made by your rational mind—and see which has the better track record. How often have you known the right decision, but made an alternate decision and ended up regretting it?

Avoid analysis paralysis. Next time I start to overthink something, I'm just going to trust my wicked intuition and step out for what I already know is inside.

TRUST YOUR WAY THROUGH THE CHAOS

Every nurse has known patients who lived when they should have died and patients who died when they should have lived. What made the difference? A nurse will say it's all about what's going on upstairs, the powerful mind-body connection. Many health obstacles are mental.

The mind-success connection is equally strong, and many barriers to our success are also mental. Your intuitive vision enables you to bypass such obstacles. Some women rely more on facts, while others rely more on feelings. There's no "right way" to be, but we all have the inborn perception to "feel" our way successfully along an unlighted path.

I learned this when I was stuck on a curb in Ho Chi Minh City (Saigon). My objective, a restaurant where my husband and lunch awaited me, stood on the opposite side of the street. Crossing the street sounds like a simple task, but my objective might as well have been the far side of the moon. Tu Do Street was crammed with motor scooters, bicycles, cyclos (pedaled rickshaws), cars, trucks and buses. The fewer wheels on a contraption, the more passengers it seemed to carry. I saw a family of five riding a Honda scooter—sans helmets, of course.

Even the center lines contributed to the confusion. Rather than dividing the traffic into two lanes, each moving in opposite directions, the yellow lane markers apparently served only to indicate that you were on a paved road. People passed, stopped, turned around and crisscrossed center lines with utter abandon. Traffic flowed both ways in the same lane, more traffic merged from side streets and even more people pushed their scooters off the curbs into the flow. Traffic bore down on me from as many as eight directions—front, back, sides and all angles— everywhere, it seemed, except from above. It was incredible chaos.

The traffic signal lights compounded my problem. In Saigon, they serve only advisory, or possibly decorative, purposes. Even when the signal light turned red, traffic continued to flow, as drivers blatantly ignored the signal. The lanes of traffic impatiently waiting at the green light would edge forward into the traffic that was ignoring the red light. At some point traffic trying to move with the green light would build up enough momentum (and vehicles) to stop the traffic running the red light. Traffic would then flow correctly until the light changed, and the whole process started again.

Above this onslaught the flashing "walk" sign serenely taunted me from the far side of the street. I was ready to abandon lunch with Tom and look for a baggie of lemonade and a roasted lizard on a stick when a mature Vietnamese gentleman took my arm.

In English, he kindly said, "Crossing the street is not a problem, but a dance." With that we stepped off the curb and into the maelstrom. My heart pounded as we walked slowly across. Instead of greeting us with blaring horns, irate shouts and screeching brakes, drivers saw and adjusted to us. As long as we made no sudden movements (like diving for the curb), we were fine. I felt like we were gracefully swimming through a school of fish. The tempest flowed smoothly around us, in all directions, and before I knew it we were across.

Tempt Mystery Not Certainty

The streets of Saigon are a metaphor for life. There's a sort of graceful chaos, everyone going in their own direction, some traveling with traffic, some across it and some against it. Buses and trucks barrel through, stopping for no one. Certainly collisions and accidents happen, but people generally reach their destinations, and life goes on. The best way to survive is not to struggle against the flow, but to approach it like a dance.

Learning to dance through the chaos of Saigon's traffic is much like learning to follow your intuitive vision. It's a combination of intention, timing and trust. Do you dance gracefully through the chaos of your life and career? Do you struggle against it, exhausting yourself, colliding with others and keeping yourself from reaching your chosen destination? Or do you detour, avoiding possible collisions altogether?

In Saigon, I chose to cross the street with my newfound guide and enjoyed the reward of a wonderful lunch. Then I plunged back into the chaos, feeling more comfortable with it all. Every day in my business I face the traffic, dance with it to the best of my ability and hope to enjoy continued success.

A professional colleague asked, "Vickie, what's next for you?" She knew I was in the middle of this book and that I'm involved in an upcoming event with Stedman Graham. "Where will these two projects lead?" My response was, "Just as I didn't know Stedman would call me to do an event together, I have no idea what will come next. I'm okay with not knowing."

I'm a very grounded person, more a doer than a dreamer. I like to plan, but there's no way I can fully plan for what comes next, especially during an unstable economy. When the time comes for me to know, I trust my intuitive vision enough to know I will know. In the meantime my job is to do the work and dance through the chaos, preparing myself to be open to the next Big Thing.

An artist friend's description of creating art describes perfectly how an intuitive woman creates her life. "When I am in the process of conceiving a new image, I have to make sure that some part of the process is unclear to me. It has to be like a mystery. There's got to be something that I don't know, don't control. If there isn't, I don't feel I'm doing anything that means something either to me or to anyone else."

Develop your intuitive vision and learn to trust it. Certainly, collisions and accidents will happen. Even when things are going well, a big truck may hurtle out of the blue, forcing you to stop or change directions or maybe running you over. But guided by instinct, emotion and cognition, you can dance your way through your chaos and find the lighted path.

RELAX YOUR WAY INTO WICKED SUCCESS

Having been interviewed on TV, radio and for print many times, I learned the hard way that there's no room for tension in wicked success.

Laura Sydell of National Public Radio's (NPR) *All Things Considered*, scheduled me for an interview on an upcoming program. When I first learned about it, I was ecstatic! It was to be my first national radio show.

I began preparing, and then the undesirable happened—I started worrying. Figuring I'd only get one chance to be on NPR, I covered every base. I thought out questions, typed out and revised my revised talking points, rehearsed and rehearsed some more.

I arrived at the NPR station on the dreaded, rainy day and sat in the lobby, relentlessly practicing and editing my perfect script. These were the same points I'd edited just two hours earlier at the office. Little did I know Laura would see through them in an instant.

I entered the soundproof radio studio through a door that wouldn't have looked out of place in an airlock on the space station. An intrusive microphone was suspended in front of me like a spider on a web of antivibration cables. Even though I was extremely prepared, I was uncommonly tense and more than slightly on guard.

A technician told me to sit in a chair, be careful to not thump the microphone and for sound quality purposes, be sure and keep my mouth no more than four inches from the microphone. I'm Italian; asking me not to move around or gesture with my hands while I talk is like gagging me.

The disembodied voice of Laura Sydell suddenly came out of a speaker near the ceiling, like the voice of the great Oz. Rather than talk about the safe, impersonal subjects I'd prepared (women in business and entrepreneurship), it turned out that she actually wanted to talk about me. I had prepared notes on everything but my own life. Suddenly, I was acting like I didn't know the subject at all: me.

After a few routine questions, this piercingly perceptive woman, accustomed to interviewing the best, accurately judged my answers to be canned, and suddenly asked me, "Are you reading notes? Do you have notes?"

"Yes." I admitted, holding onto those notes like a life preserver from the *Titanic*.

"Put them away and relax. We're just two friends talking."

Yeah, I thought, just talking over 1,500 miles of high-speed Internet cable in a dark room with an airtight door. I put my notes away, but still within arm's reach, tensing up even more.

Despite knowing the information in my notes, and knowing myself inside and out, I did just okay. I never hit the interview out of the park because I never relaxed into it. I allowed the disembodied voice coming over the big speaker in the dark room to get into my head.

I fell back on the testifying rules I'd used and had coached others in using for depositions. "Answer only the questions," I'd tell them. "Usually, yes or no is good enough. Don't elaborate. Two words are one too many when one word will do."

When Laura asked if I had a family, I answered, "Yes." I didn't say, "Yes, I have a wonderful, supportive husband and many best friends." She asked me if I had any trips or vacations planned, and I answered, "Yes." She had to follow up by asking me to where, and I said, "New Zealand and Fiji." Not, "I'm taking a bicycle trip across New Zealand then going to Fiji to scuba dive with hammerhead sharks," or anything exciting and fun. Just "New Zealand and Fiji." I must have sounded like Eeyore, the morose donkey from Winnie the Pooh cartoons.

When it was over, I asked Laura when she thought the interview would air. I still recall the lack of enthusiasm in her voice, and to her credit she didn't say, "Probably never," but she did hedge and told me she'd have to judge after it had been edited. How much editing of "yes" and "no" would be required, I wondered.

I walked out of the studio with nothing left but a wet drive home and all the eloquently structured ideas I hadn't expressed. In retrospect, I blew it. The interview was never aired, that I've heard of, and frankly I'm glad.

I thought back to all those radio programs where I'd listened to Laura have conversations that sounded like two best friends chatting over a cup of healthy green tea, and I realized my interview sounded more like I was a murder suspect being questioned on *Law & Order: Criminal Intent* for murdering my own chances of getting on NPR.

This I Believe

Later, I got a second chance to do it right for NPR when they asked me to write an essay for "This I Believe," another feature of NPR's national news program, *All Things Considered*. This time I nailed it perfectly, because I did for that essay what I've been telling women to do for 29 years—relax.

By then I had a number of national radio and TV interviews behind me and had seen behind the wizard's curtain. Dark studios and spiderlike microphones no longer intimidated me.

I walked into that same radio studio with a different attitude. I stepped through the airlock and embraced that hanging microphone. After speaking with their recording engineer, I stood in front of the mic and gave a terrific reading. You can still hear it to this day if you want.[1] I talked about my childhood and how those experiences shaped my attitude toward life and business. I hit it out of the park because, this time, I was relaxed.

Relax and be yourself. I know this is sometimes easier said than done (like having a photographer tell you to smile for the 477th time).

---

[1] Milazzo, Vickie, "Stepping Out of Fear," NPR online, thisibelieve.org/essay/22873.

But this I believe: The more relaxed you are, the more relaxed everyone around you will be. And if you're alone trying to connect with your passionate vision, you're more likely to relax right into wicked success.

PRACTICE MENTALLY EVERYTHING YOU WANT TO ACCOMPLISH

To become wickedly successful, you must first see yourself as successful. Visualize the process of attainment, embellishing your imagination with sensory details. This practice is commonplace in sports and the performing arts.

Great performers such as Alicia Alonso and most stellar athletes practice in their heads even more than they do in the physical world. A basketball player mentally throws thousands of baskets, dancers mentally dance thousands of steps. The mind can withstand a rigor the joints cannot. This mental practice is as important to success as time spent actually playing or dancing.

I was going to attend a reception which I knew Richard Gere would also be attending. I could have planned to just hang in the background, ogling him from a distance. But how often does a woman get to be in the same room as Richard Gere? So for weeks in advance I practiced mentally what I wanted to accomplish.

I imagined walking up to him without tripping, talking without stuttering and starting a conversation without drooling in my wineglass. Vividly imagining how it was going to happen built the bridge to make it happen. Because I imagined it so vividly, I actually had a great conversation with the man that other women were admiring from afar. If you think it was easy for me, it wasn't. But that's the power of practicing mentally everything you want to accomplish.

When you do see it, it's okay if no one else does. When I started my business, some of my family and friends couldn't see the future I so clearly envisioned, and they were afraid for me. I got everything but the encouragement I was expecting—warnings, all the reasons not to do it. It was my vision. I had to see it, even if they couldn't.

Do you struggle against your own vision, exhausting yourself because approval is important? Are you living your vision, or another person's concept of what your vision should be?

We all know someone who succeeded that probably should have failed. We all know someone who failed yet should have succeeded. Why does one person succeed while another doesn't? The mind-success connection: Most successes are sown in the mind. What successes are you sowing? Most failures are sown in the mind. What failures are you sowing?

Envision your success over and over again—approaching, taking action, succeeding—playing a melody on your favorite instrument, getting that promotion, building a simple table or a flourishing business. You must see the change you want to be and where you want to go. It doesn't matter if nobody else sees it.

Even if you don't believe visualizing works, even if you believe only geniuses like Albert Einstein and performers like Alicia Alonso have such powerful imaginations, or you think it's too "out there" to be useful in everyday life, try visualizing anyway. It's totally free and there are no harmful side effects.

GET DOWN WITH BEETHOVEN

I'm a big advocate of brainstorming, and often some of the best ideas for Vickie Milazzo Institute (LegalNurse.com) come from brainstorming, both formally and informally. Staff at the Institute brainstorm in the hallway, in each other's offices, at each other's desks and even in the restrooms. The ideas are sparking and the atmosphere is almost incendiary. When we come together and engage in a conversation, we raise new questions and think of things at a level we would not have reached on our own. Collaboration is genius.

Nevertheless, some of my best ideas come to me not in the midst of a passionate brainstorm, but when no one else is around and I'm writing.

I confess, I write best alone—just me, Beethoven, my laptop or favorite pen, a legal pad and a stack of sticky notes for company. Even Tom knows to stay out of my way when the pages start flying. Sometimes, I even tune out Beethoven.

I love writing not only because it releases the creative energy that fuels ideas for my business, but because it also feeds my creativity, which in turn fuels my endurance, allowing me to create longer and produce more. Plus, I'm always careful to capture any random thoughts, even those that seem unrelated, so as to not lose them. (Note to self: Get bigger sticky notes!)

Sometimes a stray idea is pure gold. Other times it's only a sieve through which to mine the gold. And sometimes it's nothing more than fool's gold—but what have you lost beside the keystrokes or a sheet of paper? The idea may not even be ripe for the time, but by capturing it, you can hold it until the time is ripe. Nothing gets lost.

Even if you haven't had any training in writing, you can still write. Buy a journal or notepad. Clear a space, sit down and take a stab at writing an opinion; or write about a recent trip, a funny experience or your last day off. Better still, just write what's on your mind. You'll be amazed how new ideas for your life or career emerge even when you're not consciously thinking about such things.

Here's a tip: Put on your iPod and play the score from *Slumdog Millionaire*, or "La Vie en Rose," or Beethoven's 9th, and write away— write now. And watch your intuitive vision soar.

ACCELERATE ACHIEVEMENT WITH HYPNAGOGIC IMAGERY

Testing experts tell us that to better retain information we're struggling to learn, we should study it 30 minutes before bedtime. Our mind absorbs the information better when at rest.

How many times have you said, "I need to sleep on that"? While you may have meant that remark as a figure of speech, it actually helps to let your subconscious mind work on ideas, problems and decisions independently of your conscious mind. That state immediately preceding or following sleep is fertile ground for imagination.

To germinate ideas, envision a desired result as you're falling asleep. Incorporate images, sounds, smells, textures—whatever comes to mind—but avoid thinking and trying to impose logic. This will only keep you awake. Simply let your mind drift off after envisioning what you want to have happen. When you awaken, recapture that vision, along with any fluttering ideas that accompany it. As quickly as possible, jot down your thoughts for your conscious mind to ponder later.

I know a writer who plotted a short story using hypnogogic imagery. Her visions were so distinct and rapid, they kept waking her. To avoid losing them, she jotted down her thoughts, then lay back down to sleep. Minutes later, she woke again, envisioning the next twist. That went on for nearly an hour. The next morning, her paper was filled with scribbles, mere threads of ideas, but salient threads, which she quickly developed into a prize-winning story.

Why not put this powerful process to work for you? Try hypnogogic imagery tonight. You'll be astonished at the outcome.

SPEED UP TO BE MINDFUL

Tom jokes with me that I have two speeds—fast and off. It's true that I work fast and that I have an innate way of grasping a concept and moving forward with it. I can also switch back and forth between complex issues with a speed and mindfulness that baffles people around me. At the end of the day though, that speed catches up with me, and I switch to off, usually right after a glass of healthy red wine. During the day, I move like quicksilver and expect the same from my staff—the business world moves rapidly and we need to stay ahead of it.

I never cared for those self-help books that claim you must act slowly to be mindful. After all, most of us can't and don't live a Buddhist monk's life in this fast-paced world. During a trip to an ancient Buddhist monastery in Kyoto, Japan, it was the monks themselves who shattered the "mindfulness" myth perpetuated by many self-help authors. Buddhist monks are the epitome of mindfulness, and on this trip I observed them mindfully walking the grounds, ringing the prayer bell, meditating, sweeping or gardening, all in the slow and deliberate manner we associate with mindfulness. But to get to that mindful state, they must first wake and eat. That's where the myth gets shattered and where speed comes in.

Well before dawn, when the waking bell rings, the otherwise peaceful monastery becomes a beehive of frenzied activity. The monks rapidly roll off their pallets, "thump," fold and store their bedding then stream down the hall to the meal room, rice bowls in hand. There they pass wordlessly through the line, receive their food and shovel it into their mouths with a speed and intensity that makes a new mother's lunch look leisurely. The monks accomplish all of these tasks quickly, but at the same time, in a fully present and mindful state—despite the speed.

That day reinforced my belief that doing something quickly doesn't mean you have to abandon mindfulness when you do it. You can be fully present in every state and at every speed so long as you have the intention to be mindful.

Practice mindfulness at whatever speed is required, even if it's the speed of light. Start practicing speedy mindfulness today, and you'll join the wickedly successful women who've mastered moving at the speed of light.

LINK YOUR VISION TO YOUR PASSION

When your intuitive vision and your passion are richly connected, your decisions will lead you quickly to success. Connect your passion to your intuitive vision in three ways:

1. **Create an environment for success.** Match your vision to something you're good at. One of my passions is dance. I love dance in all of its variations—modern, ballet, jazz, tap and even interpretational movement. I admire the strength, athleticism and ability of dancers to contort their bodies into all kinds of impossible positions. If you've ever thought those male ballet dancers don't measure up to other testosterone-laden male athletes, just ask your husband to lift you over his head and dance across your living room. Tom is still recovering from that move.

   I took dance lessons after college, and I always thought it would be cool to be a dancer. But I'm just not that talented on my feet. I had to match my vision to what I could actually do. I could be passionate about dancing, but taking it to a professional level never would have happened. Time and energy wasted and a life of disappointment.

   When your intuitive vision matches your personal strengths, you're more likely to take the necessary action to make it happen and succeed. Have you created the environment for your wicked success? Are you doing what you're naturally good at?

2. **Give every success an encore.** You're already successful. As you venture into new success, don't forget your past successes and all you learned from them. What do you do today that's easy but was hard when you first attempted it?

   When your intuitive vision challenges you to grow or change, give your past successes an encore. Anytime you need a shot of courage, relive the applause and the good decisions. Get the visceral boost you need, then apply what you learned to your new vision. New challenges put you back in the limelight, and that place can be scary, but every time you encore a small success, the applause sets you on fire and the next success comes easier.

Success promotes success. The more you succeed, the more you will succeed.

3. **Your brain doesn't remember failure; neither should you.** In growing my business, I focused on my strengths and successes, not my weaknesses and mistakes. I could write the book on the mistakes I've personally made. Maybe you can too. Now though, there's hard evidence that it's our successes that have the most impact on the brain. If you do something the right way, the brain remembers how you did it.

In fact, the study suggests that failure has no impact on helping us to succeed. That's because if you do something wrong, the brain doesn't know how to process and store it (unless there's a strong negative association, such as pain, embarrassment or electrical shock). Since we typically absorb more from success than failure, this might explain why successful people learn more from their experiences and continue to succeed often, while people who fail learn less from experiences and continue to fail often.

Think about the people around you. We all know someone who keeps making the same mistakes—in love, at work or in business. It's because they're not learning from their failures. They fail to learn as they would from a success.

Keep succeeding and stay focused on your past successes. If your brain doesn't know how to process your failures, why should you bother to relive them? I say, you shouldn't.

BE READY WITH YOUR NEXT VISION

A writer friend spent several years accomplishing the big goal of becoming a published author. She followed her intuitive vision, and attributes her success to staying focused, believing in the vision and rehearsing mentally what she wanted to achieve physically to make it happen. When success came, she celebrated and jumped into her new lifestyle with both feet running. But she became so caught up in her success that when the glory and excitement waned, she realized she had no vision of what came next.

And what happened? Nothing came next. Yes, she published more novels, but she no longer had an audacious goal pulling at her. Her career leveled off, then began a downward slide. To start the process over again, she retrieved her deepest-held passions and summoned a new intuitive vision of her literary future. Now she continues to renew and extend her visions, anticipating success to follow success.

What's the next success you passionately want to achieve? Success is a journey. Always assume more success will come, and be ready with your next vision.

CAPTURE YOUR INTUITIVE
VISION WITH THE
5 PROMISES

PROMISE 1
I Will Live and Work a Passionate Life

Begin each day imagining in detail the place where your passionate vision will lead you. Describe that vision here.

_____

_____

_____

PROMISE 2
I Will Go for It or Reject It Outright

Write down five areas in your life you will unclutter to make time and space for living your passionate vision.

_____

_____

_____

PROMISE 3
I Will Take One Action Step a Day Toward My Passionate Vision

Assess where you are in reaching your passionate vision. Imagine taking the next step. Describe what you see.

_____

_____

_____

PROMISE 4
I Commit to Being a Success Student for Life

List three times you trusted your intuition and really went for it. What did you learn from those experiences? What signs told you that your intuition was or was not on track?

_____

_____

_____

PROMISE 5
I Believe as a Woman I Really Can Do Anything

Write down one success that came from trusting your intuitive vision. From that success create three affirming statements about yourself. Connect each one to a daily activity—showering, applying makeup. Declare your affirmations every time you engage in that activity.

_____

_____

_____

>> DOWNLOAD THE 5 PROMISES FOR INTUITIVE VISION AT **WickedSuccess.com**.

MAGGIE'S VISION

*Since I was a small girl I always had a plan, and I knew
I would follow my life on my own terms. I imagined from
the beginning what I wanted—a simple, fulfilling life
surrounded by art and beauty. Obviously, my imagination
drew the path and set the milestones for every step of the way:
where I wanted to be, how fast I wanted to get there and what
I was willing to sacrifice. Early on I knew that I wanted
to be an entrepreneur. I started drawing a map, a plan.
I understood that surrounding myself with people who
had integrity, intelligence and focus would help support my
goals. I made a personal commitment to learn everything
I could about achieving success at every level of my life.*

*I started with architecture as the main focus of my career.
I tried to expose myself to significant architectural and design
work, to help feed my passion and gain inspiration.*

*As it turned out, today I'm not an architect, but a graphic
designer. I'm not leading a team of architects or construction
workers, but a design team, which gives me other avenues
to explore in expressing my vision and helping my clients.
I come from a culture where the highest-level positions and
professional respect are reserved for men. My vision was not
to be limited by that reality but to exceed every expectation.
That is not to say it has been easy—I have always had to
work especially hard to prove myself academically and in the
workplace. I am the first woman in my family to pursue a
professional career. I set out to excel as a designer, problem solver*

and entrepreneur while balancing my responsibilities
as a daughter, sister, friend, wife and mother.

I've always had a hunger to grow as a person and to learn
more from others. I have sought out role models for every aspect
of my life. I try to understand what these people have done and
apply their wisdom to my intuitive vision. I want to get there
faster, stronger and better.

Maggie, 33
CO-OWNER, GRAPHIC DESIGN FIRM

Now that you know how awesome you can be when you capture your intuitive vision, let's explore the role engagement plays in achieving your desired future.

Far away there in the sunshine are my highest aspirations.
I may not reach them, but I can look up and see their beauty,
believe in them and try to follow where they lead.
LOUISA MAY ALCOTT

If you want something done, ask a woman.
MARGARET THATCHER

What you engage and focus on is where you will yield results.
VICKIE L. MILAZZO

3

ENGAGEMENT

Engage Commitment to Achieve Big Things

Women are tycoons of commitment. The average woman has more complex responsibilities than the crew of NASA's mission control, and handles every one of them. Forget Superman, Iron Man and Batman. I'll take Wonder-Working Woman any time. By nature, women are giving and nurturing, ready to engage the devil himself when loved ones are at risk. And this natural edge is a mighty force when we engage any challenge. Because we are tenaciously faithful to the commitments we undertake, possibilities stretch to infinity.

Yet not just any commitment will do. To achieve big, you have to engage big. Women who commit to a passionate vision reach the highest level of wicked success.

Our complex society of family, friends, career and spiritual and social obligations constantly pulls us in different directions. Social media adds yet another layer of complexity, and our always-on devices give us instant access to the world via email, texting and Skype, but they also give the world instant access to us. Opportunities to commit bombard us at every turn.

That's why every woman I know is fully committed, or ready to be committed—to a psychiatric unit. Are you exhausted all the time? Just reading Jackie's commitments is exhausting: "My husband is building refineries on the West Coast while I'm at home on the East Coast growing a business, raising five boys and managing a household. While he makes great money, he works, eats, sleeps and goes out with coworkers. I run a successful business; cook and clean; do homework, teacher conferences, laundry, bills, car pools, baths; read bedtime stories, say goodnight prayers, get everybody off to school and on and on . . ."

How does today's woman juggle family demands and society's expectations and still have a satisfying career without going insane? That's the million-dollar question.

My motto is: Women *can* do anything, not women *should* do everything. This is the greatest dilemma we're facing.

Your opportunities are boundless. Women can handle a lot, and if we're not careful we find ourselves doggedly committing our energy to every person or situation that demands our time. Everything becomes a priority. Before long we have no energy left. We become victims of "one day, some day, I'll get around to living my dreams, and in the meantime I'll help everyone else live theirs."

Similarly, we can be so overcommitted in one area of obligation that we overlook other important parts of our vision. In the early days of my business, my mind and hands busily engaged every detail. Even after hiring employees, I tried to handle my own work and still oversee the details of theirs. Overcommitment robbed me of some important social events with family and friends—birthdays, weddings, hanging out for no reason—but business boomed.

Engagement starts with choice. Choose the objective of your engagement with your passionate vision in mind.

As a CEO, I encourage my staff to engage fully on a big project, to switch their phones to voice mail and close their email. Sometimes they encourage my own engagement by covering my desk with projects that "need" my immediate involvement. At those times I joke that CEO means "Controlled Entirely by Others," smile, slide their stack to the credenza and get back on focus.

Passionately believing in the path you're on helps you narrow your commitments. By making judicious choices, you engage your day, your week and all the minutes that make up your life in pursuit of commitments that reflect the fire of your vision.

ENGAGE YOUR FEARS TO CONQUER THEM

Lady Jessica in Frank Herbert's novel *Dune* taught her son, "Fear is the mind killer." Fear is also the enemy of engagement. Even when we're passionately committed to an idea or a goal, fear can stop us cold. Fear comes in many guises—fear of failure, fear of looking silly and, most interesting of all, fear of wicked success.

We worry: How will my life change? Will I be consumed by my work? Will my family feel estranged by my success? Will other people like me less? What if I actually do succeed—what can I do for an encore?

As a child, I was afraid of everything: escalators, heights, flying New Orleans cockroaches the size of dinner plates. A near-drowning experience left me afraid of water—not a good thing in a city that lies below sea level. Then, if that wasn't enough, at the age of 8 I even became afraid of Halloween candy.

Normally on October 31, my twin brother and I would step out of our shotgun house and rush to every home within a three-block radius. Most of the homes were only a step or two off the ground. Easy pickings—a piece of candy so to speak. But that year, when we approached one of the bigger houses, a house known to have the best candy, but with 10 tall cement steps leading to the front door, my fear of heights stopped me cold. My twin brother was already up the stairs, knocking on the door and yelling, "Trick or treat," while I stood frozen at the bottom.

I told myself I might stumble in the dark and drop my bag of treats. I might crash to the concrete below. I might tear my homemade fairy costume. I wanted the candy, but there was no way I was going up those stairs to get it.

That year I learned that life's treats go to those who step out to take them. I lost more than candy. I lost my confidence.

The fear of stepping out took me along the safe, no-risk route through high school, nursing school and into a secure hospital job. Six years later, I woke up to a different kind of fear: the fear of becoming like so many other no-risk nurses—tired, burned out and old before their time. The fear of eating white cake and drinking watery punch at my own retirement party became real, and I faced a decision: Step out into the unknown or spend the rest of my life at the bottom of those childhood steps, never tasting the best candy.

I wanted to start my own business. At first, afraid to step out, I settled for reading business books instead. But I kept thinking of those retirement parties. They put my fear into a new perspective. Compared to that dismal future, how bad could stepping out be?

I wasn't just leaving a secure job and stepping out into my own business—I was stepping out to pioneer a totally new profession, legal nurse consulting. I had to sell an idea that had never been sold before. My retirement-party perspective helped me to acknowledge my fear, refuse to give it more power than it already had and step out to confront it head on.

Step Out to Expand Momentum

Stepping out in my career gave me the confidence to step out in other parts of my life. Although I overcame my fear of those childhood steps, I still get panicky at cliff-hanging heights and never really saw the point in skydiving. I never saw myself stepping out of an airplane unless I could plant my two feet firmly on an air-conditioned jetway. But when two fearless, thrill-seeking women from my company decided to skydive, I chose to engage my fear and join them. After all, wasn't I always the one advocating the virtues of risk taking?

Acknowledging fear is your first step in conquering it, and mine was no fabricated fear. In skydiving, terrible things can happen, including quadriplegia or death. A prerequisite video, guaranteed to scare off anyone easily intimidated, contained no fewer than five warnings about serious injury or death. A 10-page waiver was artfully drafted to scare the crap out of anyone who actually read it before signing. The week I was to jump I learned from one of my clients that her paraplegia resulted from a skydiving accident. All my fears crowded back to waylay my commitment.

Although I was terrified, I jumped anyway. But I had one goal and one goal only, and that was to step out. No fancy aerobatics—I wasn't even prepared to jump solo like the paralyzed woman had done. Yet to meet my goal of jumping tandem, I had to step out voluntarily. Being pushed out did not qualify. The 60-second free fall at 120 miles per hour was both scary and exhilarating—and simultaneously the longest and shortest minute of my life.

I would do it all over again for the delicious high of conquering fear. Who knows what great accomplishments that fear had undermined over the years?

Take Action to Deflate Fear

Fear can also commit you to the wrong people, wrong ideal or wrong decision. You participate in office gossip because you're afraid of being left out. I've put off severing business relationships with vendors, subcontractors and employees longer than I should have, worrying about replacing them. What if I couldn't find a replacement? What if a big project blew in and I couldn't finish it on time? In the end, the worry was for nothing. No one is indispensable, and recognizing that has helped me make better decisions about doing business with people I respect and who share my core values.

Uncertainty is the sister of fear, and adequate preparation banishes uncertainty. Even to jump tandem I needed instruction.

But the best cure for fear is action. I couldn't learn to skydive merely by hanging out at the jump zone watching a skydiving video, taking a class, watching someone else do it or reading a book. The only way to truly conquer this fear was to engage it. In skydiving, you're either jumping out of the plane or standing on the ground watching others free-fall. You never experience the thrill unless you step out. I had to step out.

Before stepping out, I interviewed my tandem master, Scott, to assess his skydiving credentials. My spirits lightened dramatically when I learned he had made 4,500 jumps and competed internationally. It felt especially auspicious to learn that his first skydiving experience was in the womb at six months gestation. He was clearly passionate about skydiving, and if I was going to entrust my life to someone, Scott was a good choice.

I owned up to my fear and was heartened further by Scott's encouragement. His best advice was, "You don't have to be perfect. Your only goal today is to have fun."

Adding fun to my goal seemed like a great idea. Beyond those two commitments—stepping out and having fun—I wasn't concerned about anything. Well, other than dying.

Rally a Support Team

Even a veteran skydiver never jumps without a certified rigger to pack her reserve chute. Like skydivers, smart women engage risk when backed by a trusted support team. Your team cheers you on, holds you accountable and provides a lifeline, ensuring that you will live through the experience to engage the next risk.

Scott supported me by sharing that one of his clients skydived for the first time on her 85th birthday, again on her 86th birthday and again on her 87th, at which time she declared she wasn't sure she could wait another year to do it again.

That encouraging message triumphed over an earlier discouraging message by one of my staffers who was not skydiving but had joined several others as spectators. She voiced her own fear with, "I can't believe you're really going to do this." When I playfully reminded her she was there to encourage me, not discourage me, she said, "I'm here to talk you out of it."

Knowing she was expressing her fear from a place of love and concern, and probably worried about her paycheck in the event I crashed head first into the jump shack, I appreciated that she cared, but I chose to discard her discouraging message.

When stepping out, we should enjoy the ride along the way. We spent a lot more time on the ground that day than we did in the air. The four-hour wait seemed eerily like both an eternity and a brief moment. I was glad I had a team to party with while waiting. They definitely took my mind off my fear.

Step Out to Fly High

Once they called our jump-load, everything happened quickly. I put on my jumpsuit, and Scott helped me into the harness. Stepping onto the plane, I forced my best fake-calm face as I eyed the side door that would become my in-flight exit.

After a dreadfully slow ride up to altitude, we leveled off at 14,000 feet, and the exit door was opened. The magnitude of my engagement became very real, very quickly. I put on my helmet and goggles. Scott snapped my harness securely to his. Suddenly, the jumpers before me were gone, and it was my turn to step out.

As Scott urged me toward the open door, I remembered the instructor's motto: "Once you're in the plane, 'no, no, no' means 'go, go, go.'" Not looking down, not thinking about what I was doing and still fully conscious, I stepped out of the plane into 14,000 feet of emptiness.

When my 60-second free fall ended and my parachute opened, the pace of the experience quickly changed from a gallop to stillness and quiet. Houston is not known for its natural beauty, but the sinking sun from my sky-high vantage point never seemed more beautiful. The most exhilarating feeling of all came when my feet hit the familiar ground. I'd done it! The champagne we all shared afterward was the sweetest I've ever tasted.

Living a passionate life is a lot like skydiving. You have to engage commitment and step out into a boundless and unpredictable future if you want to fly high. This is the joy of life—when no matter the outcome, you still step out.

Two women, Sandra and Jill, engaged their career fears entirely differently. Sandra shares:

> I went after my passion for freedom when I got tired of working for a company that wanted my soul, with little to give back in return. I had been working on my business part time. Now I decided to face my fears and plunge myself into it all the way. I have been rewarded 10 times over with freedom in my life, double my previous income, professional growth and the knowledge that I make a difference. So excuses and fear be gone!

Jill, like Sandra, had been considering a career change—for three years. When I asked what was holding her back, she told me flat out that it was fear. With more than 20 years of hard-won experience, she was afraid to make a move that would affect her positively or negatively, because either meant stepping into the unknown. To Jill, and to any woman afraid to step out, it helps to redefine success.

Wicked success is not about the achievement. It's about marching boldly into the venture. It's about choosing action over caution. Every time I step out into the unknown, win or lose, I succeed. I might break a leg or invest in a losing business idea, but I won't end up at my 90th birthday party with nothing more than stale white cake and regrets. Sure, bad things can happen when we step out, but I believe worse things happen to our souls when we don't.

DITCH PERFECTIONISM

In healthcare, perfectionism is not only rewarded, it's expected. This is one part of life where "good enough" isn't good enough. A nurse makes a mistake and someone can die. I'm sure mistakes don't win any points with your boss either. But do our toilets have to be so immaculate and our lawns so manicured?

Misguided perfectionism can keep you from stepping out and going for what you want. Perfectionism can also rob you of the enjoyment of experiences. Distinguishing what does and doesn't require perfection is the hallmark of wickedly successful women.

I'm surrounded by perfectionists (lots of Virgos) at my company, and even I sometimes suffer from the perfectionism obsession. Ten drafts of a document are not uncommon.

Improvements are valuable up to a point and then they actually have the reverse effect. They keep you from moving forward to your next Big Thing. Ask, "How much is enough? If I perfect this project any more, will I get more clients and more repeat business? Will the client or anyone important even notice?"

For the perfectionist, the answer will always be, "Yes! Of course it will!" More likely, the real answer is no.

Big Things have big payouts. You never want to deliver faulty work product, but endlessly perfecting the tiniest details is simply wasteful. Move on to something big.

And don't expect perfection from everyone around you. With 23 employees, and each of us making mistakes, I feel lucky to keep the lights on and the business running. But after the crying is over, I find it's best to have a good laugh and accept the imperfections.

Embrace Imperfection as a Wicked Growth Opportunity

Step out, try new things and expect carefully laid plans to go awry. When your best efforts fail, look upon the experience to find tools for growth. If you never tried anything new, you would certainly make fewer mistakes, and fewer things would go wrong, but would you ever accomplish anything worth remembering?

If 50 percent of your ideas succeed, you're better than the average major league baseball player, who generally bats around .260, less than a one-in-three success rate. Sheryl Swoopes, known as the "female Michael Jordon," three-time Olympic gold medalist and three-time WNBA Most Valuable Player, doesn't sink every shot. Even Rachael Ray cooks up a dish that falls flat. Wickedly successful women achieve success through the mistakes they make along the way. Embrace the value and power of imperfection and failures.

As an example, after presenting successful one-day seminars, I decided to expand the seminars to three days. I booked hotels, revised the curriculum and invested in promotion, but I failed to get a profitable response.

Panic might have led to canceling the whole idea. Instead, I restrategized and expanded the seminar to six days with certification, which is what the market really needed.

I tripled the price, mailed out new promotional brochures and the new strategy exploded into wicked success. Without the mistake of trying a three-day seminar, would I ever have stepped up to the certification program that is now the bedrock of my entire business?

If you don't get the perfect job, or your boss doesn't give you perfectly glowing reviews or you don't perfectly understand that new software package, don't give up. These are perfect opportunities to grow and learn.

Perfect the Joy of Imperfection

Don't let perfectionism rob you of enjoyment. When I made the ultimate commitment to get married, my friend Beth, told me "Vickie, your wedding day will not be perfect. Something will go wrong. Don't let it get in the way of enjoying your special day."

She was way off. Not just one wrong thing happened, but lots. Our favorite minister was out of town. The replacement minister announced the wrong friend to give a reading, and she gave me her "What's up with that?" look. We arranged the reception on the top floor of a downtown Houston skyscraper, where my stepmother, who was afraid of elevators, wouldn't go and she gave me her icy "You don't want me there, do you?" look. I realized it was a bad idea to have invited my ex-fiancée when he stole a pair of my underwear and wore them on his head like a hat during the reception. Until he ran into his wife. Then she gave me her . . . well, you can imagine how she looked at me—and I had nothing to do with it! Even worse, the underwear wasn't from Victoria's Secret, but my stretched-out cotton briefs—the kind you wear *after* the honeymoon.

On another occasion, while dining with two important attorney-clients at an Italian restaurant, I was embarrassed to discover I had splashed spaghetti sauce all over my suit (sleeves, front of the jacket, everywhere). The top partner laughed and said, "You're one of us now. We never eat spaghetti without getting it all over our neckties."

Realizing that even my "perfect" clients experienced "imperfect" moments took the edge off my chagrin. Sure, in court they were perfect, but in other parts of their lives they were willing to ditch perfectionism a little (or a lot, depending on the sauce).

Today those imperfect moments are fun memories. How often have you let minor screwups rob you of the enjoyment of an experience? Think back to a situation that went so wrong you wanted to cry. Is that outcome so important to you today? Time and distance are wonderful at devolving moments of great calamity into insignificance and fun memories. Those things that went wrong at our wedding, and the spaghetti sauce—they're the memories I still laugh at.

Nothing in life is ever perfect. When we demand perfection, we rob ourselves of the pleasures of life. I try to remember this when I'm in the middle of something that has gone badly wrong.

Lighten up! Relax and ditch perfectionism. Take a breath and reach for a glass of wine to go with that sloppy spaghetti. Don't wait for the perfect moment. It's already here.

BREAK THE FEEL-GOOD ADDICTION

How does a busy woman cope with the mounting demands and pressures of achieving her passionate vision while, all around her, life intrudes? In today's world, you're constantly sabotaged by nonproductive energy-wasters. Wicked success will not wait for you to finish the dishes, or finish that already well-written report, or finish voting for your favorite on *Dancing with the Stars*.

Because we like to feel good, many of us gravitate toward what's easy instead of what's productive. I call this the feel-good addiction. We are addicted to majoring in minor accomplishments, niggling away our time, surfing the Internet, watching TV, hanging out on Facebook, losing ourselves in FarmVille or Angry Birds.

As I write this chapter, my garden is suffering from the devastation of our winter freezes. I desperately want to share my woes with my thousands of friends on Facebook. I know they'll understand, and it will feel good to read their empathic messages. Then there's the email stacking up in my box.

Even if you like to be productive, you can be addicted to straightening, organizing and reorganizing. The feel-good addiction is insidious for those who like to check things off, because you feel good after completing each small task. This addiction to check marks comes at a high price and bites you on the butt because that cheap check-mark high guarantees to frustrate, overwhelm and stress you out in the long term. You feel busier than ever, but are accomplishing less of real value.

The feel-good addiction begins with the way you start your day. "I'll knock this out quickly and strike it off my checklist." Or "I can't start my day until I empty my email box."

Is this feel-good start to your day the best use of your time? You'll be tempted to knock out each item that clamors for your attention. After all, it only takes two minutes to fire off an email or return that unimportant phone call. Since you're not yet feeling the day's time constraints, these trivia steal more attention than they deserve. Two minutes turns into 20 as one item leads to another.

Even if you set them aside, once you put your attention to them, these small tasks buzz around in your head and have the potential to distract you for hours. A colleague misquoted you in an email to your boss, or you need to locate receipts for your expense report. Although you defer action until later, the issue now agitates until you get it out of the way. Distraction diffuses your focus on important matters. Put small tasks out of sight and out of mind until the designated time to deal with them.

About the time you've completed your feel-good tasks and are ready to start in on your real work, your colleagues have completed their feel-good tasks, and they're ready to start interrupting you from the Big Things you're ready to do; or a client calls with the latest crisis. Before you know it, quitting time arrives and you haven't accomplished a single step toward your Big Thing. You'll start asking how you can be so busy yet accomplish so little of importance. Too often our important tasks fall prey to the feel-good addictions of easy ones. By majoring in minor things we never get to our big commitments.

Breaking the feel-good addiction opens the door to achievement. Start by asking yourself, Is this feel-good start to my day the best use of my time? or Are these feel-good tasks best reserved for mental breaks throughout the day?

I too am a happy checker-off-er. Working for two hours on a huge project I won't finish doesn't release the same amount of endorphins as cleaning out my email box. After two hours I need to get something checked off. That's when I indulge my own feel-good addiction and attack the stack of bills, plow into the financials or grab my mouse to viciously click through my email.

We already have precious little free time. Work expands to fill the time available, so we need to make the most of the time we have and not niggle it away.

What you engage and focus on is where you will yield results. Small accomplishments reap small results, and trivia saps the creative energy you need for accomplishing your audacious goals. When you stop engaging the fire of your passionate vision, you lose desire and motivation. The less important your accomplishments, the less important you feel. You start to believe you're not cut out to achieve the future you've imagined.

What feel-good addiction will you quit to achieve your next Big Thing?

ENGAGE ONE BIG THING AT A TIME

Engaging Big Things guarantees a different addiction—an addiction to momentum, which promises a far more lasting high than the transitory feel-good of checking off trivial tasks. Identify three Big Things that connect to your passionate vision, then choose one to schedule your day around. Start strong and you'll experience genuine elation from achieving real goals and solving real problems.

Once you're engaged in accomplishing Big Things, you'll approach routine matters with laser-sharp focus, quickly deleting and delegating and experiencing fewer distractions.

More important, your creativity and productivity catch fire and the momentum keeps you pumped. You'll glide through your day full of confidence and satisfaction from achieving significant milestones.

Engage Momentum in 12 Easy Steps

1. **Define three Big Things.** Your vision might be to get promoted, live by the ocean or achieve financial security. A Big Thing might be to take on a high-profile work project, locate and buy a property or develop a household budget. Set a target date for completing your three Big Things.

2. **Challenge your engagement.** Ask: "Am I really going for it all the way?" Or, "If it's too tough, will I quit?" Make sure it's the right engagement for you at this time.

3. **Turn cyberspace off.** There's no greater blow to productivity than breaking your concentration to reply to an email as soon as it hits your inbox. It's not a contest and there's no reward for being the fastest responder. If you're doing nothing but responding to email, you're bouncing around like a pinball.

   And remember, the purpose of email is not to generate more email. Unless a response is necessary, go ahead, let the other person have the last word. I'm not saying that email isn't important, but if you can't bring yourself to close your email box, at least turn off the sound alert and pop-ups so you won't have the annoying "ping" sound and flash notification every time a potential time-waster drops out of cyberspace and into your mental space.

   Use your triage skills like an ER nurse would. Don't start the surgery unless the patient is critical. Email doesn't bleed out, doesn't need defibrillation and, unlike a critically ill patient, won't expire if not tended to immediately.

4. **Turn off the TV to turn on your engagement.** I've got a confession to make. I'm not hooked on *American Idol*. I don't know who's been fired or not, and I've never watched any version of *CSI*, *NCIS* or *EIEIO*.

I will also confess there are a couple of exceptions. I set aside as sacrosanct an evening each for the Grammys, Golden Globes, Tony Awards, Super Bowl (for Tom) and the Academy Awards. Don't text me on those nights; I won't respond unless we're watching the same show. The other 360 days of the year, my TV is off. My Google homepage tells me the news headlines. If the world were coming to an end, my executive team would notify me and ask me to close the office early so the employees could go home and prepare for the Rapture.

On the other extreme, I know women who live and die by their TVs. Between *The Office* or *Desperate Housewives* and endless hours of anything Kardashian, they eat, sleep and work. I understand the need to let your mind coast and let your body relax. I just think a good movie, the jacuzzi, quiet time and a glass of a great red wine restore in a way TV cannot.

Every hour you sit in front of a television you're accomplishing nothing. Each of those hours is irretrievably lost. If you're struggling to let go of this feel-good addiction, start by turning your TV off one day or one hour a week. Put that time into your Big Thing. See what you'll reap from that time. You'll never again say, "I'm too busy to . . ."

If you dare to fully realize the phenomenal power of TV banishment, take a week off. I hear you gasping from withdrawal pains, and I warn you, this powerful practice is not for everyone; it's only for women determined to take back their time and make something wickedly powerful happen.

5. **Tame the social media beast.** We all love social media. For example, I use Facebook to communicate with friends, clients and prospects. I truly enjoy reading details of their lives and seeing the fun photos they post.

There's actually a scientific reason that social media feels good. Informal research is demonstrating that the rush you feel when a social media friend or business associate posts on your wall, comments on or likes your status or tags you in a photo seems more likely than not to result from a release of the hormone oxytocin (the so-called cuddle chemical). This hormone is released into our systems when we connect or experience intimacy with another person, and we feel increased levels of trust, contentment and affection. Your brain processes the electronic connection the same as an in-person connection. That's one reason social media is so addictive—it's like experiencing human hugs all day long. Now that you understand why you like it, it's time to tame the beast.

Social media can quickly move from a social communication to an obsessive-compulsive disorder. You can get caught up in all of the things to do there—the games and other ancillary applications. That's my big issue with social media. Let's face it, clicking your mouse to get points to build a hen house for your farm or sending someone virtual hugs, flowers or groceries seems like a crazy waste of time. Does "I got a new llama for my herd today" really sound better to you than "I made three sales calls on new clients"?

The way you unwind is certainly your personal choice, but while relaxation has a beginning and an end, the demands of a "virtual farm" never will.

Wickedly successful women living in the real world avoid those meaningless feel-good addictions. We spend our time growing our lives and careers, not fertilizing our virtual fields. We measure our lives in seconds, not just hours and days. Thirty seconds here and there add up.

Social media is a great thing. It's changing the way we connect and communicate. Just make sure you're using it to advance relationships and meaningful engagement.

6. **Set aside sacred "momentum time."** Most people claim to cherish their "quiet" time, but be honest: Do you create the space for momentum time? Momentum time is the only way you can stop being a slave to petty distractions. This is what gives us our biggest gains. First thing each week, schedule a substantial chunk of uninterrupted time (aim for two hours) for projects that support at least one of your Big Things. To carve out time, examine every activity and decide how to eliminate it, delegate it, hire it out or do it faster.

If part of your day is rarely interrupted (such as early morning or late evening), reserve it for momentum time. You'll finish that huge project that seemed impossible, or wrestle that new training program into comprehension, three times faster. My favorite momentum time is early morning, before my office opens, when I can knock out Big Things three times faster. I make time for my cup of healthy green tea and a workout but still use some of that time to accomplish the Big Thing. It does mean getting up early, but I'd rather reward myself with a morning under my control than sleep later and spend my day under everyone else's control.

My office opens at 8:00 a.m. Often by 7:50 there's a line of penitents forming outside my door; employees asking for my input on projects, directors telling me why they won't meet a deadline and the janitor asking me to diagnose a toenail fungus. Knowing this madness is coming, I use my quiet momentum time to hunker down and work on those projects that need the most concentration.

Keep your momentum time sacred. Use phrases such as, "I'll be available in one hour. What time after that works best?"

If you get distracted, even briefly, commit to stopping the distraction. While writing this section, I'm certain emails are flooding in, but I won't know until I switch myself into email mode and start responding. I'm in writing mode, which means all those other distractions will need to wait until this job is complete. If the office is on fire, I'm pretty certain at least one staffer will want to save me. If the company website is down, the staff knows better than I do how to get it back up.

Poor work habits won't change overnight. As with exercise, what's difficult at first becomes easy. The more progress you see, the more addicted you'll become to momentum.

Start your day with a two-hour uninterrupted chunk, then gradually add more two-hour momentum sessions each day. Claim your momentum time and you'll find those lost hours you've been looking for. Start strong and you'll finish strong.

7. **Interrupt the interrupters.** We have enough policies and procedures at my company to fill an electronic employee manual to overflowing. One of my favorites is the Institute's "Interruptions" policy. This simple practice sets up a hierarchy of reasons and times when a person working on "drive-by" (as we call a closed door) can be interrupted. The intention is to give everyone the space and time we

need to do that Big Thing uninterrupted. Of course, this policy is routinely and enthusiastically ignored.

Like any other woman, whether you're working at home with family around you, in an office with colleagues or camped out in a Starbucks with your laptop, I can guarantee you'll be interrupted. Statistically, you're interrupted every seven minutes in the workplace. I personally think there's a secret alarm or flashing blue light that goes off the moment I shut my office door to focus. It seems to be a shout-out for people to start lining up to interrupt and ask me questions, ranging from the important ("Please approve the advertising budget.") to the mundane ("Can I leave early on Friday?") to the ones that are so goofy I won't even mention them.

I handle interruptions pretty easily—I'm sure it's a result of my nursing experience. Nurses must handle interruptions with grace and aplomb and still keep cool. Plus, I know that by letting someone interrupt me, they can get the answer they need and get on with their work, which keeps them productive.

But other than all those outsiders, there's one person who is responsible for interrupting the work you're doing and keeping you from getting to your Big Thing. That one person is probably responsible for more interruptions than anyone else in your home or office. Who is the responsible party? That's right—you.

Today we're bombarded by a plethora of interruptions that we invite into our mental space—email pop-up notifications, Facebook postings, text messages, Twitter streams and blinking message lights.

It's more important than ever to work with focus and a consciousness about whether you're on or off focus. If you can interrupt the interrupter, you'll get a whole lot more done.

8. **Alternate momentum time with "weed pulling."** Miscellaneous routine tasks are like weeds in your garden; we all have them, and no matter how often we get rid of them, they never go away. Yet they do have to be handled, and pulling a few weeds can provide a restorative break from more intensive work. Categorize tasks into Big Things or weeds. After each momentum session, devote 15 to 30 minutes to weed pulling—handling email, phone calls or other minor tasks.

Don't try to tackle all your weeds at once. Prioritize. Set aside a three-hour block periodically to do the deep weeding and organizing. Deep cleaning is cathartic.

If you need a five-minute break from your Big Thing, don't tackle the weeds. They will only distract. Use those five minutes to refresh your energy with a stretch or bit of nourishment, raw nuts or a cup of healthy green tea.

Finally, Facebook and other social media used improperly aren't weeds. They're time-sinks. You may decide to hop onto Facebook and just spend a minute, but then 15 minutes evaporate.

9. **Focus on one Big Thing at a time.** When you engage in too much at once, you risk finishing nothing. Finish your first Big Thing, or at least reach a significant milestone before embarking on the next. I have difficulty following my own advice on this, and do have to tame the beast of "too many good ideas." Engage one Big Thing then the next and the next.

10. **Use technology to your advantage.** I love my iPhone; it's with me everywhere I go. It saves time. When I travel, I can get my email done before I pick my luggage off the conveyer belt. By the time I hit the hotel I'm ready to accomplish Big Things—the reasons I traveled to begin with. Likewise, I know when to turn it off. If I'm at a friend's house, I turn it off. If I'm speaking to a group, I turn it off. I used to find a hiding place to check my email, Facebook and text messages during a speaking break, but I enjoy speaking more when I focus on the audience, and they deserve my full attention.

I also love the variety of iPhone apps available. One of my favorite productivity apps is Dragon Dictation. If you've ever had a eureka thought but no paper to write it down, you'll love it too. No matter where you are, the app allows you to dictate your ideas, save them, edit them and email them to yourself or some other lucky recipient. You'll never again have to worry about reading your scribbled handwriting or decoding the cocktail napkin notes from the two-martini lunch with your favorite client.

11. **Let go of bad ideas.** Successful women can be successful at many things, so it is tempting to go after all kinds of ideas, even ones that are not so great.

When we decided to update our training curriculums for our online and live programs, we put extensive time into customizing the material to each format. Midway we realized we were creating two monsters. Every future revision meant double work. It still breaks my heart to think of the hours that went into this before we wised up and created one curriculum that works for both.

That's an example of a "great" idea that wasn't so great after all. No matter how much it hurt, we had to let it go. When a "great idea" isn't so great after all, let it go. This frees you to work on the next genuine Big Thing.

12. Safeguard your momentum. Accept that you won't please everyone. Someone is bound to be unhappy about the changes you make to focus on your Big Things. A friend gets upset because you stop meeting for lunch on Wednesdays. Your spouse complains because you won't run his errands on a weekday. They'll get over it. Stop feeling guilty and stay true to your goals. Surround yourself with friends, family and peers who support your vision. Discard all discouraging messages. This is your engagement, not anyone else's.

There's more to feeling good than feeling the feel-good addiction. The more Big Things you do, the more you'll do! Engage momentum. You can have time in your life and still have the time of your life. Make your Big Thing the Big Thing for today.

What's your next Big Thing?

GET WHACKED LIKE A BUDDHIST

Imagine yourself sitting in a Japanese-style kneeling position on a hard wooden bench in an 800-year-old Buddhist temple in Kyoto, Japan, trying to empty your mind in a breathing, open-eyed meditation. Your eyes are focused in the middle distance, seeing all and seeing nothing. The soft smell of pine and burning incense fills the air, and all around is quiet.

At that almost perfect moment only one thing stands between you and *satori*, perfect enlightenment—well two, if you count the prickly feeling of your legs falling asleep. That one thing is a smiling, bald monk in a dark brown robe standing in front of you wielding a three-foot-long stick over his head. His benign smile doesn't fool you, because it belies the fact that he is about to whack you with the stick.

Let me start at the beginning. I've always felt I was pretty good with focus. After all, I worked as a nurse in critical care. Nurses are used to working in an environment where the world around us is going haywire—people running left and right, procedures being done, orders being given (or shouted)—where lives hang in the balance while we concentrate on the task at hand. We intubate, defibrillate and resuscitate without a second thought. Total focus!

How about you? Are you really focused, or do you sometimes sleepwalk through engagement? While in an important meeting you make a note to yourself to pick up diapers for the baby, or construct your Saturday honey-do list. In the first meeting you ever attended, you were totally focused on every word, and probably apologized if you sneezed. Then maybe you moved from doing your job with focus to doing it subconsciously, maybe even unconsciously.

Can we truly focus while the past and future intrude upon our thoughts? Are we fully present or merely idling through the motions while our minds traipse away to other thoughts? Are we giving our families, spouses, bosses and clients the benefit of our full attention, or are we cheating them of our wholehearted engagement?

Back to Japan: I had come to this ancient Zen Buddhist temple in Kyoto for expert advice, to sharpen my ability to focus. The purpose of meditating with open eyes was to allow the Roshi, or senior monk, to look in the eyes of his students as he walked the room, to see who was focused and who was sleeping or daydreaming.

Now, for me, there's a short distance between meditating and napping. I also find myself following thoughts down rabbit holes instead of discarding or ignoring them when I meditate, so I was anxious for some instruction from a master. This exercise was designed to train us to stay grounded in the present.

My husband Tom and I, along with a visiting monk from another temple, sat in audience while the Roshi talked about meditation techniques. He was funny and self-deprecating, and I immediately liked him. During breathing meditation, he explained, we would observe our thoughts from outside, like watching a river. We were to count our breaths in and out. Our goal was to reach 10 breaths without having a thought other than the count. If a random (or purposeful) thought intruded, we were to recognize it and start over at one. I asked the visiting monk next to me if he ever made it all the way to 10. He nodded. "Of course, many times. Once your mind is clear it is quite simple."

The Roshi explained that to start the *zazen* session he would light an incense stick and strike a small gong. Then we'd meditate for the period of time it would take for the stick to burn through. Afterward, he'd strike the gong again, to remind us to return to the present. We settled in and I was ready to leap into the meditation. I heard him strike the match and ring the gong, and there I went, my eyes focused in the empty space halfway to the large seated Buddha figure in the front of the room. Like everything I do, I was "all in."

One breath, in and out; so far so good. Two breaths, in and out; going well. Three breaths, in and—was that Tom rustling around? Darn. One, in and out. Two, in . . . and so on. When the gong finally rang I'd never gotten past a count of four. The Roshi told me that was excellent for the first time. The visiting monk flashed me a quick smile, so I knew he'd probably gotten to 10 effortlessly.

The Roshi then asked if we'd like to do it for real. "For real?" I asked. "Wasn't that for real?" "No," he clarified. "It is easy to focus when you are alone with your thoughts in a temple such as this. But when there are outside influences present, it is not so easy."

This is when the three-foot-long willow pole appeared. He pulled it out and explained that during the next meditation he would walk around the room observing each student as we meditated. If he felt that our focus was wandering, he would stop in front of us. At that point, we were to bow and thank him. Then he would strike us on each shoulder to remind us to focus.

This is the goofiest thing I've ever heard of, I thought. How can getting whacked help you focus? I asked the visiting monk if it hurt. "That depends on you," he said, then winked and added, "Whacking does help one to clear the mind . . . after it stops stinging." Great, I thought. Too bad this guy's not old and frail. I just hope he's not trigger-happy.

Then came the test. Ever ready for a challenge, and buoyed by my past success of four breaths, I was prepared. I heard the match strike, followed by the sound of the gong. I brought my focus to center. One breath, in and out. Two breaths, in and out. In the corner of my vision appeared a bald, five-foot-six man in gray robes and slippers tiptoeing around the room and brandishing a stick like a baseball bat. Alex Rodriguez in his pinstriped Yankee's uniform holding a Louisville Slugger would have been less obvious.

The Roshi slowly crossed my field of vision, moving left to right in front of us. My eyes stayed centered and unfocused. One breath, in and out. Two breaths, in and out. Three—is that Tom giggling? Is that me giggling? I struggled to stifle myself, but it was like laughing in church with my twin, Vince, back when we were 5, only this time instead of a nun with a ruler there stood a monk with a great overhand swing waiting for me.

One breath, in and out. Back in control. Suddenly I glimpsed a movement to my right and sensed the monk next to me, bowing. Then WHACK! a pause and WHACK! followed by silence. The monk beside me had obviously failed in his focus. I tensed and wasn't present-focused either; my thoughts strayed to the future and whether I was next to be whacked. The visiting monk's failure at reaching serenity was affecting my own attempts. One breath, in and out. The Roshi passed by me moving to the left. One breath, in and out, again. Two breaths, in and out. Focus inside, focus inside.

I sensed movement to my left, then WHACK! It had to be Tom's left shoulder—seemed even louder than before. Was that a whimper? WHACK! Tom's right shoulder. Suddenly I was fully focused, not inside as I should be, but on the future. I was thinking "I'm so out of here. I am not staying around for this."

My awareness immediately snapped to the present and there he was: the Roshi and his stick. Talk about fight or flight. I couldn't very well punch a man whose life was dedicated to peace and nonviolence. Flight wasn't an option either—after all, I'd come here specifically to learn how to meditate. It wouldn't do to kick him in the shins and run screaming out of the temple with a horde of angry monks (like a bad chopsocky movie) chasing me to the nearest Starbucks for a calming cup of healthy green tea.

I remembered I was expected to bring my hands up and bow to the Roshi, in thanks for two things: first, for bringing to my attention the fact that I wasn't focused, and second, for the reminder to focus more thoughtfully. I bowed my head and then my body to the inevitable.

WHACK! It stung like the dickens. WHACK! Okay, okay, it only stung for a minute.

I bowed again to the Roshi and resumed my open-eyed meditation. It was easy to find the middle distance when my eyes were full of water. One breath, in and out. Two breaths, in and out.

Pema Chödrön teaches, pain is inevitable; it is suffering that's optional. The pain of the stick came and went. Sure, I could have focused on the past and held a grudge. Or I could have focused on the future and worried about whether the Roshi would have time to circle the room again before that darn incense stick burned out. That's the optional suffering, the wandering around in the wilderness of our thoughts. Instead, I focused on the present. Where I was and what I was supposed to be doing: meditating. I was learning a simple lesson taught the same way for hundreds of years.

Focus is important in our communications, too. After listening to a woman I was mentoring ramble aimlessly for three minutes, I politely stopped her: "I would really like to help you solve your issue, but would you please describe the issue?" After a few more attempts, still rambling, and more nudging by me to focus, she finally got to the heart of the matter and we dealt with it easily and swiftly.

As we were about to wrap up, she confessed that she still found it uncomfortable and often unsuccessful to talk to prospective clients. I knew the source of her problem. I had just lived it! It was her rambling method of communication.

People who know me, know that I tell it like it is. Businesspeople are crazy busy. They're working for a living. They're not like patients who lie around in bed with lots of time to spare, waiting for the next visit from their favorite nurse, happy for any company other than a bad reality show.

Focus is one of the essential keys to successfully communicating. Whether you're talking to your boss or a prospective client, you have to focus, focus and focus more. You cannot go into an interview or meeting unprepared or misdirected. Once you lose that person, you lose the opportunity.

When things are blowing up around you, you may need to give yourself a whacking to get it under control. Think back to that monk and remember to keep your focus in the present. Focus on what you can do now and on what you are doing now. Whether you are alone or with someone else, whack all distractions aside. By keeping your thoughts on what you can do now—not what you might do, hope to do or didn't do—you'll be the calm in the center of any storm.

I'm not sure how long I'll retain this precious gift. But as long as I'm here in the present, I'm going to put my all into being here, so l can engage big.

ENGAGE IN WHAT'S RIGHT, NOT WHAT'S EASY

If we only did what's easy, we'd still be riding tricycles. Despite your passion and belief in the path you've chosen, not everything you engage in will come easily, especially when it comes to doing what is right at that moment. Many assume the most successful and happiest people have had the easiest lives. Nothing could be further from the truth.

We rarely fully know another woman's story. But after connecting with many wickedly successful women and learning parts of their stories, I know for certain that wicked success has nothing to do with easy. I've mentored every type of woman, from women with cancer to mothers with autistic children or with sole custody and financial responsibility for their children, and you'd never know by looking at them. Wickedly successful women merely do what less successful women are not willing to do.

Yvonne worked as an executive, went back to school at night to complete a degree, and still participated actively in family life with her husband, 6-year-old son (his school events and sports), plus their extended family. It's nothing for 100 people to show up at her birthday party. How did she do it all? She wanted that degree bad enough to persevere. Sometimes you sacrifice things you don't want to sacrifice. For Yvonne, it paid off.

With only 23 employees at my company, and working as closely as we do, it's impossible not to develop friendships. I prefer working with competent people whom I also like, but this makes being a boss particularly tough when employee issues arise.

The first time I had to fire an employee, I agonized over it. For support and advice I called Mary Ann, another business owner. She said, "Vickie, you know you have to do it. I promise that one day you won't even remember that person's name. Just do it."

It sounds harsh now, but the way she phrased it got through to me. No matter how much I dreaded firing a person I'd grown to care about, it was the right thing. The next day I terminated her. That night, in bed with Tom and a glass of wine, I cried and laughed about how tough it was, but it was done. The nudge from my friend helped me do what was right, not what was easy.

Buck Up at Camp Buck-Up

I never hire a girl to do a woman's job. Women who expect their lives and careers to be easy just need to buck up. That's why I'm thinking about starting a new camp and calling it Camp Buck-Up. This camp will be for any woman out there who needs to be told to "buck up" on a regular basis. This includes more than just the people who continually forget their responsibilities ("Why are the laryngoscope batteries dead?"), the whiners ("You really want me to make those copies for you?"), and the complainers ("This is the second time this year I've had to work on a Saturday.").

What's the point of this camp? It's to get people to do their jobs, without complaining. I'm sure you all know a couple of candidates for Camp Buck-Up. I can think of several already. And to tell the truth, I need the occasional visit to Camp Buck-Up myself.

At Camp Buck-Up, we'll start each day with healthy green tea, followed by PE drills, such as shouldering and carrying a heavy load of responsibilities, pulling your own weight in meetings, running an obstacle course of objections while juggling a complex project and climbing a wall of disasters, all without complaining. Easy activities like fire-walking are for those feel-good camps—not Camp Buck-Up.

Everyone will spend the week without gossiping or complaining about anything or anybody. It's easier to moan and groan than it is to put our noses to the grindstone. But we'll straighten that out. Anyone heard gossiping or complaining will get a second week at Camp Buck-Up, at no additional charge.

I'm even thinking of creating my own line of camp T-shirts, with catchy phrases like: "Lead, follow, or get out of the way!" "We were all born crying—time for you to outgrow it." And, "Whining and complaining are not competitive sports."

At Camp Buck-Up, everyone will have at least one good belly laugh a day, and it won't be from schadenfreude; it'll be from the genuine pleasure of having fun working and laughing together.

We'll close each day with a sundowner of healthy red wine, thanking our lucky stars we're at Camp Buck-Up.

I haven't started mandatory Camp Buck-Up for my employees yet, but I'm thinking about it. I've already filled the guest list for my first Camp Buck-Up with people I think need it most. If you want to sign up, I'll be happy to put you on the waiting list; just let me know.

ENGAGE THE DETAILS

So often I'll hear someone ask, "Why is that woman successful? I'm just as talented, skilled, and inventive as she is, so why not me?"

Reality check: The vision is the easy part. The fun often lies in dreaming the dream, fleshing out the vision in your mind. Then come the late nights, early mornings and working weekends, getting your hands dirty with the details. That's when the casually engaged fall slack while the tenaciously persistent grab the prize and run.

Dreaming about my new business was easy. Engaging the thousand details to convert that vision into reality was tough. How many good ideas never get off the drawing board? Wicked success doesn't materialize from nothing, even when fueled by passionate vision. Wickedly successful women aren't focused on the rewards of success; they focus on engaging the details that collectively complete their vision.

When people ask me how I managed to get a major newspaper like the *New York Times* to write my story, my response is, "Two decades of engaging the details every day."

One of my staff members, who confesses she's not the most detailed person, observes,

> Vickie believes that if you're sloppy with the little things, you'll be sloppy with the big things. The real danger of ignoring details doesn't stop with you. If you're sloppy about details, your subcontractors, vendors and employees will take that as a cue that they can be sloppy too. A missing term in a contract, poor grammar in email and paying bills late all stem from not engaging the details.

At first I was worried about how vendors would perceive us. But vendors have told me they appreciate our attention to detail because it challenges and inspires them to do their best work.

Vickie taught me that when you engage the details you reach a higher level of engagement, one that reaps benefits in many other ways.

Wicked success starts with passionate vision, but engagement in a hundred thousand tiny details is the difference between wicked success and failure. That's what women who are wickedly successful know.

SHRUG OFF RESTRICTIONS

We all experience setbacks. While you can't simply ignore your weaknesses, you will get more value by focusing on your strengths. Improving every minor deficiency reaps little benefit. Focusing on weaknesses only creates mental restrictions. "I wasn't trained to do this. I've never done this before."

Shrug off the restriction of pessimism. A study found that optimists are more successful than pessimists in their careers. Optimists succeed not because they're more competent or experienced, but because they're more likely to actively engage problems and positively reframe, rather than be restricted by, challenges. They don't expect issues to resolve themselves; they attack those issues with true grit.

Optimists disengage from courses of action that don't work and engage new strategies. Optimists are also more fun to be around. Wouldn't you rather hang with positive, happy people than someone for whom the sky is always falling? Is it truly a surprise that optimists are more successful? Not to me.

Some of the most optimistic people are Cirque du Soleil artists. I can never get enough of them. They do everything so exquisitely well— costumes, acrobatics, acts, clowns and music. I always come away awed.

One show has the biggest aerial acrobatics act these performers have ever done, and the distances they cover are some of the most difficult in the world. This act took place much higher in the air than I would ever willingly climb. Muscular men were swinging from hanging aerial platforms, launching themselves into space and landing either on a tiny center platform or being caught by the hands by another acrobat. The entire audience held their breath while the men were in the air and cheered and clapped at their daring.

The acrobats took our enthusiasm as a stimulus to challenge each other to attempt more and more daring feats of twisting, turning aerial acrobatics. Suddenly, one of the acrobats mistimed his jump and missed the outstretched hands of the man swinging to catch him. We all gasped as he fell into the safety net far below. He landed, leaped up (just like a guy) and was climbing back up the rope ladder as quickly as he could.

As this optimist climbed, the audience erupted into louder shouts and cheers, not just for the audacity of what he attempted, but also for the fact that he went right back up to do it again. Restrictions? What's that to a Cirque du Soleil aerialist?

In life and career, just like in acrobatics, there's no 100 percent success rate. Wickedly successful women know they can't let a weakness or setback restrict them. The more you're wired for getting right back up after you stumble or fall, the more tenaciously you will engage.

DON'T BE A COMMITMENT QUEEN

Women are queens of commitment. In fact, I'm cautious when speaking to women about engagement, because they tend to overengage. We can also be tenacious about overcommitting to the wrong people and the wrong goals. We martyr ourselves beyond reasonable engagement.

When I first started my seminars, I engaged to the point of exhaustion. I taught all day, and I always had lunch with the students. At day's end, they invited me to dinner, and I'd go, which was not a relaxing affair because I was still the teacher and they wanted to pick my brain. Finally, my sister Karen asked me, "Vickie, why don't you say no, take some time for yourself and relax a little?" Eureka! I started setting boundaries. At first, I felt guilty, but I soon learned that people are usually okay with them.

No wonder women are so exhausted. Your boss wants it yesterday, your kids want it today and your spouse wants it tonight. What's interesting is that once I set the dinner boundary, people stopped inviting me to dinner. It was as if I had sent a subliminal message. They got it. They easily accepted it.

Stop being a commitment queen and martyring yourself beyond reasonable engagement. Shed the guilt. Stop committing your energy to every person or situation that demands it. You need to set your own expectations of what you want to accomplish. Don't let your career or life take a backseat to everyone else's. Yes, you have responsibilities to others. You've also got a responsibility to yourself.

Just Say No

"If I don't do it, nobody else will" is the most insidious myth women are brainwashed to believe. Learn to say no. It's the most powerful word in the dictionary. Practice saying no to this request and that request, people who drain you and any other cause that distracts you from your passionate vision. And the tough one: You have to say no to the people you love most, no to doing all the laundry, all the housework and all the errands.

The reality today is that even as women are building incredible careers they're still battling the stereotypical roles of traditional wife and mother. When you walk in the door after a long day of work, do you grab the remote or play on Facebook while your husband makes dinner, watches the kids and cleans the house?

Women still do more housework than their husbands. One study reported that having a husband adds an additional seven hours to a woman's weekly housework load. Stop the insanity. Women are exhausted by the battle of repeatedly asking and reminding their husbands to pitch in. Rather than rock the boat, for some women it's easier to do it themselves; but that's a trap. It leads to generations of exhausted women while men reap the rewards of extra leisure time and career advancement.

When Edie's husband told her "I don't do laundry," she replied "That's okay, neither do I." Today he helps with the laundry, all because Edie knows how to use the no word.

It's okay for your husband and kids to do some of the housework or wash the dishes. It's not going to kill them; but it is going to kill you if you keep doing it all. Everyone benefits—especially your significant other, since you'll be a much happier person when you join him in bed at night.

Draw your man in. Ask him to take a walk and tell him how much you appreciate him. Then explain you're feeling overloaded. Discuss the long list of all your responsibilities. Together, decide on joint responsibilities and all the ways you can handle them—dinnertime, for example: cook, eat out, eat prepared foods and so on. Invite your husband to offer his own solutions, and be open to his ideas.

If that doesn't work, stand up for yourself. Don't say yes by default. Only say yes when it works within the balance of your career, family and passionate vision. By refusing to commit to every person or cause that comes along, you gain a new freedom to achieve your goals, not everyone else's.

Camille, a very successful sports medicine doctor, says, "I'm a fantastic mother, wife and doctor, but I don't cook, I don't bake cookies and I don't decorate the house. I'm totally fine with not being able to and not wanting to do it all."

Engagement doesn't require giving up yourself and subordinating your dreams to help friends and family achieve theirs. We all need to set boundaries on our willingness to engage.

It's no mystery that successful women engage big. The more success you have, the more success you will have. Winners want to hang out and engage with winners. This is the secret that wickedly successful women know.

ENGAGE TO ACHIEVE
BIG THINGS WITH THE
5 PROMISES

PROMISE 1
I Will Live and Work a Passionate Life

What Big Thing must you engage now to live your passionate vision?

_____

_____

_____

What commitments must you let go?

_____

_____

_____

PROMISE 2
I Will Go for It or Reject It Outright

What fear must you overcome to accomplish this Big Thing? How will you use momentum sessions to break the feel-good addiction?

_____

_____

_____

PROMISE 3
I Will Take One Action Step a Day Toward My Passionate Vision

Identify three action steps you will take to accomplish your Big Thing. Specifically, when will you tackle your momentum sessions each day? Which tasks will you designate as weeds?

_____

_____

_____

PROMISE 4
I Commit to Being a Success Student for Life

What areas of training or knowledge would assist you in accomplishing your Big Thing? How and when you will gain this knowledge?

_____

_____

_____

PROMISE 5
I Believe as a Woman I Really Can Do Anything

Identify a fear you overcame and the risks you took to do so. What did you learn that will help you achieve your Big Thing?

_____

_____

_____

➤➤ DOWNLOAD THE 5 PROMISES FOR ENGAGEMENT AT **WickedSuccess.com**.

LEIGH'S ENGAGEMENT

A bookstore owner I met early in my publishing career invited me to my first Houston Financial Council for Women luncheon meeting. The women who gathered for this networking meeting wore perfect accessories and drank wine. They all seemed so sophisticated and self-assured. I was in my 20s and not one bit sophisticated. I wanted to be like them, so I applied for membership. I wasn't a powerful networker, but I attended every meeting, and that got me noticed. A huge part of success is showing up, but I didn't know that then.

A member I admired was elected president and asked me to serve on her board. Who, me? I was flattered but unsure, having never served on any board, but she guaranteed I could do it. That was the beginning of my commitment to advance professional women, and I became totally engaged.

As program director, I brought in Ann Richards, before she was elected governor of Texas, to speak to our small group. As vice president of membership, I created information packets for potential members. I discovered the reward of always giving a little extra. As president, I introduced our organization into a larger arena, the Federation of Houston Professional Women, an alliance of women's organizations similar to ours.

Again, I showed up. I volunteered on Federation committees and proved I could be counted on. Just nine months after joining, I became a member of their impressive 20-member board. I gave hours to my cause when I didn't have money.

As membership director, I spoke to women's associations all over Houston to encourage them to join. My passion to engage women resulted in 18 new member organizations—twice as many as previous directors had brought in. When I lost my first bid for president, I continued my engagement and served on the winner's board as newsletter editor, where I expanded the format, increased the number of pages and sold more ads than anyone else. Four years after joining, I was elected president of this 6,000-member organization.

I get a charge out of making interesting and valuable connections for women. If someone mentions that she needs an interior designer or banker or computer repair, I know who she can call. I am continually engaged in promoting the success of businesswomen in our community. Engagement is easy when you are passionate.

Leigh, a woman who doesn't tell her age
MARKETING DIRECTOR

Engagement gives you momentum to live your passionate vision. You'll engage momentum at ever higher levels using the Feminine Force of agility, which we'll explore next.

Do something every day that scares you.
ELEANOR ROOSEVELT

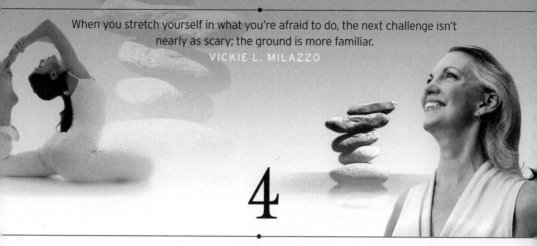

If we don't change, we don't grow. If we don't grow, we aren't really living.
GAIL SHEEHY

When you stretch yourself in what you're afraid to do, the next challenge isn't nearly as scary; the ground is more familiar.
VICKIE L. MILAZZO

4

AGILITY

Flex Your Agility to Grab New Opportunities

Women's bodies are naturally more flexible than men's. Just go to any beginner's yoga class and watch the men. Then watch the women. Men have their own strengths, but women are naturally engineered for agility.

This inherent agility extends to our thought processes. Women excel at multitasking. How many things can you do at once? How many things can your spouse or significant other do at once? Chat up any group of women with a variety of talents, emotions and intelligence and you'll find most of them are juggling a dozen different projects, a handful of important relationships and at least one pressing dilemma.

Flexible and adaptable, women handle unexpected change gracefully. We're not thrown by 10 things hitting us at once—that won't wreck our day. We're wired for agility.

In prehistoric times women and men participated almost equally in hunting and gathering. As agriculture developed, women had to use both sides of their brains to prepare food, make clothing and care for children, while also plowing fields, harvesting crops and tending animals. Later, as people gathered into cities, women kept many of those "prehistoric" responsibilities and also sold or traded goods in the marketplace. So very early on we developed the agility to be well rounded in our expertise.

A constant reminder of women's agility greets me each morning as I drink my first cup of healthy green tea and look out to the silhouettes of giant timber bamboo that surrounds our home. Easily reaching heights of 60 feet, the bamboo stalks sway gently in the wind, like ballet dancers in the predawn light.

Even the slightest breeze will prompt their graceful movement. A strong wind sets off a dramatic modern dance performance accompanied by the sounds of giant wind chimes. I love hearing the stalks clacking through the stillness.

Like a woman, bamboo is unnaturally strong and flexible. And like a woman, it will bend almost double before breaking. Rather than crack in the face of a strong force, it flexes and twists, reactively buffering any changes in weather and wind direction. After a hurricane, Houston was blanketed with downed trees and broken tree limbs. Bamboo leaves littered the ground, but almost no bamboo stalks lay in our yard.

A passionate, agile woman never says "I can't" when it comes to achieving. She knows that success comes in "cans," that when faced with strong forces, every "can't" she utters will undermine her agility and limit her ultimate wicked success.

Though strong, bamboo is slender and lightweight. It reminds us to keep our lives and careers trim, fast and agile. Being trim and fast like bamboo, a woman can change directions quickly, take advantage of opportunities and try new alternatives.

Hand a woman an iPhone and you turn her into a captain of high-tech industry. She'll set appointments, answer email, snap and send photos to friends and family, update Facebook, arrange a party, make dinner reservations and text her husband to pick up the dry cleaning. We've learned to bend technology to fit our needs, and extend our agility for handling more complex situations at increasingly higher and faster levels.

Agility is the path to a deeper, richer experience and agility is the strength that gets you to bigger, more audacious goals. The more we stretch, the deeper we're able to go into our passionate vision.

This is true not only with our bodies, but with our minds and the goals we pursue. When we challenge ourselves to stretch, our physical, mental and emotional energies rev up to make anything possible. Agility can snap us out of rigidly held commitments (a job, a relationship, an attitude) that are no longer congruent with our vision. Agility shapes us for the only constant in a woman's life: change. Agility is the strength we wield to initiate imperative, but often dangerous, changes.

With agility we can look at an old situation in a new way. When we change, we make easy that which was formerly difficult. Agility lifts us to the next level, where each new challenge expands and strengthens our agility for moving through life with ease and confidence.

SHAKE IT UP

In a Buddhist monastery in Bhutan I witnessed two monks working on a mandala. Intricate and brilliantly colorful images are "painted" with colored sand laboriously trickled onto a horizontal "canvas," almost one grain at a time. Monks will spend countless hours creating these highly detailed sand paintings.

Once the mandala is completed, you might expect the monk to proudly display it or at least savor its beauty. Instead, as soon as the exquisite work of art is finished, he destroys it, in recognition and celebration of the impermanence of life.

Like a monk creating a mandala, we may painstakingly and lovingly craft a dream, pouring our passion into it and attending to every detail. For some women the dream manifests as a perfect spouse and family; for others it's career advancement, a promotion to vice president or steps to retirement. Surely, we tell ourselves, this is the dream that will satisfy.

Wickedly successful women fully understand the saying: "To make God laugh, make plans." Even the best dream is as impermanent as a mandala. A dream, any dream, is simply the first step on the journey. Once we create the perfect dream, before we know it, it's time to destroy it and start over.

To be wickedly successful at anything, you must be willing and agile enough to go new places, change directions and shake things up, even to the point of destroying a very comfortable state or a perfect dream. Risking even minor change strengthens your agility to go where you need to go next and prepares you for major challenges later that will undoubtedly require even more change.

I wake up every day with a plan. But I also wake up fully intending to bust that plan. Wicked success cannot be managed tightly and neatly. Wicked success is messy, welcoming an occasional gentle shake-up or, sometimes, a massive tremor. Agility is the strength that welcomes surrender to the myriad unplanned opportunities that come our way.

Stedman Graham contacted me to do a business presentation with him, but Stedman wasn't part of my company's 65-page strategic plan. When the universe summoned, agility is the strength I used to refocus resources, money and efforts to make that presentation happen.

When I find myself resisting change or disruption, I try to remember that soon I will see this challenge as the barrier that, once crossed, opened a gate to new perspectives, new opportunities and new choices. I will look back and see how risking this change presented an opportunity to become more agile.

More and more women today are using their agility to shake up their careers and embrace technology, some even creating their own high-tech start-ups. I'm not one of those women. I'm the least computer-savvy person in my office. When technology invaded my company I felt all shook up and just wanted the whole techno-world to vanish. I had to relax my resistance and rely on my strength of agility to appreciate how technology could advance my company to a whole new level and galvanize my genius into learning wicked new skills.

Since I founded Vickie Milazzo Institute, we've moved from a single DOS-based desktop computer to 30 Windows and Mac computers, used for everything from running our CRM software and managing our customer relations to editing our videos and creating complex graphics. The single server that sat in the corner has morphed into a climate-controlled, secure server room filled with a rack of SANs, servers and hosts running a minimum of 11 virtual machines at any one time on a variety of platforms, our VoIP equipment and all the switches and other paraphernalia required to make everything work together. Now that we're turning to the "cloud," a lot of that equipment and software will go away.

Who knows where technology will take us next? I'll have to stay agile enough to find out.

Agility demands courage to create effective change. Courage is not the absence of fear, it's the confidence to agilely shove fear aside and act despite it. It's simply another choice we make.

Every morning, while showering and getting dressed, ask yourself, "What's not working as well in my life as it could? What might work better? And how can I change it?" Then employ your strength of agility to implement that positive change, no matter how small.

Overthrow Your Natural State

When we welcome change and expand our agility, we realize that what we thought of as our "natural state" will never return to its former stiff and monotonous self. We find ourselves in a new space, one of unlimited options.

It's easy to believe that only a certain type of charismatic person will be wickedly successful. But I remember as a child being teased about my imaginary classes. My sister and twin brother thought I was the nerdiest kid ever—quiet, reserved and serious, while they were more outgoing. I always had a mission. My girlfriends changed their baby dolls while I plotted to change the world.

As I took more and more risks, diving deeper into areas I'd never been, I lost that timidity. When you accept the challenge of change, you stretch yourself in what you're afraid to do, and that feat of agility builds reserves of courage that will expand with each new stretch. The next challenge isn't nearly as scary, because it isn't out there so far. The ground is more familiar, the obstacles don't loom as large and you're more agile in scaling them.

FLEX YOUR CURIOSITY

I've already confided to you my fear of water. A near-drowning experience when I was a child left me wary of swimming and totally unwilling to go deeper than snorkeling along the water's surface while safely wearing my inflatable buoyancy vest. That's why I had no plans to scuba dive with Tom when we went to Fiji.

Several years earlier, on Maui, I tried learning to dive. On that first attempt Tom, my 14-year-old nephew Matt and I started our lessons in the pool. As soon as the water closed over my face mask, and I struggled with the weight of the tank dragging me to the bottom and the BCD vest that was supposed to help save my life, but instead was threatening to drown me, I climbed out of the pool and didn't look back.

On the safety of the shore, I enjoyed a massage instead. While the guys took to the ocean like fish, exploring coral reefs, shipwrecks and the limitless variety of sea life, I clung to my beach chair with my self-help book, *Mastering Your Fear for Dummies*.

On later vacations Tom and I worked out a compromise. He would dive, then return to snorkel with me. Although not much of a swimmer, I was a great flailer. I snorkeled in the shallows, where I could stand up when I tired from flailing or needed to adjust my mask. Yoga practice had prepared me for proper breathing and body control, and over time my confidence grew. So did the quality of my flailing. To this day my nephew still calls me shark bait.

Back to Fiji: I watched a young girl with a mental disability go out doggedly every day to learn to dive, while I stayed safely on the surface, afraid to leave my shallow comfort zone for the deeper unknown. I wondered who had the greater disability, she or I. Hers was real, mine only imagined. Who was more agile?

Every morning, Tom regaled me with stories of turtles, lionfish, hammerhead sharks and the vibrant coral he saw on his dives while I continued flailing about in the shallows. But each day I snorkeled into deeper and deeper water until, finally, on day four, I built up the confidence to approach the edge of a 300-foot wall. Looking into its depths I was suddenly no longer content to observe from the surface. My curiosity engaged, I longed to dive deep and envelop myself in the dark wonders below. I resolved to try diving again.

My first dive was in a shallow bay. I clung to the bottom, pulling up sand and sea grass 15 feet below the surface. Easy. Being close to the bottom gave me security and perspective, and the small success encouraged me to go for more.

The second day I dove longer and deeper, to 25 feet. Upon arrival at the reef, the first thing the dive master talked about was sharks. "This is their world. They're in control. Don't approach or move toward them. Respect them. Respect their space."

Actually, sharks didn't scare me at all. I was too afraid of the water to worry about sharks. First I had to get into the water. Then I'd think about sharks.

On my third day of diving, we boated to a sandy ledge that led to the 300-foot wall I was ready to explore. The boat rocked on 5-foot swells.

Tom and the dive master rolled off the side of the boat backward—the standard diver's show-off entry. When the dive master instructed me to do the same, I said, "No way!" and waddled down the narrow stepladder designed for deck shoes, not fins. No easy feat. Tom said it was typical of me to take the hard way down.

After the initial roller-coaster ride associated with equalizing my ears and my anxiety, we swam along the shallow bottom to the precipice of the wall, slipped over the edge and slowly dropped into the abyss. Surprisingly, the stability and quiet of being underwater was a wonderful respite from the swells that bounced the boat on the surface. Anyway, it does no good to scream underwater, no matter how claustrophobic you feel, with 45 feet of water between you and the surface.

Soon I was keenly observing the sea life. Coral heads, bulbs, fans and thousands of fish, all sizes and temperaments, from the diminutive clown fish bravely defending his anemone home to the shy 35-pound sweetlips that disappeared into his coral cavern at the first sight of us.

As my breathing relaxed I began to hear the sounds of the sea life. Midway, Tom joined me, held my hand in celebration and I lost all sense of time, depth and my childhood fear, even when the menacing 10-foot reef sharks swam past us. While I'll never be a fish in the water, I was now enjoying their world. Even more, I was enjoying my newfound agility.

CHALLENGE A FIXED VIEWPOINT

Where would I be if I hadn't challenged my fear of water? Probably where I am now, but with less confidence. I believe the happiest people are those who continuously grow and stretch. The only way to grow is to question, challenge, probe for new answers and new viewpoints and remain agile enough to try new experiences.

In business, you grow or you die. Most of us are willing to stretch when it comes to our careers. It's expected. You strive for a bigger paycheck, a bigger office, more influence or more power. Why don't we do the same in our personal lives? One always affects the other.

In life, as in business, when you neglect growth and cling to inertia, the passion inside you cools. Plan not only for a bigger house or a snazzier vehicle, but for muscling up your inner strengths. Strive to reinvent yourself on a regular basis. Why wake up five years from now greeting the same person in the mirror when you could see a smarter, stronger, bolder woman who has transcended former boundaries? Refusing to grow and stretch keeps you in the shallows, just as not taking that dive might have kept me out of the depths of the underwater world for the rest of my life.

Don't Inject the Heroin

When we believe the fixed viewpoints of those insidious mantras—"I can't . . . ," "I don't . . . ," I wasn't trained for that"—we set up our own failure. In nursing school I worked with heroin addicts—not exactly the most fun or inspiring bunch of people to be around. Not having an addictive personality myself, I couldn't understand the forces that drove them. I wanted to shake them and shout, "Just because you've inserted the needle doesn't mean you have to inject the heroin," but I knew it wouldn't mean anything to them.

Tina, struggling with the fast-paced training of our seminar, became upset when she couldn't keep up. I encouraged her to relax more and embrace the opportunity these struggles were offering her. After it became apparent that wasn't working, I offered to let her take home the DVD version of the program and study at her own pace.

She refused the offer. Instead, she sat in the front row the entire six days, talking to herself, escalating her frustration and not listening to a word of what she'd come to learn. For six days she injected the heroin over and over again. She was one of only a few students who failed the certification examination, simply because she sabotaged herself with her fixed "I can't" viewpoint.

Have you ever started down a path and discovered your direction or viewpoint was not working, but you kept going anyway? Then a sudden flash of insight—just because you inserted the needle didn't mean you had to inject the heroin.

The next time you notice yourself inserting the needle filled with rigidity and resistance to change, take a minute to think about what you're about to do. Ask yourself: "Do I really need to inject the heroin or is there a better way to do this?" You might be surprised when a new perspective from a better viewpoint appears to you in a flash of insight.

Agility enables us to recognize what's not working and fix it. When employees come to me with company problems, I say, "Don't just tell me the problem. Challenge your fixed viewpoints and give me the solution."

I didn't always own a company. I grew up selling Avon, working at Burger King and eventually working in hospitals as an RN. Making the transition from registered nurse to entrepreneur was a long stretch. Entrepreneurship constantly challenges my agility and has taught me this attitude: "Wherever you are, make the most of it by questioning, probing and challenging fixed viewpoints."

I had to challenge the fixed viewpoint that nurses don't own businesses; they only work for hospitals. I had to challenge my own fixed viewpoint that I didn't have time to start a business with a full-time job. Decades later, I had to challenge the fixed viewpoint that social media and blogging are not for CEOs. More recently, I had to challenge a fixed viewpoint I shared with my financial director, that we were an education company, not a finance company. Financing a portion of our clients, knowing we wouldn't see a self-sustaining return or cash flow for almost three years, felt like corporate suicide. A radical change, but it worked.

In a tough economic environment that has made it difficult for many people to own a house, a car, books or even a bicycle, the new business model of sharing challenges the fixed viewpoint of ownership. College students and young adults have long shared apartments and lodgings— nothing new there—but Vélib' in Paris has made bicycle sharing an affordable and convenient alternative to owning and parking a bike. This concept is spreading to the United States for both bikes and cars. Today, Zipcar is making car sharing easy for those who either cannot afford their own cars or for whom ownership is impractical.

Websites appear almost daily that promote sharing everything from rides to books to baby clothes and babysitting cooperatives. Young people may see sharing as a last resort, when they can't afford to own, but this is a cleverly agile generation who may view it as a new and sensible way of life.

What fixed viewpoint is preventing you from stretching? Inside every woman is the agility to be anything she wants to be and to do everything her passionate vision demands.

STRETCH TO INTENSIFY AGILITY

I thought scuba diving to 45 feet was a big deal until I learned there are divers who go more than 11 times deeper—without scuba gear. Imagine taking one huge breath and plunging hundreds of feet into the ocean, so deep you need a light to see where you're going. Just try holding your breath for six minutes!

Some free divers ride a weighted sled to the target depth and swim back to the surface—all on a single breath. The no-limits women's record was set by Tanya Streeter in 2002, who dove to 525 feet and back in 3 minutes 26 seconds—deeper than many submarines reached during World War II.

Natalia Molchanova set a record depth of 331 feet for women's constant-weight diving in 2009. A constant-weight free diver uses only a pair of fins to propel herself alongside a guideline to her target depth. She swims entirely on her own strength, using minimal oxygen and exertion, each movement as graceful and fluid as a dolphin's. She wastes no energy; every scrap goes into pushing toward her goal.

Like Natalia and Tanya, strong, agile women are willing to dive deep into their dreams, visions, desires and fears. Challenge yourself. It's important to have realistic goals, like losing five pounds or selling five percent more, but you should also have a stretch goal that's out there on the horizon. Stretching intensifies agility. I'd much rather set one audacious goal and not quite reach it than set all my goals too low. Expanding and intensifying agility prepares you for the bigger opportunities you'll encounter as your new passionate life unfolds.

DIVE DEEPER EVERY DAY

Record-breaking free divers practice their skills until they become automatic. A free diver's amazing agility comes from setting aside a huge portion of their lives for training, planning, preparation and execution.

To survive such extremes, to break records and safely return to the surface, a free diver pushes to new limits on deeper and deeper training dives. For a dangerous dive lasting mere minutes, she might endure 10 months of training. She runs, lifts weights, diets, practices holding her breath and achieves startling levels of concentration to extend one breath even further than ever before.

I attribute the growth of our company to our continuously going deeper through training, planning, preparation and execution. We make sure we're working smarter, not harder. We constantly ask ourselves if there's a better way to do what we're doing. Can we be more flexible, more responsive to opportunity? Are there new technologies we must master and incorporate into our business? As a result of this constant agility training, we can dive deeper with every breath.

We never settle for ordinary when another stretch might take us to extraordinary. Fifteen percent growth in one year is great, but the real gain comes in the cumulative effect. Growing even 7 percent, personally or in business revenues, might not sound like a big deal, but do that every year for 5, 10 or 30 years and you'll find yourself in an awesome place that's not crowded.

What are the skills that will take you to the next level in living your passionate vision? Like free divers, you must be willing to invest time and energy in training until your skills become deeply ingrained, then maintain those skills so that you can access them with agility, as needed.

For a free diver, taking the correct action instinctively, with the lightning speed that a prepared mind is capable of, can make the difference between survival and drowning. When you face a challenge in your personal life or career, your skills and knowledge will serve you well—if you've practiced until you instinctively make good choices.

To dive deep you must focus on a few things, not on everything. My company, for example, could create continuing education in hundreds of nursing specialties, but we choose not to. We train and certify registered nurses as Certified Legal Nurse Consultants. That is our passion and that is what we do best. And because we don't dabble all over the place, our students trust us as the true experts we are.

In today's world we are bombarded with so many options that it's difficult to choose where to focus. The deeper you dive, the narrower your choices. Choose a few areas in which you passionately want to improve your agility, and focus on diving deep to reach them.

What new agility will propel you to dive more deeply into your passionate vision?

SCHEDULE AN AGILITY BREAK

The value in routine is that it conserves energy. As we learn from our mistakes, we develop routines that facilitate speed and accuracy. Routine can be a source of confidence as we accept new risks. Attacking new problems with a familiar and successful system saves time and other resources. We get into a groove.

One of my favorite Broadway musicals will always be *Jersey Boys*. I've seen it five times, four with the original cast and have had the pleasure of sharing it with many friends.

Two of the lead characters, Frankie Valli and Bob Gaudio strike a deal to collaborate and share everything 50/50. They sealed their deal with a "Jersey contract"—also known as a handshake. This happened in 1961, early in the group's history—a time that brought us many hit songs including "Sherry," "Big Girls Don't Cry" and "Can't Take My Eyes Off of You." Their Jersey contract thrives today.

I recently entered into a Jersey contract with the owner of a company. I've known him for a long time and always felt we had a bond that transcended business. I was thinking we'd be like Frankie Valli and Bob Gaudio.

I always joke that I like to break the rules, and here I was in typical fashion violating one of my own, which is to have a contract in every business relationship. Questions and issues that should have been covered in a contract came up and needed to be resolved. It became obvious to both of us that the only way to clear things up was with a contract.

Luckily, we have enough respect for each other and a strong enough relationship to withstand revisiting our deal and committing it to paper. We arrived at a contract favorable to both, but along the way there were a few tense discussions and potential for damage to the relationship we'd nurtured for more than 20 years.

So as much as I admire Frankie Valli and Bob Gaudio, I have to admit it's not 1961; and in 2011, I resolved not to break my rule concerning contracts ever again. No more Jersey contracts for Vickie Milazzo Institute. It's not a matter of trust—it's business (even if you're in Jersey).

But routine can be the enemy of your agility. At the gym, if I do the same workout, without adding new challenges to my muscles, they get so used to it that I stop advancing. I have to shift, do a different exercise—five different types of planks instead of the same one.

When I work out with my trainer, every session is different. He never repeats a routine. Not only is this more fun and interesting—my body is more awake to the benefits of exercise. We need to be agile mentally and emotionally, as well as physically. Routine can quickly become a rut that we dig deeper and deeper simply to avoid risking a new path.

To strengthen agility, be spontaneous and break your routine by doing something you wouldn't normally do. Think of an activity you've always wanted to try but resisted. Break out of your ordinary world and experience what else is out there.

Be a Glutton for Punishment

Hang out with people who are different from you. One of my best friends from high school asked me one day, "Vickie, did you ever wonder how we got to be such great friends when we're so different?" While I excelled in business, Missy excelled in being a great mom. While I'm excessively neat, she doesn't mind a little clutter. She might say that I have better taste in men; I'd say she has a better gift of gab. Totally dissimilar but totally in sync with each other.

My twin brother Vince and I are very different, and not just in gender. In one of our favorite baby photos he's playing with a ball and I'm reading a book. That sums it up. Even as babies, we're unconsciously grasping the totems that mirror our separate paths. You'd think we'd have nothing in common, but he's my best pal (albeit a rough one), and the reason is because we know we're different and we accept those differences.

Wickedly successful women know to surround themselves with individuals who expand their imagination. One of my staff members sees everything from a totally different perspective than I do. Every time I ask her to review something for me, I think, "I'm a glutton for punishment." Before I know it, instead of sitting and discussing, I find myself standing up, defending my ideas . . . but also refining those ideas. She gets my imagination going, and I get to where I need to be. When you're around stimulating people, people who challenge you and who think differently, you may resist at first, but ultimately your mind will go in new directions and agilely snatch the choice opportunities.

When choosing your support team, consider people of varying ages, interests, attitudes, talents and educational and social levels. They will shake up your thinking, encourage you to step out of your routines, fortify your courage to take new risks and introduce you to new ideas and new ways of solving problems.

Dare to Appear Foolish

At our conferences I walk down the aisle of a ballroom and up to the stage amidst rock music, rotating lights (I nixed fireworks after the hairspray and sparkler incident) and confetti-firing cannons, to lead our mantra-cheer in front of an audience of hundreds. To some, I probably look foolish. The majority, though, love it, and when we chant our mantra, we rock the house! What once felt foolish now feels perfectly normal.

As we say in Texas, there's nothing in the middle of the road but yellow stripes and dead armadillos. The neutrality that middle-of-the-road routine creates is rarely a formula for wickedly successful women; daring to look foolish is. Whichever side I pick, you can be sure I'll rock the house with my foolishness.

What agility break will propel you to rock your house and dive more deeply into your passionate vision?

ADD THE RIGHT TOOLS TO YOUR AGILITY ARSENAL

I'm on the road about 20 weeks a year for business and vacation. That means I'm on a minimum of 40 flights a year. Yes, I do have elite frequent flyer status that affords me upgrades, but sometimes all my elite status guarantees me is early boarding and sitting near the front of the plane behind the Platinum and Million-Mile members. I'm close enough to see them up in first class, sipping champagne and eating a succulent rib eye steak, at least until the flight attendant pulls the velvet curtain that separates "us" from "them."

Lately the airlines have been stingier with their upgrades, and as I write this section, I'm sitting in a coach seat, 9C. Thanks to fewer and more crowded flights and extended ground times, I've been sentenced to more than three and a half hours of false imprisonment. The airline industry seems to be one of the few that excels in getting worse instead of better. What I really want to do when I'm flying coach is weep. But what good would that do? Instead, I use my strength of agility to turn crowded confinement into a tolerable, if not enjoyable, experience.

Soon the cabin door will close, and if I'm lucky, the person next to me or across the aisle won't hack up a lung or kidney. For the next 10 minutes I'll listen to the woman in the row in front of me with the cell phone voice tell her friend about her frightening medical condition while I dodge carry-on bags and backpacks as I people-watch during the boarding process. Watching people board is sort of fascinating, in the way that it's fascinating to watch a train wreck.

Upon preparation for takeoff, no fewer than two surly female flight attendants came by to tell Tom, in no uncertain terms, that he was threatening the safety of not only all the other passengers, but possibly the destiny of the free world, because he still had his headset, iPhone and laptop turned on. And, if he didn't want to say hello to the business end of the air marshal's Sig-Sauer pistol, it was time to shut things down.

As luck would have it, at that exact moment, my iPhone rang; it was a call from the one person I really needed to talk to, so I answered it. This put me on the watch list for the next three hours. As a consequence, not only did I *not* get my four ounces of TSA-approved fluids, I also was on the receiving end of that special "inattention" that only a hostile, angry and otherwise unsatisfied-with-her-career flight attendant can provide.

I can deal with that. I've learned to flex my agility to be self-sufficient. I travel with teapot, table and tent. I've got my water and snacks. But what I really want is . . . quiet. Once in the air, I have about three hours to work on whatever I want, without interruption.

Flexing my agility, I plan ahead for any contingency and bring along the right equipment. Bose noise-reducing headphones and fresh batteries are a must. *Check.* My fully charged iPod, loaded with Green Day and all my favorite music, a trash novel—*oops,* I mean a piece of classical literature in the original Greek—and plenty of magazines for takeoff, landing and layovers. *Check.* Two person auto-inflating life raft, personal flotation vest and two weeks of freeze-dried foods in case of an unforeseen incident. *Check.* (Just making sure you're still reading.) *Uncheck.* Laptop computer. *Check.* Sterile handi-wipes to clean the seat, tray table, armrests, restroom and airline burrito prior to consumption. *Check*—sort of. (I'm a nurse, so I know infections lurk everywhere and prefer to let my immune system deal with them.)

Adding the right tools to our arsenal increases our agility for handling difficult and unforeseen conditions. My strength of agility always cushions my flights. Oh, and I forgot to mention—I always start my flight with Green Day's "Novocain," so for those first three minutes I won't feel a thing.

AGILITY IS A TWO-MINUTE INVESTMENT

I like to move, and anyone who knows me knows I can't sit still for long, unless I'm having my morning tea or enjoying a theatrical performance. Even in my office, I'm on the move all day. Frequently getting out of my chair helps me sustain both my mental and physical stamina. I probably log a couple of miles a day just moving around the office.

That's one reason being on an airplane seems like false imprisonment. Confined to my seat, I quickly become restless and uncomfortable. Shortly after takeoff on an eight-hour red-eye flight from Amsterdam to Nairobi, I realized I had to do something about my uncomfortable seat or I'd be miserable for the rest of the flight. I wanted to arrive in Africa in better condition than my luggage, and there was a solution in the overhead bin: a small lumbar cushion I'd packed in my carry-on bag. I tossed Tom a huge smile and asked him to pull down my bag, which was wedged behind his.

Tom is normally a bundle of energy, but when we're on an airplane he's a perfect candidate for blood clots. As soon as we board, he hunkers down and builds himself a nest in his seat, surrounded by his books, tech magazines, Bose headset, iPod, iPhone, bottle of water and laptop. If I don't remind him to move, he won't budge or even look up until it's time to deplane. This is great if he's in the window seat, because he never climbs over me. But it also makes him severely resistant to any requests that involve rising once he's nested.

You can imagine Tom's response to my plea for assistance. In textbook husband-speak: "Are you really sure you want to pull that cushion out of your bag?"

Years of marriage allowed me to quickly translate what he was really asking me: "Now that we're seated and I've perfected my nest, are you sure you want me to get up, haul your bag out of the overhead, take everything out of it and dig out that small cushion stashed in the very bottom, just so you can see if it will make you comfortable? And are you really sure you want me to put down my work, shut my laptop, fold up my tray table, unbuckle my seatbelt, stand up and go to all that trouble, only to have to get up again, as soon as I've settled back in, and repeat the process to repack the bag and then wedge it back up there?"

My response was an unqualified, "Yes! The two minutes it will take us to do this is a great trade-off for eight hours of comfort." Tom grudgingly agreed and the entire process required much less time than I spent thinking about it and Tom spent trying to talk me out of it. A two-minute investment paid off with eight hours of comfort.

Of course, it might not have worked at all. The point is, I was willing to invest my time (and Tom's reluctant energy) in attempting a solution. Agility often means experimenting today in hopes of wicked success tomorrow. Agility comes from a willingness to try something different.

Are you investing today to ensure your future comfort and growth? Or are you resisting a simple change that could pay off big down the line? Stop the insanity of excuses for why you can't, won't or shouldn't do something. Today is the day to commit to one small action. Whether a shift is large or small—a simple step toward comfort (like getting my cushion) or a major shift in your life or career—that change is often just two minutes away.

Invest two minutes today, five minutes tomorrow. Small investments in your growth can pay big dividends when you need that agility later.

DON'T BE A RELIC OF PAST SPLENDOR

Angkor Wat is the relic of an ancient civilization that was far advanced for its time. On a trip to Cambodia I was blessed to spend three days exploring the ruins of this magnificent complex of temples, many built more than 900 years ago. These relics of past splendor were constructed with stones carried from far away, and without modern machinery. Yet the structures have withstood the ravages of time, weather and humankind.

In contrast, on my last evening in Cambodia, I took a boat ride through Chong Khneas, a floating fishing village. This loose collection of more than 700 families of fishermen and a complete support community live on boats and travel Tonlé Sap Lake following the fish and the rainy season. To reach it we drove along an unpaved road through villages with primitive living conditions. Bamboo shacks stood on spindly poles to withstand flooding. I would have been afraid to roll over in my sleep in these houses, much less raise a family or ride out a monsoon in one. Electricity was nonexistent, and the only running water was the stream we were following to the lake. The only nod to the twenty-first century was the existence of televisions, running on car batteries and prominently displayed in glassless windows.

The floating village consisted of hundreds of boats, some no bigger than 20 feet by 8 feet. Entire families lived on each boat. Cages suspended underneath the boat served as impromptu fish farms. The back of the boat held a primitive outhouse. Children bathed in the lake while old women cleaned fish or cooked noodles in water dipped from the front of the boat. The lake served not only as a source of food and drinking water, but as the bathtub and septic system, as well. Outboard motors, used to power the fishing boats onto the lake each evening and those ubiquitous televisions were the only lifestyle changes in the last 200 years.

The bamboo shacks and floating village were light-years below the standard of living enjoyed by the Cambodians who designed and lived in the temple complex at Angkor Wat. All of those past splendors seem lost to the Cambodians of today.

What lesson can we learn from this study in contrasts? How did these people lose touch with the agility of spirit and intelligence that made Angkor Wat possible? Instead of stretching forward, they idle in place.

Once we cease to learn, build, create and stretch, we not only stop gaining or growing, we allow the rest of the world to pass us by. Ask yourself, frequently, "Am I moving forward or simply drifting?" The lesson I learned in Cambodia helped me, especially during the most recent recession: Use your agility so you never become a floating relic of past splendor.

GET IN SYNC WITH AGILITY, NOT INSANE WITH DIVERSENESS

Agility also encompasses the way we interact with the world around us and the people in that world. For 29 years I've been a student of business, and during that time I've encountered many management theories obviously written by university professors or solo consultants who have never managed a functioning business for a single day in their lives. It's like getting relationship advice from someone who's not in one.

I don't profess to be a management expert. Managing employees is probably the most challenging thing I've ever done. Believe it or not, managing conferences with 1,000-plus attendees and celebrity speakers is a piece of cake compared to managing my staff of 23.

I never expected to find myself involved in management. In fact, when I worked in the hospital as an RN, management was not one of my ambitions. What I've learned from my experiences is that managing a business is like being in a giant laboratory. Sometimes your experiments work, sometimes they catch fire and sometimes they blow up in your face.

While I don't know everything there is to know about management theory, here's what I do know: I've got five executive directors and every one of them is distinct. Their differences make for a stronger company, but also demand that I be agile in the way I manage.

When they're successful, my company is successful. So I'm extremely motivated and called upon all day, every day to flex my agility muscles and interface differently with each executive director. Some perform at their best when I'm totally hands-off; others perform best when I'm very hands-on and at least one performs best when I'm somewhere in the middle (one hand on, one hand off). If I tried to manage each individual the same way, the outcome would be disastrous.

You may not automatically think of yourself as a manager or director, but if you're a woman, you are. You manage your life, career, family and probably most of the people involved. I'm sure you've noticed by now that every relationship in your life requires some form of management. Whether it's your spouse, mother-in-law, parents, children, coworkers, boss or even your dry cleaner, they all have to be treated differently.

Check the Water Level of Your Relationships

People are like orchids. My twin brother Vince loves animals, and he's always trying to get me to buy a horse or a dog. Whenever he does, Tom chimes in with, "This is the woman who kills plastic houseplants."

Historically, every plant I've brought into our home was dead or dying by the time I returned from one of my trips. It got so bad that I started expecting them to be dead. After my last cactus croaked, I almost gave up for good.

Then I discovered orchids. I love their delicate beauty, their range of colors and their various shapes. But like many first-time orchid owners, I had no idea how to treat them. At first I fed them too much plant food. They survived being overfed, but I could sense a rebellion was about to take place. Next I overwatered them. I could practically hear their roots gurgling, "Please, no more." Next I neglected them, allowing them to tell me when they needed attention—usually by starting to wilt or wither. Finally, I learned to strike the perfect balance between care and neglect.

As it turns out, orchids are the perfect plant for someone like me, because they thrive so well on their own and don't even mind being neglected. Orchids have the agility to survive despite hardship or smothering. Today when I return home from a trip, my orchids are there for me, just as beautiful as when I left them.

Just like orchids, you can overwater a person with too many phone calls, too much contact and too much of too much. It's a delicate balance. You must retie the connections with clients or friends, but constantly commenting on their Facebook pages, or texting or emailing them for no good reason, may be too much. Put yourself in their "pot," and ask yourself how much "water" you would need.

I gave my second client the same level of information I was giving to my first client, whose philosophy was, "Tell me everything you know." I figured if the first client liked it, so would the second. It turned out I was overwatering the second client. He thought I was flooding him with information he didn't need. Right or wrong, I learned through this experience that people come in all shapes and sizes, and I learned which ones needed extra water and which ones thrived on small amounts.

Likewise, if you're not paying enough attention to the people important to you and your passionate vision, it's like neglecting your orchids. An old client or friend no longer hears from you because you're not retying the connection. The relationship withers and fades.

People are as precious as orchids. Use your agility to treat them like these stunning flowers, and your relationships will blossom and grow.

Agility Sustains Odd Couples

A big test of my skills in managing my own agility came shortly after I started my business. The first attorney I consulted with was serendipity. Everything I did was perfectly in sync with him. We hit it off like best friends. With my goal to turn my business from a part-time venture into a full-time business, I concluded, "I've got it all figured out. I know exactly what attorneys want, and this is going to be easy." Boy, I could not have been more wrong.

When Andy went to his partner Jim (who literally wrote the book in Texas on medical malpractice trial tactics), and said, "Jim, you have to start using Vickie," use me Jim did. He rode me like my brother rides a thoroughbred horse—hard and fast.

Jim was the smartest attorney I've ever met, and he turned out to be my most challenging client. In contrast, Andy was fun and respectful and treated me like a lady, while Jim was 100 percent good-ole-boy. He thought women had their place and should stay exactly where they belonged.

When I moved to Texas from New Orleans for nursing school, I had steered clear of the good-ole-boys. The one and only time I went country western dancing with my friends, some urban cowboy clamped his hand around the back of my neck to lead me like a horse onto the dance floor.

"That's it! I'm out of here." I never went country western dancing again.

To this day I don't like pickup trucks or men in cowboy hats, and country western music still gives me a pain in my neck. (Apologies to all country music fans—please don't let my regrettably bad experience stop you from reading the rest of the book.)

Working with Jim was like being right back in that cowboy dance hall again. After a particularly difficult Jim encounter, I figured if I could survive growing up with my twin brother, who taught me to buck up at an early age, I could survive Jim.

I knew I could learn a lot—that is, if I had the agility to avoid bashing Jim on the head with one of his big cigars. I haven't mentioned the cigars and the way he'd smoke them everywhere he went. He figured that when your name is first on the door, you do what you want—and he did.

This "odd couple" (like Brooks and Dunn) were amazingly effective together. Jim was the courtroom showboat, strutting his brilliance for the judge and jury, while Andy was the street fighter, slugging it out behind the scenes in depositions and motions. Together they created an enviable record and legend. That in itself was an agility lesson for me.

The experience with this formidable pair taught me that if I was going to build something big, which was my intention for my business, I needed to be agile enough to respond to odd relationships, to get in sync with them instead of going insane.

Jim set the bar high, expecting everyone to leap over it; and we all did. His partners, associates and legal assistants all rose to his challenge. So I bucked up, and Jim and I did our dance, through clouds of cigar smoke, glasses of whiskey, dirty boots up on his desk during brainstorms and along the way he taught me more about medical malpractice than 95 percent of other attorneys will ever know.

The teaching went both ways, though. In my buck-up style, I taught him that women professionals didn't need to be led around by the neck. Jim and I reached a truce and our own level of understanding. He made me a better consultant. I like to think he'd admit that my work product made him a better attorney.

Here's the real surprise: Like Andy, Jim will always be one of my favorite attorney-clients. But hey, maybe that's not so surprising, after all. I love a challenge to my agility, don't you?

LEAVE YOUR OLD COMFORTS AT HOME

When packing for a trip to the deserts of Morocco, I noticed that I was cramming in an awful lot of American comforts. Here we go again: teapot, table, tent and hair dryer—plus two Sherpas to carry it all. Having invested my time and money in the adventure of exploring this exotic destination, I had to admit, "If I'm going to bring the United States with me, I might as well stay at home."

By replicating my homey comforts on the road, I'd actually miss what I was traveling in search of—an exciting, unpredictable experience that would enliven my senses, stimulate my creative juices and move me out of my comfort zone so that I could return home rejuvenated, with increased agility to deal with all the challenges of life and business. I didn't need my hair dryer to ride a camel and sleep in the Sahara desert. By leaving such items behind, I packed lighter and was able to immerse myself in the Moroccan culture with a more complete sense of adventure.

Isn't this how we often approach life, dragging old baggage into new situations? We decide to travel to a new place—a new career, a new relationship. But we carry along old attitudes that deny us the new experience.

In your passionate new life, you'll be traveling to a new place, so leave your old comforts at home. The less baggage you carry, the more opportunity you'll have to flex your agility. Pack a lighter bag.

FLEX YOUR AGILITY WITH THE
5 PROMISES

PROMISE 1
I Will Live and Work a Passionate Life

In what way do you need to be more agile to dive deeply into your passionate vision?

_____

_____

_____

PROMISE 2
I Will Go for It or Reject It Outright

What risk will you take to stretch to your new level of agility?

_____

_____

_____

PROMISE 3
I Will Take One Action Step a Day Toward My Passionate Vision

Write down two action steps you will take to stretch to the next level.

_____

_____

_____

PROMISE 4
I Commit to Being a Success Student for Life

Define a third level of growth, a stretch that seems unattainable. How, when and where will you attain the knowledge or training to reach this advanced level of agility?

_____

_____

_____

PROMISE 5
I Believe as a Woman I Really Can Do Anything

Focus on your highest aspiration. See yourself enjoying the attainment of this highest goal, then reach out with your inner being for a tangible symbol of attainment. What is that symbol? Write it down. Listen with your inner ear to the praise and congratulations of your peers, family and friends. (Reject any negatives.) What are they saying?

_____

_____

_____

>> DOWNLOAD THE 5 PROMISES FOR AGILITY AT **WickedSuccess.com.**

BLANCHE'S AGILITY

I learned so much from my mom, especially how to make do, how to be agile. We didn't have a lot of money, but my mom was a very strong and agile woman. We raised chickens and sold eggs. My mom made dresses out of feed sacks for me to wear. She loved to sew. I had all these fancy dresses, which made everyone think we were rich. One day, I asked my mother, "Are we poor?" She replied, "No, you will never be poor. You can be broke but not poor. You are rich because you have family, love and food to eat."

My husband passed away six months ago from strokes he'd had for years. Before that he was ill a lot. Every day was a challenge for him, and for me as I figured out how to help him eat, walk and communicate. I had to entertain and humor him, keep him emotionally stable.

We all have choices in life. I chose to stand by him no matter what. It wasn't easy. I worked as a dental assistant for 34 years and was the sole supporter of my family. I did what I had to do. Surrounding myself with all the kids in the neighborhood kept me young and agile. You can either make life good or not. I try to be agile and open-minded, try to see humor in everything. You've got to have lightness and darkness. How would we know what lightness feels like if we didn't have darkness to remind us?

I'm a woman; I'm strong and rich in the ways that count and I know how to do more than just get by. I choose to

celebrate even when I feel like crying. That's agility. I guess
I'm lucky I grew up in New Orleans, where you don't need
a reason to celebrate.

Blanche, 74
A LOVER OF LIFE, PEOPLE AND TREES

With agility you can tackle a world of options as you follow
your passionate vision. The next Feminine Force, the genius
inside every woman, can make your vision a brilliant reality
and lead you to truly wicked success.

Those curve balls are always coming. Eventually,
you learn how to hit some of them.
QUEEN LATIFAH

The especial genius of women I believe to be electrical in movement, intuitive in function, spiritual in tendency.
MARGARET FULLER

Genius is not fixed, but elastic.
VICKIE L. MILAZZO

5

GENIUS

Intensify Your Intelligence for Accelerated Success

Study after study shows that, overall, men and women are equally intelligent, despite men having 4 percent more brain cells, about 100 grams more brain tissue and an annoying ability to memorize the most inane sports statistics while forgetting their anniversaries.

Interestingly though, women's grade point averages in college are generally higher than men's, no matter what field they study. Women have outstripped men in completing college and obtaining graduate-level degrees, and the lead is widening.

Although equally intelligent, men and women possess different kinds of intelligence. Women have smaller, more compact brains with 10 times more white matter, which tends to improve the integration and assimilation of information. Men have six times more gray matter, which makes them more adept at spatial tasks and thus enhances their map-reading and directional skills. (Could that be why they never ask for directions?)

Women typically develop better language-related skills. During childhood, girls' vocabularies develop faster than those of boys; and by the time they're adults, women speak 20,000 to 25,000 words a day, compared to a man's 7,000 to 10,000.

Women use their holistic intelligence to accumulate knowledge in a variety of areas and to synthesize that material. In the "total immersion" process of learning, women take it in all at once, through their eyes, ears and intuitive senses.

What does all this mean? It means that despite historical data citing more male "geniuses," women can do anything intellectually that men can do. We simply do it differently.

COLLABORATION IS COLLECTIVE GENIUS

The secret to a woman's genius is collaboration. Instead of solving problems in isolation, we evolved to connect and collaborate. The success that comes from this process provides sanity, support and genius solutions.

Tom and I went fishing in the Colorado backcountry with a group of CEOs and their spouses. I was one of only two women CEOs in the bunch. One evening we played a game, the men against the women. From opposite sides of a blazing campfire, each team asked the other trivia questions about the opposite gender. The men might ask, "Who's Earl Anthony?" The women, "What's GWP?"

The two teams used completely different approaches. The women huddled and collaborated on the answers as well as the questions. "Tom's going to know that GWP means 'gift with purchase,'" I whispered. "Every time I buy cosmetics I show him my gift and brag, 'I got my GWP!'"

The other women chimed in, and together we strategically decided which questions to ask. In contrast, the men studied their list of questions individually. When a man's turn came, he asked the question he perceived to be hardest. No collaboration, and total astonishment when the women got the answer right.

One question was about weight lifting. As soon as a man asked it, Tom exclaimed, "Arghhh!" He knew I'd know that answer, but since the guys didn't collaborate, Tom's information was useless. The men also popped off their answers without collaborating.

A team of highly successful CEOs against mostly homemakers—wouldn't you expect the men to have the intellectual edge? The men lost miserably because they failed to collaborate. They were so surprised, they demanded a rematch, which we promptly won too.

In my office, the women collaborate naturally. They're in the hallway, in each others' offices, at each others' desks. The ideas are always sparking. In a man's world, collaboration may be viewed as a weakness. Have you ever noticed how determinedly men resist asking for directions, and how many miles out of the way you travel because of that resistance?

Collaboration must be done in concert to be effective. When we route a "live" project from one desk to another, each of us thinks about it on a level that reflects our own knowledge, viewpoints and experiences. It's only when we come together and engage in conversation that we raise new questions and think of possibilities at a collective level we would not have considered on our own.

The rise in the use of wikis and other collaborative software indicate the rapid acceptance of this need to share knowledge, ideas and energies. Office technology has advanced to provide a platform for sharing, reviewing, editing and completely rethinking documents or graphics. Documents that once routed in brown office envelopes from desk to desk for sign-off can be accessed by workers anywhere there's a computer. As our workforce has gone global, software has permeated the vacuum created by our inability to meet in person simultaneously.

Collaboration is not just connecting with people. It's also an attitude of helpfulness. The anonymity of the Internet is fostering a very rude world. Wickedly successful women get it that playing nice is a sign of strength.

Even if someone else in your collaboration doesn't take the high road, take it anyway. Being nice always pays off, and in no way implies that you are weak or have to kowtow to someone else's whims. One of my favorite greeting cards pictures a charming little girl in boots. She's smiling sweetly, but the sentiment reads, "Your boots may be made for walking but mine are made for kicking your ass." That pretty much sums up my attitude about competitors, yet I'm always professional, even when they're not.

While I ultimately make my own decisions, collaboration is one of the secrets to the wicked success of my company. Inside every woman is a natural collaborator. That's a wicked advantage we have as women, an intellectual edge we can leverage for using our genius at the highest possible level.

LEVERAGE PEOPLE WHO ARE ALREADY
WICKEDLY SUCCESSFUL

Leveraging other people's talents and connections is collaborative genius. I've worked with women who say, "I want to do this all on my own. I don't want my husband's, colleagues' or friends' help."

My response: "What! Are you crazy? Ride the horse of anybody who has what you need." None of us arrived where we are completely on our own. That's impossible.

Look around and you'll be surprised by the talent that's already available to you. Evie sums up my attitude about leveraging skills and brain matter in our company:

> Vickie is the master of using her staff's strengths. She exploits us—in a good way. Many entrepreneurs only use their staff according to their job descriptions. Vickie says that's a waste.
>
> Vickie taught me that you don't just use your support team for what they think they can do. Instead, she urges me to notice their other talents, then to help them stretch beyond their self-imposed limits, to develop and use those additional talents. The result is more career satisfaction for the team member and more productivity for our company.
>
> When I was a brand-new employee at the Institute, Vickie would ask us to present book reports to encourage learning. I'd never given a presentation in my life, yet I found myself selling the idea of mind-mapping to the entire team. I loved it.
>
> At the end of my presentation, Vickie asked me to give a talk for 250 people. I said, "Sure, I can," even though I was thinking, "Oh no, what have I gotten myself into?" Vickie saw a strength I didn't see in myself, and she immediately put it to use. Vickie mentored me through the entire process of becoming a confident speaker. Since then I've spoken to audiences of 1,000 or more with ease.
>
> Most entrepreneurs would have treated that first presentation as just a book report. In fact, most entrepreneurs wouldn't have their staff doing book reports at all. But Vickie is all about helping her staff learn and grow, mentoring them as they feel their way into new and more challenging roles, and then getting the best out of them. That's genius.

Even when I worked solo from home, I leveraged other people's knowledge and talents to accelerate my success. I hired a part-time bookkeeper, seven of my typist's children as assistants and other nurses as subcontractors. I woke every day asking, "What can someone else help me with today? How can I leverage the strengths of others to build this business?" Through leveraging others I grossed $1 million before leaving my home office and staffing up for real.

Whether you own a business, manage others or just manage your own day, leveraging the talents of others is just plain smart.

Push Past Success Apartheid

Just as you become a better tennis player by playing with those who are better than you, so too will you become better at your career or any endeavor by interacting with people who are already wickedly successful in that area. But here's the rub: Successful people like to hang out with other successful people, so sometimes you may feel like you're on the outside looking into this private club of "The Wickedly Successful."

In one association I belong to, the majority of the members pull in five-figure incomes. At the other end are a small number of members who pull in the six-figure and seven-figure salaries only dreamed of by the others.

When it comes to socializing and collaborating, the specter of success apartheid raises its ugly head, as the larger group is excluded by the smaller. At the end of the day, if you can't help the ones at the top, they probably aren't looking to help you.

As a mentor to other women, and a natural collaborator, I find this distressing. Likewise, it's helpful to remember that getting into the club requires that you too have something to contribute. Successful people owe you nothing. When they give of themselves, consider it a gift. I've had people angry with me or worse, publicly trash me, because I won't give them my time or a slice of my pie for free. Time is a precious commodity, and wickedly successful women understand they're responsible for their own success.

Don't Chalk Up Failures to Experience

None of us likes the "F"-word (failure), yet mistakes are an inevitable part of success. While we do need to free ourselves to fail, not all mistakes are created equal. Running out of catalogs because your new ad doubled the usual response rate could be classified as an intelligent mistake, and a nice problem to have. Having the wrong phone number on a catalog because you didn't proof it before printing cannot be categorized as anything but negligence. By leveraging the knowledge of others, you're likely to make fewer mistakes, or at least to make more intelligent ones.

I mentored a woman who violated the principles I had taught her about getting a contract and retainer before starting a project with new clients. After completing the project, she had difficulty getting paid. When she contacted me for mentoring, I asked her to describe her plan for solving this issue.

"I guess I'll just write it off and chalk this one up to experience," she responded. That was exactly the wrong thing to say to me. I was all over that like a goose on a bug.

"No, you don't chalk up an obviously preventable error to experience. The time you want to write off you will never get back, and would have been better spent solidifying your relationship with clients, marketing to grow your business and working on more projects. Lost time is lost money. Sometimes you have to chalk up a mistake to experience, but this is not one of those times. Why? Because you didn't make a mistake. You consciously chose to do something you knew you should not do. With that conscious decision comes an obvious price."

I am all for making mistakes. I make them every day. After all, people who never make a mistake never make anything. But I am not into making just any mistake—especially not mistakes that are obvious and avoidable. Instead, I aim for making intelligent ones. Making a bad choice and expecting a different outcome isn't a learning experience, it's insanity.

I teach that when you do X, you will get Y result. I take the Xs very seriously. If you choose to do Z, do not expect to get Y, and don't be surprised by the resulting pain from Z. Only chalk up to experience that which grows you.

NOW THAT YOU'VE GOT THE ADVICE, BE GENIUS AND HEED IT

I love to mentor entrepreneurs. I think it's in my DNA, and I like knowing that the advice I'm giving doesn't come from a textbook. I've lived it for 29 years, and I pride myself on the fact that my advice is real and grounded—there's no fluff. Of all the mentors at my company, I'm probably the toughest. I've always lived a buck-up lifestyle and don't like it when people make excuses for why they can't do what they know they have to do to succeed.

I'm also never afraid to say I don't know, or that I have to research a question (a skill I learned from working with attorneys). But my advice is only as good as the recipient's willingness to do something with it.

Here are the stories of two different entrepreneurs and their very different reactions to my mentoring. The first has been in business for 10 years. This entrepreneur asked me to critique an audio recording promo he'd created. When I communicated my input, I started by saying that I wasn't sure if he wanted to re-record the promo, but that my feedback would require him to do so. His response was, "Absolutely, I'll do it!" and he did.

The other is a student with zero years of entrepreneurial experience. She has bombarded me and other company mentors with question after question, all without putting any of it into practice. With every piece of advice offered, she instantly jumps in to say why the advice is wrong for her and won't work.

If I can borrow and paraphrase Danny DeVito's line from the movie, *War of the Roses*, "When someone who gets paid $400 an hour wants to give you free advice, you should listen." When you've asked advice from an expert, whether you're paying for it or not, be ready to listen. It doesn't mean you should blindly follow it. I've gotten advice from high-powered business experts that was clearly wrong for me, but I at least considered it before rejecting it outright.

When an expert's advice isn't right for you, you don't have to heed it, but at least first receive the advice with openness and curiosity. If the advice is from a credible expert, ask yourself why you're resisting it. Is it because the advice is not a right fit for you? Or are you rejecting it because it will require you to stretch yourself or do something inconvenient or outside the comfort zone you've built around yourself?

People who covet what someone else has worked hard to achieve, whether it's losing weight, composing an award-winning song or making a six-figure income, often hesitate to analyze what it took to achieve those results, because the answer often involves hard work and discipline.

A common question people ask me is, "Vickie, where do you get the energy to manage your company, speak, exercise and write books too?" It's true that I'm a high-energy person. I start at 4:00 a.m. and go strong all day long. But I don't magically wake up every morning in overdrive. There's a discipline to achieving that energy level—exercise, weight control, a good night's sleep, eating the right foods, a glass of healthy red wine. It takes the whole routine.

Yet when I tell people about that simple discipline I can see their eyes glaze over. They expect a magic potion, a quick fix, like pulling out your lipstick for a touch-up. They've learned my secret, but instead of applying what they've learned, they often look for an easier route. You don't have to get up at 4:00 a.m. to be wickedly successful, but you do have to get up. Take my advice on this one, and I won't even charge you the $400.

GENIUS HEARS OTHER VOICES

While I don't need to take a majority vote on every issue, I've learned that I care more about being successful than being right. That requires listening, collaborating and even seeking opposing viewpoints. My staff is strong, opinionated and sometimes even mouthy—just the way I like them.

We naturally navigate toward people who agree with us. But the person who disagrees will force you to think at a higher level. Consensus almost always leads to weakened decisions. Some of our best ideas are spawned from discussing an opposing viewpoint. Surround yourself with people who challenge you. And reward their outspokenness by listening, even when you decide not to heed their advice. These other voices might be hard to hear when their suggestions lead to more work or more expense, but it's worth it.

We call one extraordinary woman in our company the "other voice." When the rest of us are hot on an idea, she presents alternative ways of thinking. Without being negative, she challenges our paradigms.

Recently, I sat down with our conference team to discuss the curriculum, expecting the discussion to go quickly. We'd forgotten our other voice. She didn't like one of the decisions we made. Her dissenting opinion at first made us moan with the realization that her suggestions meant more work; but after the groaning died down, we revisited our decision, adopted her ideas, made the change and arrived at a much better result.

When we shortchange collaboration and the dissenting viewpoints that come with it, we're missing an important piece of the performance process. Diverse opinions spark new thoughts and atypical directions, and one plus one suddenly equals a lot more than two. You arrive at a place no individual would have reached alone, and your project rockets to a new level. Even when I disagree with a collaborator's viewpoint, I try to extract something of value from it.

Actively seek out individuals with opposing viewpoints. Do you typically hang with your best friends who never disagree with you on how you handled a situation with your boss? Do you eat lunch with the same person every day or sit next to the same person in every meeting? Do you only hang with people your age? I recommend doing the opposite—get with people who have the potential to challenge you.

Stop Sucking Up

If you can't express opposing viewpoints without fear of recrimination or retaliation, or you work for someone who doesn't care about your ideas, it may be the wrong job for you.

But when we hire new employees, I sometimes notice they're reluctant at first to give opinions that are different from the majority of the outspoken staffers. Not only are they slow to speak up, when they do it's obvious they're just tagging onto the others' opinions. It's like the new hires are afraid to get off the fence and jump down on either side until they know what side everybody else is on. Here in Texas, if you're sitting on a fence in a pasture full of longhorn cattle, that may be a good idea. But when you're in my conference room, it's not a tactic for success with me or my staff.

If you don't buck up and speak up, you'll get zero credit for your contribution. If I or your boss wanted a parrot, we would have hired one. Instead, we hired you for your expertise. We want to hear your opinion—whether we agree with it or not.

Successful businessowners don't want to be surrounded by yes-people. They're used to thinking for themselves, and they expect the same of you.

They don't need you to suck up; they need you to buck up and intelligently articulate your thoughts and opinions.

CHALLENGE THE EXPERTS

There are experts all around us, and it could be those very experts holding you back. This is why you don't want to limit your collective genius to just the acclaimed authorities. They're often wrong.

What happened when the nutrition experts convinced an entire nation that a high-carbohydrate diet (including processed carbs) was healthy? Increased obesity and alarming rates of diabetes, in not just adults, but also our children.

My success, like that of many entrepreneurs, is built on challenging the experts—not relying on them. Our founding fathers weren't experts at governing for freedom. Many of our best inventors weren't experts. America was built by a handful of amateurs, and many of our greatest achievements came from the "genius" of tinkerers and inventors constantly poking, prodding, testing, then discarding what didn't work, until they hit the magic formula.

To be wickedly successful we often have to act contrary to what the experts advise. When I pioneered the field of legal nurse consulting I was challenging the experts. The whole concept was contrary to what attorneys accepted as an industry standard. Typically, they relied on doctors to try to make sense of medical records, yet it's widely known that most doctors don't read the medical records. So how could attorneys possibly be getting what they really needed? Not to mention the fact that physicians were charging way too much for their time and weren't always giving the attorneys objective opinions, because they are often too protective of each other.

I had to go against the experts and educate attorneys that the registered nurse is the only healthcare provider who knows everything that's going on with the patient. We were the ones with hands-on information, with 24/7, face-to-face contact with patients; and, most important, we're the only healthcare providers who ever read the entire medical record. RNs not only have the expertise to uncover vital facts and key pieces of information that can make or break an attorney's case, they're cost-effective, too.

When James Cameron created the movie *Avatar,* he did everything contrary to the experts. The conventional wisdom Hollywood experts clung to warned that audiences "won't go see an intelligent movie," that they only want gross-out, teen-oriented comedies or star-driven vehicles. Cameron ignored the experts. He penned, directed and produced a movie that required a viewer's full attention, because he put its leading characters into unrecognizable avatars.

The experts say the attention span of audiences caps out at 90 minutes, that moviegoers won't sit for a film running 162 minutes. Cameron ignored that expert advice and cut the movie he wanted audiences to see. Again, the experts were wrong—to the tune of more than $2.7 billion worldwide!

Experts also believed that audiences weren't ready for full-length 3D movies other than children's animated films or the occasional IMAX spectacle. Cameron ventured out on a limb and filmed his movie in 3D anyway. This turned out to be the viewing method of choice for *Avatar* audiences. And since the release of *Avatar*, 3D is breeding in the movie industry.

Contrary to what most people believe, it doesn't take an Einstein to spawn brilliant ideas. The reality is that there are very few Einsteins out there and a lot more ordinary people like you and me. We all wake up with ideas; some are brilliant, some are ordinary and some are just plain dumb. But even an ordinary idea can pay off huge.

In my company, I encourage everyone, expert or not, to speak up when they have a new idea and to verbalize their objections when they think something isn't working. Sometimes the person who knows the least about the subject asks a question that helps us make the biggest breakthroughs. In fact, I always know we're onto a truly innovative idea when one of the experts offers up his or her good, old-fashioned, safe, conservative advice and says, "You can't do that, because . . ."

I frequently gather our staff around our big conference table for a focused, all-day brainstorming session. These sessions have contributed tremendously to our wicked success.

I've shared this strategy with CEOs who say, "I can't afford to shut down my business for the day and sit in a room with $15/hour nonexperts." My response: "I can't afford not to, knowing how many genius ideas I get for launching new services, products and better service for our clients."

How many multimillion-dollar ideas are stuck in the mailroom? Brilliant ideas are generated by the most unlikely individuals—and you'll never know if you don't ask. Ethically "embezzling" my employees' ideas for 29 years makes me look like a genius.

To advance your career or business, listen to nonexperts as well as the acclaimed authorities. If not for renegade visionaries who followed their own minds despite the advice of experts, a lot of wonderful things we take for granted today wouldn't exist, because the experts said no one needed them or nobody would buy them.

What expert have you challenged lately? What nonexpert have you listened to? Embrace this renegade strategy, and no one can stop you on the fast lane to wicked success.

REMOVE YOUR OWN BURRS

During a trip to Africa I went hiking with Colin Francombe on his Kenyan game sanctuary, Ol Malo. The trail varied between rock and brush. Colin's dog Uzuri came with us, sometimes running ahead, other times following behind. Well into the hike we encountered a section of trail infested with burrs. Soon Uzuri limped up next to me on three legs, obviously having picked up a burr, and I stooped to help.

When I asked Colin the best way to remove a burr, he replied, "Oh, I don't do that. I let her sort it out. Otherwise, I'd spend all my time picking burrs off her." I put her paw down and, sure enough, moments later she ran alongside us again on all fours, the burr gone and forgotten.

As we hiked, I considered Colin's attitude. He lives in a brutal country where self-reliance is a necessity, not a luxury. African people and animals must be strong and independent or they'd never survive in the hostile African bush. My sympathy for Uzuri almost caused me to intervene, to her detriment. If I'd helped her, I would have made a friend. Instead, Colin encouraged her independence. The next time she picks up a burr, she'll handle it like a pro. She won't limp back to the main house looking for Colin or me.

This bush survival principle also applies in our world. When we find our own solutions, we grow stronger. Excessive reliance on others for our success weakens us. Soon we shy away from challenges we once might have conquered with relish and ease.

Consulting mentors, leveraging the talents of others, and listening to other voices won't protect you from every burr, or help you every time you get one. Intelligent women know when to ask for help in removing burrs too big or thorny to manage alone and when to enjoy the sweet victory that comes from their own efforts. Toughen your intelligence by removing your own burrs.

TRUST YOUR OWN VOICE

We all have an inner teacher (our own voice) ready to show us the way, as long as we're willing to be a student of our own intelligence. In yoga class the teacher is essential, but the reflection in the mirror is the best teacher of all.

Are you a reflection of your own ideas, or someone else's? Doing what others tell us to do is often a way to avoid accountability. Even though I highly appreciate brainstorming sessions and use them extensively in my company, I don't always go with the crowd. My staff teases that we're not a democracy; we're a semibenevolent dictatorship. I laugh, because I'm fine with that.

In a meeting, when I've gone against the crowd and made a decision contrary to their collective advice, somebody will invariably pipe up and say "It's unanimous!" and we all have a good laugh. It's not that I don't listen to the crowd, but the crowd isn't always right. Neither am I, but at the end of the day, the decision, responsibility and the name on the company are mine, and it has to feel right to me.

Always trusting the groupthink is herd mentality. Blending into the herd is not a strategy for wicked success. It's only a strategy for staying alive if you're a zebra or wildebeest. Agreeing with the majority doesn't make you right; it just means you hang out with a lot of people of like mind. They might be so busy agreeing with one another that they miss the errors in their thinking. In a world jam-packed with information, ideas, options and opinions, you have to be willing to assess, decide and trust your own voice.

As I mentioned, a related industry association formed after I pioneered the industry of legal nurse consulting. And the strangest thing happened: I started getting negative messages from them—"Vickie, you're saturating our market." "Vickie, you can't do seminars in our city."

"Vickie, you can't do this; you shouldn't do that." My reaction was, "I'll do it my way, thank you very much."

When I offered to help them develop a set of standards, they said, "We don't need standards." Later, I noticed they had adopted my published standards as their own.

When our industry further matured, I offered to help the association create a certification. They again said, "No, we don't need that. We're not ready for that."

I didn't agree. And after what had happened when I offered to help them develop standards, I knew that sooner or later they would take my idea, probably use my curriculum and develop the certification without me, since I wasn't a member of their herd.

I decided to create the certification I knew our nursing specialty needed. Today our association thrives, while theirs continues to shrink in membership. Their limited and often negative mind-sets drive away prospective members. We advocate freethinkers while they foster an atmosphere of groupthink rigidity.

Wanting too much to be accepted as a group member or striving to please others can detract from thinking for yourself. Audaciously successful people often stand contrary to what the world believes is right, and they don't care if their ideas upset people. Of course your goal is not to upset, but to express your opinions uncensored, in your truest voice.

Be willing to stir things up, stand out and maybe tick off a few people. Let other women "go along" and have their middle-of-the-road successes. Just don't let one of those other women be you.

STOP HANGING WITH THE BIGGEST LOSERS

I have a friend who's overweight and really wants to lose the extra pounds. She has tried just about everything—the grapefruit diet, the cabbage soup diet and the Atkins, South Park, South Beach, Long Beach and Muscle Beach diets. Each one lasted less than a week. She's now considering lap band surgery and joining yet another weight management support group.

When I did psych rotations in nursing school, I thought, "How can group therapy possibly work?" Well, it usually didn't, and that's because we persist in putting a psych patient who has a particular problem in a group of other psych patients with like problems. Then we wonder why they don't act normal. How can they even know what normal looks like?

I wonder if the ultimate peer pressure is to not rise above a group but to remain at the same level as everyone else in the group. I'm going to take a position here that's controversial: I don't believe the best way to achieve something is by hanging out with people who haven't achieved their own goals—whether shared or different from yours.

If you want to lose weight, you're more likely to succeed if you hang with people who have successfully managed to maintain or lose weight, instead of people who haven't. Just like if you want to learn to play golf, you don't hang with a bad golfer. You take lessons from a professional, or at least someone with high-level skills.

My overweight friend has fallen into what I call the culture of losers. Rather than do the hard work of getting on an exercise program, regulating her diet, cooking healthy foods at home and exercising self-discipline, she's found a support group of other "dieters" with similar issues, who sit around together, acting empathic about failing week after week. As much as American society loves winners, individually we seem to be more comfortable identifying with a culture of losers. Think reality TV.

This also applies to your workplace. Generally there are two groups of people: the successful movers and shakers who work hard and get promoted, and the coffee-klatchers who spend their time complaining and whining about anything and everything.

Let's face facts. People who are successful tend to hang with other successful people, not with losers who whine about someone else's success.

Which way do you gravitate? I go to a number of professional conferences each year. At one of my favorites, I typically see three clearly defined groups: (1) worked hard to become successful and are; (2) working hard to be successful and probably will be, and (3) working hard at complaining, and will probably never be successful.

Group three always gives me pause. You can easily spot them by their glum, dour looks. You'll hear them exchanging failed strategies and denouncing proven strategies. Why aren't they hanging with any successful people from group one? Where they are, they won't learn a thing other than how not to be successful.

An entrepreneur I know needed to fill a vacancy in a department and hoped to do so internally. She had the perfect candidate in mind, perceiving her to have untapped potential. But there was one drawback: The candidate had never expressed any interest in increasing her knowledge or growing beyond her current position. Also, she never socialized or interacted with people outside her department.

When the owner suggested this woman to the department manager, the manager rejected the recommendation outright, explaining that she'd never noticed the employee do anything other than what was expected of her. Unaware of all this, the castoff candidate still works her original job, doing what she was hired to do, lunching with the same people and hanging with that same group at company functions. She'll never know the opportunities she missed out on by hanging with the same people day after day.

Back to my friend with the weight issue. She has every skill she needs to lose her additional pounds. I know her family, and she's certainly the exception to her family's rule. Her issue isn't genetic; it's motivational. It's time for her to change her support group, from a lack of support for change to an active support to change. Instead of going to a meeting where everyone understands and commiserates over how they needed that extra pint of Häagen-Dazs dulce de leche after a less than stellar performance review, and how they'll do better next week, she needs someone who will support her in taking responsibility for her weight and hold her feet to the fryer when she doesn't.

The view from the top is meant to be shared. Find someone who's there to share it with, not someone who's never seen it.

GENIUS COMBINES IQ AND HARD WORK

Wicked success is not about genetics, and intelligence won't get you out of doing the hard work. Occasionally someone will be in the right place at the right time, but you may as well start buying lottery tickets if you think it's that easy.

Thomas Edison, who failed thousands of times at producing a working lightbulb before he hit on the perfect model, said: "Genius is 1 percent inspiration and 99 percent perspiration." Our advanced technology might speed up the process a bit, but hard work is still a big part of the success equation.

I learned a humbling lesson from my thesis advisor when she gave me a B in a course, even though I had turned in A work. When I challenged

her, she said that while the result of my semester's work was certainly
A quality, I was capable of doing more than I had done. And she was
right. I tried to skate through that last semester solely on my intelligence,
thinking she wouldn't notice.

I was upset that she busted my 4.0 average for my master's degree,
but looking back I know she did me a favor. This intelligent woman
taught me that being smart is not enough. To excel in life, we have to
merge IQ with a strong work ethic.

The team who works for me knows that to get the same performance
evaluation rating the next year, they have to be stronger and swifter.
That's right; the same behaviors year after year won't cut it for them
because it won't cut it for the company and our clients. In today's
fast-moving world, just to get the same results year after year requires
new behavior. Just think about what your world was like five years ago.

Talent Is Overrated

According to Geoffrey Colvin in his book *Talent Is Overrated*, high
achievers are not just talented (i.e., have an inborn ability); they might
not be talented at all.

So what separates wickedly successful women from the rest of the
pack? They don't need someone to watch over them or push them. They
buck up to reality of what wicked success demands: repetitive, focused
and deliberate practice designed to specifically improve performance.

Now, if that sounds like hard work, it is. If you've ever watched
American Idol or *Dancing with the Stars*, you know it's not always the
most talented who advance. Time after time, the winner is the one who
puts on the best show. And to put on the best show requires repetitive,
focused and deliberate practice.

That's why honest and competent self-analysis is so important. Act as
though you're on the outside looking in, an active observer of your own
behavior. We all know it's easier to analyze someone else than to aim
that harsh scrutiny in our own direction. The ability to analyze yourself
objectively is truly a wicked trait.

For example: If you're about to interview for a promotion, you don't
just show up, you apply repetitive, focused and deliberate practice to
make that interview the best one yet. Once the interview commences,

you need the intuitive perception to recognize if you're off target and the agility to pull your act together swiftly.

You must be able to self-analyze at the very moment something is going wrong, so you can rescue the situation. If you can't competently self-analyze, not only will you fail in that interview, you'll just keep making the same mistakes over and over again in future interviews.

It's no surprise that people who fail, fail often. And people who succeed, succeed often.

Practicing the answers to interview questions over and over is an important action step to mastering your self-analysis skills. But that only works if you're practicing the correct responses.

Practicing the same bad tennis swing over and over just produces more bad tennis swings. Repetitive, focused and deliberate practice is worthless if it's the wrong practice. At first you need a tennis coach to straighten out your swing. Then you'll be able to tell for yourself when your swing is off.

As Vince Lombardi said, "Practice doesn't make perfect. Perfect practice makes perfect."

A woman who works out at our gym literally throws herself into her weight-lifting routine with an intensity that would put women half her age to shame. She's disciplined, dedicated and hardworking, but she's not getting any discernable results.

Why? Because her form is off. She flails around, spastically moving her arms and legs as if she's just been hit by a Taser. When she's working out, we all give her a wide berth because we never know in which direction she'll suddenly lurch.

My trainer Jerome is almost a form-fascist. Fortunately he never saw my form when I was working out with my previous trainer—he might have rejected me outright.

When I move a weight, no matter how heavy or light, Jerome chants a mantra of "shoulder blades, abs, glutes, adductors," or whatever muscles or body parts I'm supposed to be engaging for stabilization, strength and form. He constantly teaches me how to exercise my muscles correctly. Jerome's philosophy is that the workout is not how much weight I'm moving; it's about doing it with correct form.

Working hard or long doesn't always predict the quality or quantity of your output. Correct form reaps astonishing productivity. To achieve the form that will provide the results you want, you must practice good work habits.

The woman at my gym is a glowing example of why "working smarter not harder" became such a success mantra. She's working hard without paying attention to those "smart" details that could give her the results she so obviously craves and is willing to work so hard to obtain.

Choose your mentors and advisors carefully. Inept coaches don't just fail to help you, they actually help you to fail.

I recently invested eight months mentoring a woman in my company through repetitive, focused and deliberate practice on a job function I wanted her to master. I required her to do the job herself first. Then I gave her feedback, so each time she was doing it more and more correctly.

Sometimes we don't know what we don't know. That's why appropriate mentors are so important to the process of learning how to self-analyze competently.

I didn't just give this woman feedback; I would ask her to tell me what she needed to do differently the next time. I wanted her to analyze herself, before I mentored her.

My goal was that she would become me during her self-analysis. It would be like Vickie was standing over her shoulder guiding her every step of the way. I wanted her to be able to assess herself in the same way I would.

Time-consuming and sometimes painful for both of us, this investment has paid off in hundreds of thousands of dollars each year. She tells me she still occasionally looks over her shoulder to see if I'm there. And sometimes I am! But not to correct her, just to ask her how her day is going.

Move with Stillness

During a polar-bear-spotting trip to the Svalbard archipelago, one of the naturalists, Richard, was usually the first to spot a polar bear. Now, if they're sitting next to the ship or licking the bow, that's pretty easy, but Richard could spot a white bear in a white environment as far as two and a half miles away.

While the rest of us were scanning the ice flows for anything that looked like it might be alive, Richard would spot a bear and say something like, "It's lying on its belly, off the bow at two o'clock, about a mile out, just past the two ivory gulls and to the left of the walrus with the cavity in its right tusk."

Everyone on the ship was in awe of him and his talent. He had a slight advantage because he was a birder. In comparison to spotting and identifying tiny, quick-moving birds, 8-foot-tall, 1,500-pound polar bears are relatively easy. What no one commented on, however, was the fact that Richard relied on more than just his talent.

Observing Richard spot wildlife, I noticed why he was so successful. He was working harder than anyone else. He never stopped moving and searching. A combination of constant movement and absolute stillness, Richard started on one side of the ship's bridge, searching, moving to the other side, searching, moving outside to the freezing cold of the observation deck (in his flip-flops) and searching some more. When he was moving, he moved quickly, but when he was searching, he was a portrait in stillness.

Richard achieved the perfect balance of action and observation, one that I certainly envy—not just for polar bear spotting but for everyday work. Other passengers and crew were also looking for wildlife, but without the success rate Richard achieved because they often gave up after half an hour or so.

The wickedly successful women I meet aren't the lucky ones. These successful women are the ones who work the hardest—day in and day out.

Apply repetitive, focused and deliberate practice to your passionate vision. With such genius behavior, you might even become legendary. Any woman can, because, after all, talent is overrated.

EMPLOY THE GENIUS OF EINSTEIN

A genius for all times, Albert Einstein once said, "You can't solve a problem with the same consciousness that created it." When I first read this, I contemplated its meaning and thought, "It is only a problem if I allow myself to view it as such."

Applying Einstein's statement in a practical way to my everyday life and career, I decided, "To solve a problem I've obviously helped to create, I need to start with a new and fresh mind."

For example, a woman thinks, "If I can change my job, my life will be better." Possibly. If her job is truly the problem, she might be right, but what if she carries her old attitude into a new job and finds that life hasn't changed at all? More often, this is what happens. If we persist in doing and thinking the same thoughts as always, nothing new or fresh ever gets in.

For many of us, myself included, the Pavlovian response to new ideas and solving problems is, "The problem with that is . . ."

Well, the problem with that is precisely what Einstein knew—that we can't solve problems as long as we perceive them as problems. Unless you change your mind-set, your thoughts or your self-talk will get you the same results. Every problem will be a problem instead of the opportunity it could be.

If you want to effect a change, get outside yourself and look at the situation with fresh eyes. See how you might assess your problem using a different mind-set. Oversimplification? Perhaps. Career or business applications? Infinite.

One of the things that makes my husband Tom good with computers is that he doesn't see a computer problem as a problem. He simply views it as a fun puzzle to solve. I've watched him call tech support on an issue and then help the techie resolve it, simply because Tom approaches it with a different mind-set.

Education is wonderful, but so is forging new ground. Even though I have a string of degrees, I don't have any formal business training, which often works in my favor. I don't feel the constraints that a classroom of MBAs all trained to think alike might feel. Not having their training, I'm free to go in any direction I choose, right or wrong.

Use the next 10 sections to think with a different mind-set and improve your own in the process.

Break Patterns

Insanity is often described as doing the same thing over and over and expecting a different result. Your mind is made up of neural pathways that are like roads connecting bits of information. Most of us have found ourselves driving home only to jolt alert and wonder how we got there. The road is so familiar we follow it automatically. The same thing happens in your mind. Once you learn a thing and do it over and over, you follow that pathway from one thought to another automatically, which allows you to give a speech or swing a golf club.

The mind likes patterns, and it's not always easy to break a pattern. But breaking a pattern presents an opportunity for finding a new solution to a recurring problem. Merely brainstorming ideas with a different person or working in a different environment can give you a new mind-set.

At my company's brainstorming sessions all our employees participate. We constantly change the composition of the small breakout groups. By changing the patterns, we ensure that we get different approaches every time, because it's never the same minds working together.

Tom and I got free coffee from Starbucks for two weeks straight. How do you get free coffee at Starbucks? Easy—go to the one where the staff has developed the bad habit of not being ready when the doors open.

I don't know if it's a Starbucks corporate policy, but it's certainly a policy at this local Starbucks that if you show up at 5:30 a.m. and they haven't yet brewed those steaming hot cauldrons of coffee, they'll give it to you for free once it's ready. This policy consistently worked to our advantage for two weeks because the morning crew was unfailingly late.

If insanity is doing the same thing over and over and expecting a different result, isn't it also insanity to make the same mistake over and over and expect a different result?

What bad habits have you developed that are causing you to give away the equivalent of a cup (or pot) of free coffee? Do you push the envelope on your commute and then act surprised when you're late? Do you fail to return calls promptly and then act surprised that an important client is unhappy? Each of these bad patterns represents a free cup of hot, steamy, expensive Starbucks coffee, ready to be served to the person you've let down.

The hardest thing about a bad habit or a pattern that no longer advances you is recognizing it. Honestly evaluate your habits and patterns, then work at breaking one bad habit or pattern at a time.

Seek New Patterns

Mark Zuckerberg is widely credited for creating Facebook, and at the same time widely accused of stealing Facebook. Social networking sites existed long before Facebook, but what Zuckerberg did was take a hard look at the existing ideas and preconceptions of social media and apply new ideas to improve the social media experience.

He believed that Facebook's true value was in keeping users informed about their "friends." He sought new ways to do this, adding the news feed (which was originally detested), privacy options and photo-tagging. Most important, he made Facebook easy to use for everyone, no matter how primitive or advanced their computer skills, so all Facebook users share the same experience.

Seeking new patterns from old ideas, Zuckerberg created a new and unmatched paradigm for social networks. He reinvented social media and changed forever the way we communicate.

Change a Small Action or Behavior

Taking action, even a small one, will often automatically change your thoughts. Instead of going immediately to your computer, if that's your habit, stop instead to write out a short list of what you want to accomplish. Then power up. You might awaken your mind to sensational new possibilities.

New behaviors are also essential to keeping your brain healthy and young. Brain plasticity allows you to add new synapses and new brain cells by learning new tasks. Brains can get lazy and adjust to routines, much like muscles do on a static workout program. Challenge your brain to learn and you extend its life and memory.

Challenge Your Obstacles

Let go of the notion that you don't have enough time, energy, money or discipline to do what it takes to succeed. Ask yourself frequently, "What beliefs, ideas and behaviors are obstructing my progress? What must I change to abolish these obstacles?"

My biggest obstacle is time, specifically, that I don't have enough to accomplish everything I want. When I challenge my belief and just start doing what I don't have time to do, I magically make it happen.

Become Your Own Other Voice

Law school taught me to consider both sides of a problem, the validity of opposing ideas and that there is no black or white, just shades of gray. The perfect answer is somewhere in that gray.

Like boxers who anticipate their opponent's every punch, successful attorneys spend as much time in the mind of their opponents as they do in their own. The more you anticipate opposing ideas, their not-so-obvious direction and their impact, the better you can strategize for success and avoid fatal blows. Whether it's a career issue or a personal problem to solve, practice considering alternative ideas by being your own other voice.

Ditch Unnecessary Complexities

Complexity in and of itself is not negative. When what you do is complex, someone else can't copy or replicate you so easily. But complexity for complexity's sake wastes your genius.

In one of our staff brainstorming sessions, I asked everyone to identify unnecessary complexities, with the focus on being more efficient and eliminating processes that were no longer needed. Together they identified 48. I was stunned. Of course we triaged the most important ones to tackle first, but many required very little effort. Doing away with the frozen margarita machine in the lunchroom, however, generated numerous heated discussions.

Raise your complexity consciousness by asking yourself the following questions:

1. What am I doing that I no longer need to be doing?

2. Why exactly am I doing it this way? Is it simply because that's how I've always done it?

3. What am I doing that gives me little or no payoff?

4. How can I simplify this process and do it faster and/or cheaper?

5. What technology exists to automate or simplify this process?

Ditching unnecessary complexity opens your complexity consciousness for engagement in Big Things.

Influence Mind-Set with Simplicity

An attorney taught me that there is no value in trying to win a case by proving 10 points if you can prevail by proving only three. Piling on the points can actually backfire because a jury may be counting the points and get distracted from the more important issues.

Similarly, the danger in presenting too many variables for your most important communications is that your listener or reader might lose focus and miss the entire message. Avoid making minor points that render an explanation too complex and confusing. Identify the strong points and keep coming back to those.

A well-known trial attorney I consulted with proves this point. The young guns from the opposing team announced to their colleagues that they were "unimpressed" with this famous attorney's unpretentious trial arguments. Yet that attorney won a $12-million verdict. What failed to impress these less experienced attorneys was the power of simplicity.

This attorney succeeded by condensing the case to the basics, pointing out the obvious, never straying from it and making the difficult appear simple. Twelve million dollars' worth of simple, "unimpressive" communication.

Words have power. Break complex situations down to the most basic level and deliver a focused message. Consciously observe if you are making a simple question, statement or issue more complex than it really is. If someone asks you the time, don't tell them how to build a Rolex.

Do you quickly get to the essence, or are you cluttering unnecessarily? Do you come up for air while answering a question? Do you occasionally pause to receive feedback or clarify questions? Or do you go on until the person you're talking to starts fidgeting to escape? Pay attention not only to how you communicate, but how you think. Assess for yourself how you analyze a problem.

The more we simplify and focus, the more our listeners or readers will comprehend. The process of clear communication starts and ends with us. Simplicity is genius.

Less Is More

I've eaten just about every variety of food in restaurants around the world, from standing in the rain at tiny *Blade Runner* noodle stands at the Tsukiji Fish Market in Tokyo to the humble carts of street vendors in Bangkok to the "best restaurant in the world," the highly idiosyncratic Noma, in Copenhagen, but I keep returning to one chef's place every chance I get. I can't tell you the name of the restaurant or chef because reservations are already too hard to get. The food is such a sensory experience that I devour every dish he places in front of me. One amazing creation is a one-bite crab salad.

Before you say "Vickie, that's ridiculous; why would you want just one bite of a crab salad?" let me add: This crab salad demonstrates one of the chef's most important success secrets—less is more.

You won't find an overflowing bowl of pasta or a slab of ribs on his table. His dishes are so small that each one can usually be eaten in a bite or two, and they burst with intensity. The experience starts when you first see the dish, continues as you smell its aroma and savor the too quickly gone burst of flavors and ends with your hoping no one is looking so that you can lick the plate clean.

The chef's goal: he never wants you to be satiated. In other words, after you've had that bite or two, he wants you to crave more. I've dreamed about having more of some of his dishes. I would gladly scrub pots and pans in his kitchen for just another bite of one oyster dish he creates.

That's a goal you should strive for in your interactions. You want people to always want more of you, to never feel they've had enough or too much.

When you meet in person, never overstay your welcome. If you're on the phone or Skyping, remember, time is valuable.

Come up for air, and don't talk more than you have to. Never use 10 sentences when two will do. In your communications, written, electronic or vocal, and in your work product, give relevant detail, but don't go down rabbit trails commenting on irrelevancies.

Tune Up Your Voice

A study published in *Speech Management* magazine shows that when meeting someone for the first time, 62 percent of a person's effectiveness can be attributed to voice and delivery and only 38 percent to content.

Delivery is the way you talk—your speech mannerisms, the sound of your voice and even how you change your posture as you speak. What you say is important, but the way you say it affects listeners as much as three times more. Your voice is a vital communication tool.

Having grown up in New Orleans, I joke that in America you can talk funny and still be wickedly successful. While I have pretty much shed my New Orleans accent, my voice does have its own distinctive qualities. Analyze yours to discover what needs improvement. Do you whisper or mumble? Do people constantly ask you to repeat yourself? Do you find yourself using your parent or cell phone voice in normal conversation? Do you sound interested or bored? Do you race like a runaway train, providing no opportunity for the listener to speak? Do you needlessly punctuate your speech with ahs, ums, hmms, sighs, "like," "I mean," "you know," or other fillers?

Most of us are not aware of how we sound to others. If we were, we might talk a lot less. I've appeared on radio, television and video often enough to know all too well how I sound. This process has taught me that the best way to learn your own verbal "tics" is to video-record a conversation and then watch and listen to it. This enables you to hear how you really sound and see how you really look when you speak. Review the recordings as objectively as possible and honestly assess what you need to improve. Then do it.

With only a little practice this important tool of genius will gain you instant credibility, visibility and profit while you achieve your goals. Ignore it and you might never realize how many opportunities you've lost just because of your voice. Even one is too many, so start tuning up your voice today.

Improve Your Memory with a Legal Pad

People often compliment me on what a great memory I have. While my memory's respectable, what's even better is my note-taking prowess. That's my real secret. I am a voracious note-taker in every business situation.

I always have a legal pad and pen handy, even in the most informal of meetings. They serve as my external memory, one that doesn't get erased by sleep, an office crisis or a box of hot glazed donuts. One of my executive directors boils it down to, "The person with the best notes wins."

Have you noticed that as a society we are becoming less skilled at listening? You can't afford to be, or risk becoming, a poor listener. When you're talking to your boss, clients or colleagues, they must be the center of your attention, and you should appear smart, alert and "all in" the conversation.

Think about the last time you were talking to someone who was looking past you over your shoulder, checking her iPhone or appeared to be daydreaming. Remember how you felt? You also risk missing a key communication, such as an important issue or deadline. Just as taking notes in school improved your exam scores, taking notes in business situations will dramatically increase the number of points you score.

If you switch conversations to a different subject, switch to a different page. You might slay a forest in your lifetime, but it's simpler and ultimately more efficient to have notes for only one subject per page. That way, when you get to your office, you can file appropriate pages with their corresponding files without having to rewrite a single note.

You might be thinking, "I can do the same thing with my iPad or laptop," but when you're on a device, people believe, rightly or wrongly, that they have lost you to cyberspace.

The more you practice efficient note-taking, the more natural it becomes. Soon you'll be able to talk, maintain eye contact, smile and take notes all at the same time. The people in my office who see me take notes all day, every day, in every meeting or hallway conversation, are the same people who credit me with a great memory. The note-taking becomes invisible, and all they remember is that somehow, day after day, I remember everything we discussed. Note-taking is a business power tool for wickedly successful women.

Beginning today, think frequently about which consciousness you have working before you tackle a challenge. Your problems won't disappear, and you may not find a solution instantly, but new patterns, new thinking, new behaviors and new communication will awaken the genius within you.

INTENSIFY YOUR GENIUS WITH THE
5 PROMISES

PROMISE 1
I Will Live and Work a Passionate Life

List three intelligent minds you will engage in collaboration to help you pursue your passionate vision.

_____

_____

_____

PROMISE 2
I Will Go for It or Reject It Outright

What new mind-set would enable you to passionately go all out in living your vision? What thought or belief is holding you back?

_____

_____

_____

PROMISE 3
I Will Take One Action Step a Day Toward My Passionate Vision

From your passionate vision, select a complex idea you want to communicate. Describe it.

_____

_____

_____

Now describe it from a different viewpoint.

_____

_____

_____

PROMISE 4
I Commit to Being a Success Student for Life

Invest in a book on a topic you want to know more about. Read 30 minutes a day from that book. What is your first topic?

_____

_____

_____

Subscribe to a publication outside of your industry. Read the first issue before the next arrives, and apply one thing you learned to your career. Which publication will you choose?

_____

_____

_____

PROMISE 5
I Believe as a Woman I Really Can Do Anything

What is your spark of genius that will carry you to your passionate vision? Write down three ways to expand that genius.

_____

_____

_____

>> DOWNLOAD THE 5 PROMISES FOR GENIUS AT WickedSuccess.com.

CHRIS'S GENIUS

My grandmother never knew the valuable gift she gave me. Sewing or quilting, she always had a needle in hand and fabric scraps around her feet. I used a scrap to sew my doll a pair of pedal pushers—today they're called capri pants. Even at age 10 I knew enough to cut both a front and back and to leave a seam allowance, but the pants wouldn't go on. They could easily fit a paper doll, but not a doll of any dimension. My grandmother showed me how to cut a proper pattern, which required four pieces, not two, and in those few moments I formed the first piece of a basic understanding that would direct all my future education. I realized that everything in life consisted of patterns. All I had to do was find the right pattern and I could do anything, from baking a cake to one day tearing down the engine in my Datsun and replacing the head gasket.

A good student, I brought home all A's, except in gym; but before completing the eighth grade I dropped out to marry. By the time most girls my age were trying on high school graduation gowns, I was giving my attention to three toddlers. While I never missed the social aspects of school, I did miss the learning process, and in those early years of motherhood I hit upon the second piece of my education theory. I realized that teachers taught from books, ergo I could learn anything I wanted to learn by reading the right books. Which I did.

Along with cooking and sewing, I taught myself the concepts of design and literature. I passed the GED high school equivalency test; then, in my early 30s, I enrolled in college to get that degree I coveted. After two semesters, I looked at what I'd learned and knew that college was much too slow. I could have read dozens of excellent texts in those nine months, and learned far more than I was taking away.

I never returned to college until I became a teacher, but I expanded my theory of learning to include asking questions and listening. I have been a graphic designer, illustrator and marketing consultant. I've owned a business and mentored other business owners. I've published three novels, coauthored nonfiction books and taught an adjunct mystery-writing class. I've built basic furniture and fences and painted murals. I've created and conducted seminars in writing, graphic design, photo composition and small business advertising. Every aspect of my education and the process I use to educate others has involved patterns. Thanks, Grandma.

Chris, 60
WRITER AND EDUCATOR

The genius inside every woman accelerates wicked success, but only integrity will keep you at the top. Let's explore the Feminine Force of integrity in the next chapter.

The thinking of a genius does not proceed logically. It leaps with great ellipses. It pulls knowledge from God knows where.
DOROTHY THOMPSON

Character builds slowly, but it can be torn down with incredible swiftness.
FAITH BALDWIN

Integrity is fragile. If you compromise, even in a small way, you become broken.
VICKIE L. MILAZZO

6

INTEGRITY

Practice Uncompromising Integrity for Authentic Success

The most trusted profession is dominated by women. According to Gallup, that profession—for 11 years in a row—is nursing, which is 94 percent women. One of the least trusted professions, car sales, is less than 7 percent women.

Women make up 9 percent of the prison population, which tells us that, on the whole, women can be trusted to abide by laws and do the right thing. I cannot believe these powerful facts are accidental.

A Chinese proverb says, "If you stand straight, do not fear a crooked shadow." Perhaps women stand straighter than men because we're more emotionally analytical. The emotional "why" tugs at us, and, based on our interpretation of cause and effect, we form opinions about how to act. Our interpretations feed our integrity.

As you pursue your passionate vision and reach higher, more complex levels of accomplishment—especially in your career, but also in your personal life—your integrity will be continuously tested in new ways. Think about what you would do in these situations:

- Coworkers at your new job get together at lunch and complain about the boss. The conversation makes you uncomfortable, but you want to fit in and be part of the group.

- You discover that your best friend is cheating on her husband, a man who trusts and honors her in every way.

- You decide to host a party for the people who live on your street. You don't like one couple. Do you invite them into your home because it's expected?

Integrity-based decisions are not always easy. On a trip to Poland, I stood in the gas chamber at Auschwitz and walked through the women's barracks at Birkenau. Visiting these horrific places, I was struck by how easily our hold on humanity can be stripped away—possessions, success, health, dignity, privacy and even individuality—until the only thing remaining is our personal integrity.

I'd read the memoirs of Viktor Frankl prior to the visit and thought I had a grip on what to expect. But actually standing where so many had lived and died changed that perception straight-off. Each day in the midst of unspeakable cruelty, Holocaust victims had to decide how to treat others and handle themselves with integrity. Without integrity, even living through those conditions would not guarantee surviving the memories afterward. I couldn't help wondering how my own integrity would have held out in that situation.

Our choices determine whether we live a free life or a life imprisoned—and I'm not talking about a physical jail cell. No one would voluntarily imprison herself and be her own warden, yet every time we breach integrity, we sentence ourselves to a mental jail.

Integrity has the final say in whether we will rise or decline, be whole or broken. When uncompromising integrity is our guide, success is authentic. And the joy of success is authentic.

BREACHING INTEGRITY BETRAYS OPPORTUNITY

One of our seminar instructors, an independent contractor, was selling her own products to our students while being paid to interact on our behalf. This not only violated our contract, it also violated all personal trust.

She didn't see it that way. In her mind, she was making the most of a business opportunity. When faced with a choice, to pursue quick personal sales to this ready market, which we had made highly accessible to her, or to honor her commitment and represent herself fully as our instructor, she elected personal gain. She was baffled when I put a halt to what she'd been getting by with. She didn't see her actions as a break with integrity.

I had to sever our business relationship entirely. Her weak character betrayed any future opportunities she might have had with us. To this day, she remains bitter about the outcome, without gaining insight or accepting accountability for her actions.

If you've ever doubted the economic value of integrity, there is compelling evidence that ethical companies last the longest. The collapse of corporations such as Enron, and financial institutions such as Bear Stearns, Lehman Brothers and Merrill Lynch is an example of the correspondingly high cost of the lack of integrity.

Temptations abound in business and in life. At the most basic level, taking a few extra minutes for lunch each day, steering a contract to an inferior and more costly vendor who sent you the best wine at Christmas and Facebooking, surfing the Internet or doing online Christmas shopping while at work are breaches of integrity. No matter how complex a decision appears on the surface, when stripped down to basics, it's usually pig-simple: Do what's right, not what's most appealing.

I've had the opportunity to work with thousands of women. While success is influenced by myriad variables, one fact stands clear: Women who persistently breach integrity don't just betray opportunities, they are broken and destined for eventual decline.

EVERY ACT COUNTS

To quote a favorite Buddhist proverb: "Even the smallest act should not be underestimated, for even tiny flakes of snow falling one atop another can blanket the tallest mountain in pure whiteness." Integrity is fragile. If compromised, even in a small way, integrity is swiftly broken. Once broken, integrity slides like an avalanche—it won't stop. Cutting a corner here leads to cutting another corner there . . . and there, and there.

We may not decline to extremes such as burgling houses or robbing banks, but don't we roll through stop signs, flirt with a stranger on Facebook, cheat on our taxes or pocket office supplies from work?

Little things, such as not giving your all on a work project, may seem insignificant initially, but over time these small impure "flakes" gradually smother your passion and obscure your vision. Once lost, the opportunity to demonstrate integrity can never be recaptured. A relationship that took decades to nurture can be destroyed with one frivolous breach. A career opportunity can dissolve in an instant.

Integrity compels 100 percent congruence. You can't say "I'll have integrity tomorrow, but not today," or "I'll have integrity in other situations, but not in this one." When any part of your life is out of congruence with other parts, you feel incomplete and out of sorts. Integrity is the strength that makes you whole.

Let's say you passionately accept a promotion that requires you to work excessive overtime and give up your vacation. You're also passionately committed to your family who needs you and to friends you enjoy socially. Your 70-hour workweek eats into your social time, causing you to break commitments; then it chomps away at family time, causing you to break the unspoken promise of being involved in important family activities. If you somehow manage to hold it all together, chances are you're cutting back on personal health commitments. By accepting the commitment to your career, you've broken integrity with other important parts of your life.

Maintaining unwavering integrity can be tricky. Enticements and fears do sneak up on us. But at the end of the day, no matter what we've lost or gained, we need to know that our integrity is intact. We may lose our health or our money, we may outlive all our friends and family, but if we live true, we'll have the comfort that we left behind a snowy-white legacy of integrity.

STAND UP FOR YOUR INTEGRITY

Congruence in integrity also applies to everyone who touches our lives and careers, and to holding them accountable. When we accept other people's breaches of integrity, we're compromising our own.

I'm sure every business owner has a favorite example, but in my business, hotels are the worst. They always expect us to come through 100 percent on our contractual obligations, yet many of those same hotels think nothing of taking part of our contracted space or not letting us into the ballroom at the contracted time—all in the game of snagging more business. When this happens, my response is to nip the bad behavior fast and hold the hotel accountable.

A client who represented a substantial amount of Lynne's business gave her an ultimatum: stop working with certain clients he perceived to be competitive, or risk losing his business. If she gave in to his demand, she would keep his business—but at the cost of losing her integrity. She believed her other clients had nothing to do with him. Plus, if she gave into his demand, what would his next one be? I encouraged her to stand up for her integrity. When I hung up the phone, she was still troubled and undecided.

A month later she called to share she had made the choice to be true to herself and to what she wanted for her business. She was happier, more relaxed and successful on her own terms.

A CEO came to our company to promote his services on a significant project. He charmed our staff and promised the moon, but when it came time to deliver, he sent work product that was unsatisfactory and full of errors. When he was challenged on the failure to deliver, his response was to crawl back under his bridge or wherever it is trolls live.

I'm sure you've run into this kind of troll. The person who called you every day to make the sale, but after the sale suddenly was unavailable, out of the office or on a mission trip to Lower Handstandastan; or lost his cell phone, had the swine flu or was at the funeral of yet another "close" relative. (How many grandparents can you really lose?) Eventually, you get a call back, accompanied by more promises followed by more disappointment.

The vendor and I somehow managed to end our relationship professionally. I wished him future success, knowing full well he was destined for failure. How do I know? Because now I'm being serviced by someone whose integrity is unimpeachable.

You cannot afford pretenders in your life. Join me in ridding ourselves of the trolls.

CONSENSUS ON INTEGRITY IS ELUSIVE

In the Female Fusion event I describe in Chapter 10, strong opinions emerged about the meaning of integrity. That discussion reinforced my belief that integrity is not easily defined. I found some of the comments provocative.

Jan: It bothers me to tell even a "white lie." I was trying to explain to my nephew that you don't tell someone who has cooked dessert for you that your aunt makes a better dessert. You also don't tell her this is the best dessert you've ever had.

Vickie: Sometimes integrity means not blurting out the truth, but finding a truth that's respectful and more positive. Being overly solicitous isn't the answer either; it can backfire. The mother of one of my friends is a terrible cook. This is not my New Orleans palate talking; she's just bad. Unfortunately, we often eat at her house because she likes to host family events. Everyone tells her how good her meals are—through gritted teeth. Not wanting to hurt her feelings guarantees more bad spaghetti dinners, and I never believed there could be such a thing as bad spaghetti.

Jan: Integrity is learned by example. If you're around people who lie and scheme, you pick up on that. Kids are picking up so much negative behavior via television.

Susan: A friend in advertising sent me an inspirational piece which reads, "Integrity is saying what needs to be said, not simply what people want to hear." I really had to think about that. I'm naturally a huge people pleaser, but as an interior designer, sometimes I too have to say in a gentle way, "That looks like crap."

Chris: Following through with integrity doesn't always feel good, because you often make people unhappy.

Susan: It's going out on a limb.

Vickie: It needs to be tempered with compassion. Rose Franzblau said, "Honesty without compassion and understanding is not honesty, but subtle hostility." I find it helpful to assess my intention. We've all been the victim of the honest but mean verbal jab—it never feels good.

Chris: Expecting integrity from others, especially the people we love, is equally important. I loaned money to my grandson to repair his car.

Evie: Integrity is different for everybody. What I do might not be perceived as the right thing by someone else. Certainly there's right and wrong, but every coin has two sides. One person might seem to have integrity, then when you hear the other side, that person also has integrity. That's where I struggle with it.

Maggie: For me, it's not just about right or wrong or truth or fault. It's about living according to your standards. What is right for you might not be right for me. What you believe is good might not seem so good to me. It can be very abstract.

Vickie: In medicine, the highest principle is "first, do no harm." I think that's the basis of integrity. However, each person's idea of what is harmful may differ. That's why society creates laws that set behavioral standards no matter how right a person feels about her actions.

Chris: It's interesting the way we demand upholding the law, yet believe that if a certain law is not right, it's okay to break it. We tend to cheer the lovable rascal, the charming cat burglar who steals only from the rich. He's part of our fictional culture. But we expect even a criminal to have some measure of integrity. If he kicked a dog, we wouldn't like him anymore.

Vickie: Maybe we cheer the lovable rascal because we know deep down that no matter how good our intentions, we're not perfect. Show me one woman who has never transgressed and I'll nominate her for sainthood.

Maggie: Here in the U.S. an old lady was put in jail because she shot a burglar in the back. He was not facing her, so she had to do her time. In Honduras, an old lady shoots a burglar and she is a hero. The bad guy always has to go down. So what is integrity? You are saving your life in both examples, but in two different worlds.

Evie: Integrity is usually set by the social, cultural and religious environments. One example of my confusion with it all is something that happened to my stepfather from Mexico. When he was a young boy, his mother dishonored his father by cheating on him. It was published in the newspaper, and she was outcast by the whole community. If she had been a male, it would be just another occurrence. But they ran her out of town; and the grandmother, the husband's mother, forbid the children to ever see their mother again. I'm sure the grandmother thought she had high integrity, but to this

He didn't finish the car repair and he also didn't repay the loan. I brushed it off, but I never lent him money again.

Then his twin brother called and asked for money to retain a lawyer for a DUI. When he started to say, "I'll pay you back," I stopped him. "Here's what we can do: If you ever get behind the wheel of a car again after having a drink, pay me the money immediately. If you never have another drink and then drive, you owe me nothing." My intention was to avoid what happened with h brother and to also engage his integrity.

Vickie: This sounds minor, but parents set a bad example when they slip their old popcorn bag into the movie theater to get a free refill for th bag they paid for at the last movie. Integrity is not part time. You car be semigood at playing tennis, but integrity is all or nothing.

Leigh: You don't realize how much integrity means to you until you lose it. I worked for a company built by a man who had incredible integrity. His integrity pervaded the whole company. Then a different director without integrity came on board. The company is pitiful now, down to a few people. It was sad to see that company fade. When I interviewed for a new job, I knew I was not going to work for another company without integrity.

Martha: Integrity requires discipline. My grandson Cody is 12 and lives in Colorado. The last time I visited I mentioned paying the airline $75 for an oversize bag. Cody said, "Omah, you have another $75? I want to fit into your suitcase when you go back."

Cody is home-schooled, and I decided to work with him that day. He has terrible handwriting, which I'm picky about, and I made him write things over. When he read to me, he would say "a" instead of "the" or make other mistakes, and I'd tell him to read it again. It took a lot of discipline to maintain my integrity and listen to the same story three times. When we were finished Cody said, "Omah, you can spend that $75 on something else."

Leigh (laughs)**:** He'd had enough of your integrity and discipline, and was not going home in your bag.

Susan: What about having integrity with ourselves? Sometimes I sell myself out, like when I promise myself Saturdays off and then make a Saturday appointment. If I break one of my personal goals, I'm breaking integrity with myself.

day the children are so filled with hate for their mother that they won't get to know her. That's a conflict of integrity. It's not easy to know if you really did the right thing or if you just did the right thing for you.

Vickie: Integrity is public, not just private. I think of Hillary Clinton, who had so much power to speak to women and be a role model for strength and for her daughter. She copped out when she stayed married to Bill after the marriage was flagrantly violated. Women are often counseled to leave a husband who repeatedly betrays the marriage—but not, apparently, if the husband is rich, successful or president.

Martha: If it had been Hillary cheating, it wouldn't have turned out that way.

Leigh: I went to a breakfast meeting where I was appalled at the foul language these smart professionals were using. It was dreadful. Afterward, when everyone at the table commented on the meeting, I told them what I thought, and that I was glad they didn't have a guest speaker that morning to be subjected to such language. I never went back.

Martha: There might have been others who felt like you but didn't honor their integrity and speak up.

Susan: Say what needs to be said, not just what people want to hear.

Martha: I was born in Switzerland, the oldest of eight children, and was the caretaker. I had little opportunity to play, so my siblings were like my dolls. I was proud to help Mom, but I was also determined to get what I wanted, and sometimes a little rebellious. Having responsibility for these siblings, if they did something wrong, it was my fault. This responsibility stayed with me.

Now I am a very strict instructor. I want the students to get it right. The massage method I teach, lymphatic drainage, is difficult to learn, takes a lot of dedication and must be performed precisely for optimal results. My students do not always like me during class, since I correct their hands so often, but they survive my class and like me afterward. I tell them, "It's either right or wrong. I simply call it the way it is."

Vickie: Some young women today are setting back the integrity gains made by the feminists and other women who strove for equal pay, equal rights and equal respect for women in the home and workplace.

Stripper pole parties, sexting, music videos and movies are returning women to roles as sex objects, not equal partners. Wickedly successful women have created a world where young women can aspire to be presidents of major corporations. Instead of building on these gains, I see some women trading their integrity for entry into a VIP room in a club, vanity and selfishness, aspiring to become more like Paris Hilton or Kim Kardashian. I hope this doesn't become a trend.

EVERY PROMISE COUNTS

With the best intentions, we extend ourselves in one area, perhaps our career, which causes us to unintentionally slight another: our family, our financial well-being or our physical well-being. If you promise yourself you will absolutely take that vacation this year, yet fail to follow through because you overcommitted in another area, you've betrayed your promise and yourself.

Some people might even see you as a hero for putting others' interests ahead of your own. But that failure is like the first domino in a line— one falls against the next, which falls against the next, and so on until none is left standing.

Parents learn quickly that every promise to a child counts and not to overpromise. When a child asks, "Can we go to the beach this weekend?" an astute mom avoids promising and says, "We'll see." Otherwise, if the weekend comes and conditions aren't right, the child still expects delivery on the promise.

The need to avoid overpromising in all relationships is a lesson I learned at high cost. When my sister and her husband came into my business, I made a promise I later could not keep. I was working out of our home to keep the overhead low. I set up a reward incentive: as the company grew, we'd all get paid significantly more. I wanted these people, who were important to me, to benefit from our success. But that wonderful incentive was based on keeping the business in my home forever.

It worked great at first. But as the company grew beyond what any of us expected; we had to move into expensive office space and add more salaries, which translated into lots of additional overhead. My shortsighted promise became financially impossible to keep. That was a rough time for me. I didn't feel good about my inability to deliver and didn't want to break my integrity, but I had promised a future I couldn't deliver.

A promise is usually made based on certain conditions, and conditions change. I needed to act to protect both my integrity and my company's integrity no matter how painful that would be. We eventually arrived at a mutually satisfying solution, but that painful experience and the hurt we all suffered taught me to promise within boundaries. Are you overpromising to someone? How will you stop it?

BE ACCOUNTABLE TO YOUR INTEGRITY

Sometimes we promise ourselves to do something and we fail to deliver, not because we lack integrity, but because we lack a proper plan, one that makes us accountable. For example, if you own your own business and set a goal of marketing to five prospects each week, you could meet that goal without accomplishing any results. While this goal sounds like a good one, the objective of simply meeting the goal is in no way accountable to you and your business. Instead, develop an objective that provides accountability for a specific result.

Here's an example: "I will market to obtain one new client monthly." This results-oriented objective not only propels you to act, but requires you to act until you achieve the desired result. Attach a target date to complete each objective and hold yourself accountable for hitting it.

Integrity is not just about accountability to others; it's also about accountability to your goals and passionate vision.

DO THE RIGHT THING WHEN NO ONE IS LOOKING

The expression "action speaks louder than words" is never truer than with respect to integrity. Most of us can talk a good game, but what happens when we're alone, unobserved and our integrity is tested?

Every day people surf the Internet or interact on Facebook on company time, blanking their screen when the boss shows up. They work a lot slower than they're capable of, persistently take longer breaks, arrive late or sneak out early without permission. Everybody does it, so what's the big deal?

An Australian software entrepreneur told me he missed older employees with strong work ethics. He felt the younger employees believed it to be their right to post on Facebook, text or talk on their cell phones during work, and that if he didn't allow them to do so, he wouldn't be able to retain anyone. I explained that we have a zero-tolerance policy during work hours. If you want to text a friend or beat your high score on Angry Birds, you must do so during your lunch or break. People would rather waste your time than sacrifice their own, and that speaks volumes about their integrity.

Luckily, our corporate culture doesn't support this behavior, and the natural selection process moves those with less integrity out of there fast. I heard a guy say "They call it work because that's what you're supposed to do while you're there." I completely agree.

One of my employees asked me, "How do I know if I've violated company policy?" I told him it was simple: "If you wouldn't do it with me standing beside you, then you know it's a violation." You don't have integrity if you only have it when someone else is looking.

Kelly, a young mother who has physical limitations, was grocery shopping one day. Along with her basketful of goods, she purchased a heavy case of formula. After reaching her car, buckling her baby into the car seat and unloading the groceries, she realized the clerk had not charged her for the case of product. Someone else might have thought, "Their mistake, my advantage. I'm tired, my leg hurts, I'm going home." Despite her discomfort, Kelly got out of her car, unloaded the heavy case, unloaded the baby, went back into the store and paid for the goods.

If she had not acted on her integrity, who would have known? She would. When we have a break with integrity, the biggest break is with ourselves.

Integrity is not only the bedrock of your relationships, integrity is your strength. And like cracks in a foundation, every small compromise in your integrity weakens the structure of your life. Invest integrity in every situation, even when there is no one to notice.

Women also need to know when to forgive their transgressions. Just because we breach integrity doesn't mean we're not allowed to move forward. A woman who had an affair confided, "Integrity is something you have to have all of the time and I don't have it all of the time, so I don't have it."

When you do or say what you know is wrong, rectify it. If you can't rectify it, at least learn from it. Then forgive everything about yourself and move on.

DON'T BRING AN ELEPHANT INTO THE ROOM

One of our vendors, Matthew (the name has been changed to protect the guilty), recently dropped the ball. Because he has a great track record, all he really needed to do was acknowledge his lapse and we would have gotten quickly back on track. But instead of owning his mistake, he chose to ignore it, apparently just wishing it would all disappear.

So a week later when we met, he brought a companion—what I call the "elephant in the room." The elephant in the room is the shame and discomfort that comes with knowing one is wrong, but not having the guts to own it. There we all sat around the table: Matthew, me, a couple of staffers and a very large elephant.

At first, Matthew's interactions were so strained it was laughable. The elephant just kept growing until it seemed to be taking up half the conference room. Finally, someone said, "Matt, just own it." At that moment he looked almost relieved. "I'm sorry I let everyone down," he said. "It won't happen again."

We all looked at him, said thanks and went on with the meeting. The elephant left the building as fast as it arrived because Matthew summoned the courage to finally acknowledge it.

Sometimes integrity can feel like an extreme sport, like in Dale's situation:

> Early in my career as a Certified Legal Nurse Consultant I researched a case and concluded it was meritorious. Well into the case, what I thought was impossible occurred. The plaintiff started to improve, and the damages started to disappear before our eyes. The case was not as tragic and not quite as slam-dunk as I had led my attorney-client and myself to believe.
>
> Once I overcame my embarrassment, I immediately confronted the issue and was honest with the attorney. He was obviously not happy. Based on my opinion, he had put a lot of his own money into the case. I told him that I had not foreseen a recovery and that

I would assist him in developing a new strategy. We altered our strategy for damages by focusing strictly on the losses during the shorter time the plaintiff had been affected. The strategy worked and the case was resolved.

My client shared that because I was honest with him about what I should have done differently, and because I tried to help him resolve the dilemma, he was able to trust me, and to this day we still work together.

Have you ever brought an elephant into a situation? You may have dropped the ball and, like Matthew, need to own up to it but can't seem to summon the courage to do so. Even if the other person doesn't mention it, the elephant won't go away on its own, and the pain it causes you will be much greater than the pain of acknowledging you screwed up. Plus, every second that the elephant is in the room is a strain on your integrity and relationship. I can pretty much guarantee that at some point in your life you'll walk into a room followed by a large, relentless elephant. You'll have a choice: 'fess up and leave the elephant in the zoo, as Dale did, or like Matthew, let the elephant take up all the space. You decide!

REFUSE TO BE AN INTEGRITY VICTIM

As the victim of another person's lapse of integrity, you feel violated and hurt. But you can still refuse to be a victim.

Two employees seriously breached our company's integrity standards, and I had no choice but to fire them. It hurt to discover that these two people I cared about were manipulating sales reports. After having my pity party, what did I do? What Donald Trump does once a week: "You're fired." If someone acts less than ethically, it's best to disassociate. That's hard because it can mean losing a highly skilled professional or a valued resource, but if you don't, you make yourself an integrity victim.

Sometimes breaches of integrity feel like personal assaults, which for me often come from competitors, the occasional Internet scam or slam artist or terrorist, or someone trying to stand on my shoulders to profit from my market. The more successful I am, the more I become the target of vicious, personal attacks—amusingly, by people I've never met and who certainly don't know me.

There's a T-shirt I love that says "Love me or hate me, either way I'm on your mind." Instead of fretting over why someone would act this way, I choose to laugh about how much energy they spend on me and my company. Our strategy is to shrug it off and refuse to engage in a counterattack. It's not that I pretend competitors and undeserved attacks don't exist, but I avoid being reactive; and instead of focusing on the attackers, I focus on my passionate vision. When anyone repeats a tactless remark a competitor has made about us, I just say, "You might consider that the comment came from a competitor," and leave it at that.

Women often feel compelled to explain themselves too much. You want to look right, and in the process you make another person wrong and risk making yourself look even more wrong. I would rather let people judge me wrongfully than explain myself in a way that compromises my own integrity.

Any time we're falsely accused or others are making us the "bad guy," we can't help feeling the weight of it, even if they're totally wrong. However we remedy the situation, we have to ask ourselves, "Did I breach integrity in some way?" If so, own up to it. If not, then own up to that, too.

Demonstrate your own integrity by being more concerned about who you are than who you're reputed to be. Be less dependent on praise, and criticism will sting a lot less.

AVOID THE LURE OF MANIPULATION

Now divorced, Barbara, told me she could never get her former husband to attend to any project around the house—until she learned to manipulate his responses. He was handy enough to fix a window or repair a wall, and would do it—at some future time of his choosing. When she wanted a cabinet built for her kitchen, months passed and she still had inadequate storage space. Finally, she waited until he was at work, bought the materials and tackled the cabinet herself. When he came home, she was busily nailing boards together. He said, "That will never stand up. You're not doing it right." He took the tools from her and finished the cabinet. In the future, when she needed his attention on the house, she knew exactly how to get it.

Unfortunately, this positive outcome reinforced a negative concept: manipulation. It's only a small step from manipulating your spouse into doing those pesky tasks to using manipulation without integrity. When you start manipulating, you're on a slippery slope.

Perhaps you manipulate acquaintances to wangle favors. Eventually you find yourself manipulating friends, spouses, children and coworkers. What happens to these relationships? Where are the trust and mutual respect? Then you "gently" manipulate sales figures to show more attractive results. Avoid being lured into manipulation. It never leads to authentic success.

PUT YOUR INTEGRITY WHERE YOUR MOUTH IS

Any time a person makes a negative comment about someone not present, that's gossip. Gossip is not just mean; it's a break with integrity, and that hurts us as much, if not more, than the object of the gossip. Gossip also wastes time and energy. Even though it often feels enjoyable, it serves no positive outcome. When you're gossiping, your focus is not on your passionate vision; it's on someone who probably isn't thinking about you.

Perhaps you have the integrity to never initiate gossip, but then when others start gossiping, you can't believe the words coming out of your mouth—the things you're agreeing with. It's easy to get sucked in. And it's hard to be the one who speaks up and brings gossip to a halt, but that's exactly the right thing to do.

Like most people, I'm challenged by the commitment to never gossip, so I created a way to not get sucked into it. When confronted with gossip, I will say, "Well, you know, Mary's not here to defend herself." That remark will usually stop the gossip cold, without putting anyone on the spot. I say it in a fun, friendly manner and with a smile on my face, but it clearly lets the gossiper know I don't intend to go there, and if she does, she'll have to do so without me.

Be an honest observer of your thoughts and actions. Learn to quickly recognize a breach of integrity and stop it cold. Disrupt it. When I catch myself starting to gossip or say something negative, I quickly change the end of the sentence. Or I trail off with the comment, "I forgot what I was going to say."

Women in any kind of career advancement or leadership position, including motherhood, must absolutely avoid falling into the gossip trap. It belittles you, sends negative messages, detracts from your influence, and kills opportunities for career advancement. Reclaiming your integrity, once it's compromised, is about as easy as unspreading butter.

I'm no angel, and like most women I need to vent my feelings, so I give myself permission to have one trusted person as my "gossip buddy," my "second mom." Blanche's integrity is unquestionable. I feel totally free and secure talking with her about anything. Sharing a troublesome situation with this wise woman helps me clarify what happened and prevent repetition.

I'll ask her, "How would you have handled this?" Then I try to turn the negative experience into a learning opportunity. Spiritual without being rigid or hypocritical, Blanche, who's in her 70s, has the life lessons and a perspective that enables her to mentor me, in my 50s, to make good decisions.

Do you put your integrity where your mouth is? Do you surround yourself with people who glow with integrity? Never tolerate people or groups who are intentionally gossipy, mean or hurtful to you or anyone else. Have you ever noticed what happens to a bag of apples when one apple goes bad? If you leave it in the bag, all the other apples will rot too. Remove yourself from "bad apples."

If you find yourself in an environment that's putting you down, don't put up with it. Don't let rotten apples sour your fire and vision. Eleanor Roosevelt said: "Great minds discuss ideas; average minds discuss events; small minds discuss people." I'm striving to be a great mind. How about you?

KISS OFF COMPLAINERS

As part of my preflight ritual, I went for a cross-airport walk to Starbucks. Early in the morning I'll gladly trek through two time zones to get my coffee. The young guy working at Starbucks looked and sounded like he hadn't had his coffee yet and was complaining to another barista about how he wasn't up for standing on his feet all day. After repeating my order at least twice, I received a semblance of my "black eye," a doppio espresso dumped into a Venti, bold coffee of the day. From there I headed to grab my standard preflight spicy breakfast at Popeye's Fried Chicken. The woman working the counter at Popeye's was complaining in Spanish on her cell phone to a friend about having to be the one who had to be there early to open the store, three days a week.

When I got to my gate, three uniformed airline employees (including a supervisor) were complaining, somewhat loudly, as only a group can do, about a systems problem with the airline—all within hearing distance of the customers. I was at least glad I wasn't overhearing a safety issue.

I was trying to figure out if it was just my day to ride the complain train or if there was some other message, when it hit me: The people who'd been complaining all day were doing it without regard for who was listening. Maybe they just didn't care.

What about you? Do you ever complain about someone in public spaces, or worse, use your cell phone voice to have a 72-decibel private conversation?

Complaining is counterproductive, and it rarely has an outcome in mind—unless you complain appropriately to the person who can do something about it. The airline employees weren't brainstorming the problem; they were just making sure each of them was as aggrieved as the others in dealing with it. What a waste of energy, not to mention brainpower.

Why do some people complain, even when they know better? Because complaining is easier than taking action, and much easier than exhibiting integrity. Nothing will degrade your integrity in a more pernicious way than complaining and hanging out with complainers. Complaining can masquerade as a harmless, trifling behavior, but before you know it, complaining leads to gossip and wasting time—time that could be funneled to your passionate vision. In the workplace, complaining can also lead to poor performance. ("I'm going to get my boss back for making me work overtime.")

Colleen demonstrates how the only real victims of complaining or hanging with complainers are the people participating:

> In a vain attempt to vent rising agitation and stress, my peers and I sometimes stoop to negative accolades each time we are together. I finally realized how counterproductive this bad habit is. While attempting to console each other on our miserable plight, we

are actually just reveling in negativity. This does nothing to decrease our stress or improve our plight in the least. The saying "Misery loves company" is so true. However powerful this camaraderie feels, it is a pitiful veneer at best. I intend to search for positive solutions that would actually address the core problems which, in turn, would reduce stress and empower me in my job. At the very least, refusing to complain will stop fueling the fire.

Anne shares how perspective can put a stop to complaining:

In my work as a hospice nurse I have learned that my very worst day . . . is still pretty good! Believe it or not, I have heard nurses complain to families of dying loved ones about traffic, getting the wrong order at a fast food place and other silly things.

Twenty-nine years ago I was hanging out with my fellow nurses whining and complaining about the bad state of hospital nursing. Then one day, the eureka moment hit. I stopped complaining, and life's opportunities suddenly started pouring my way.

But even today I have to be on the lookout for these integrity vampires. Just yesterday I found myself in the company of a complainer and, to my horror, found I was letting myself get sucked into it. What do you do when you find yourself getting sucked in by people who like to complain but don't really want to solve their problem?

Instead of joining the complaining party, detach and use your precious time to solve your own problems or to enjoy your life as intended. Even 10 minutes given to a complainer (family, friend or colleague) are 10 precious minutes you could have been doing something for you—minutes you'll never get back.

The next time you find yourself snared by a complainer, detach and interrupt the complaining. Before you give 10 precious minutes away to someone else's soap opera, ask yourself if you'll really be making a difference by listening or joining in. Or are those 10 minutes niggling at your integrity?

I recently severed a professional relationship with a complainer. Life is too short to be around one, and a lot more fun without them. As Barbra Streisand sang, please "don't rain on my parade."

KEEP YOUR INTEGRITY PUBLIC AND YOUR DIRTY LAUNDRY PRIVATE

Whether you like it or not, online life has created a public figure out of you. Every time you send an email, Tweet or post on Facebook, you're leaving behind a digital trail that can be followed back to you. What sort of trail are you leaving behind? And how is your Integrity holding up along the way?

We all know Facebook can be a place where people let down their guard, speak freely and, unfortunately, sometimes behave badly. Did you just congratulate your child for getting an A? Or did you complain about your ex? Do you talk favorably about your job, or whine endlessly? Does your profile photo look like you're posing for *Playboy*?

Would your mom and dad, your future boss, your significant other and your children be proud of, or embarrassed by, the woman you portray online? If you found yourself in a lawsuit, would your online presence make you look like Snow White or the evil and slightly sleazy stepmother?

Not only are all of your email, Facebook postings, Tweets and electronic communications potentially discoverable in lawsuits, but employers are monitoring them and colleges are reviewing them when making admissions decisions. Think before you post. Those photos from the stripper pole party might seem like fun to share today, but could cause huge pain and regret later.

I often think of racy comments or posts I'd like to make, but a comment made to best friends over dinner is almost certainly guaranteed to be taken out of context when it gets in the hands of the wrong people. That's why I try to guard my online legacy carefully. I can't control what people post about me, but I can certainly control what I create about myself. We're all leaving a vast and permanent digital footprint. Let's live with integrity by keeping ours clean.

Is there an integrity issue (about you or someone else) that is preventing you from living your passionate vision? Practice uncompromising integrity to enjoy more authentic success.

PRACTICE UNCOMPROMISING
INTEGRITY WITH THE

5 PROMISES

PROMISE 1
I Will Live and Work a Passionate Life

Is there an integrity issue (about you or someone else) that is preventing
you from living your passionate vision? Describe it.

_____

_____

_____

PROMISE 2
I Will Go for It or Reject It Outright

How does this integrity issue impact your commitment to your passion?

_____

_____

_____

What can you do to soften that impact? Can you rectify a past misdeed?
Is there someone to whom you need to apologize, have a long talk with
or repay a debt? Is there someone you need to stand up to? If so, set a
target date to handle the transgression, absolve the guilt, or confront the
problem. Then move on.

_____

_____

_____

PROMISE 3
I Will Take One Action Step a Day Toward My Passionate Vision

Write down three ways you will practice uncompromising integrity.
Beginning today, vow never to break this covenant with yourself.

_____

_____

_____

PROMISE 4
I Commit to Being a Success Student for Life

Write down the name of a person with uncompromising integrity who
has something you want (more peace, more success, etc.). Study how she
handles compromising situations and model her.

_____

_____

_____

PROMISE 5
I Believe as a Woman I Really Can Do Anything

Recall situations in which you demonstrated integrity, possibly when
others did not. Write down as many as you can recall. Notice how you
feel, and write down your feelings.

_____

_____

_____

>> DOWNLOAD THE 5 PROMISES FOR INTEGRITY AT **WickedSuccess.com.**

JAN'S
INTEGRITY

*I struggled through school, and I don't do well on
standardized tests, and my counselor made it quite clear
that I wasn't college material. Talk about a breach of integrity!
Couldn't he have looked more closely at my skills and
found a way to encourage me?*

*Well, I had to prove him wrong. I completed college,
became a teacher, and obtained a master's degree. Teaching
is my passion. I love kids. The pay isn't lucrative, but I love
the work. I also take special kids on field trips during the
summer. The parents are usually excited about it, and with
that trip I can make the extra money I need. These special
kids have a wonderful summertime experience they
might otherwise have missed, while the parents also
get a much-needed break.*

*I often think about that counselor. If I had the chance,
I would tell him, "Thomas Edison's teacher foolishly thought
he was addled. You can do your job with integrity and,
at the same time, give kids a sense of value."*

Jan, 52
LEARNING SPECIALIST

As you practice uncompromising integrity to achieve success, learn how the next Feminine Force, endurance, can take you the extra mile in living your passionate vision.

Break one thread—through evil intent or casual carelessness,
by deliberate action or mere inattention—and the whole fabric
defining you will unravel.
S. J. ROZAN

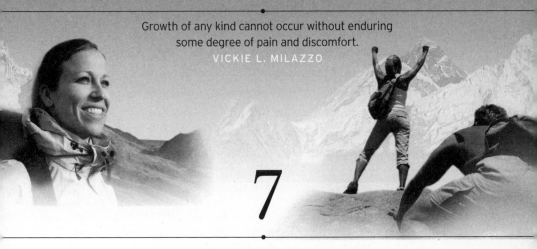

Growth of any kind cannot occur without enduring
some degree of pain and discomfort.
VICKIE L. MILAZZO

7

ENDURANCE

Fuel Your Endurance to Energize Your Performance

Women outlive men by an average of five years, which is surprising given our endless commitments and responsibilities. Among centenarians, people 100 years or older, women outnumber males two to one. That's endurance.

Male fetuses are at greater risk of damage, deformity, premature birth and death than female fetuses. Medical science attributes this increased risk to the male fetus's response to a mother's release of the stress hormone cortisol during pregnancy. Women always say they handle stress better than men, and this statistic may not prove it, but it sure is interesting.

Many women who choose to become mothers endure 14 or more hours of labor. That's 14 hours of pain. And while we might assume that mothers-to-be have no idea what to expect the first time they're picking out tiny pastel onesies, over 70 percent of them go back and do it again.

But endurance is about more than longevity or pain. It's about having the stamina to do what it takes to achieve wicked success, like working 12-hour days. Endurance is true-grit strength, a potent and positive Feminine Force we use to push onward toward a vision that

191

may seem so far in the distance we often wonder if our passion will hold out.

Endurance is about having the inner strength to sustain commitments you make to yourself and others, even when you'd rather quit. How many women do you know who have gone to an online school to obtain a higher degree even while working a full-time job and raising a family? Like Sharon, who decided to become a lawyer even though she hadn't finished college. In six nonstop years of night school, she did both. Women every day endure long hours of work, family responsibilities, study and sleep deprivation to create the career and life that fulfills their passionate visions.

Endurance is the strength necessary for being successful during good times and bad—even a recession. Endurance is the strength that makes you more than a one-hit wonder. Instead of achieving one promotion, you rise progressively from teller to vice president at the bank. Instead of just launching a business, you're still growing yours 30 years later. These achievements happen only when you have endurance.

Dance the Endurance Dance

One of my favorite endurance allegories is about an East African tribe that became famous for its rain dances. This tribe was unique in all of Africa because its rain dances always succeeded. Other tribes in the region had low or mediocre success rates; this tribe alone was 100 percent successful.

Members of rival tribes jealously studied this phenomenon, theorizing that the tribe had better dancers, special steps, more powerful chants, or more sincere prayers, or that their costumes, feathered accoutrements and masks, made the difference. Finally, they claimed it was simply luck that made the gods smile on this one fortunate tribe and not on their own.

After observing the "lucky" tribe's practices, an anthropologist uncovered the secret to their 100 percent success rate. He was surprised that it was so simple. They had no special powers, no magical interventions. They simply danced their rain dance until it rained.

They never quit, never gave in to their exhaustion and never grew despondent over how long it took for the rain to come. They expected it would always rain when they danced, and their experience supported their belief. They just kept dancing, knowing that sooner or later the gods would be satisfied and reward their persistence with rain. Rewarded they were—every single time.

This is one of the most basic and simple secrets to wicked success. It's always easier to quit the dance, but much more rewarding to dance on. All it takes is endurance.

KEEP DANCING YOUR PASSIONATE VISION

Endurance is also about having the emotional intelligence to wait for success. When I was young I wanted to change the world, and I wanted to do it *now*. That unrealistic goal resulted in frustration, until I learned to chill about the outcome. At times, the space between reaching for an objective and realizing it seems unendurable, but I endure the wait because I know the moment will arrive, and it will pass all too quickly.

Today I'm content with growing my business 5 or 10 percent; our growth rate doesn't have to double or triple each year. And I don't have to change the whole healthcare system. I keep myself plenty busy while enduring the space between desire and fulfillment. As a result, I'm not fighting my own frustration.

Have you ever watched a woman who has a background or talent similar to your own become wickedly successful while your efforts stalled? Have you ever coveted another person's wicked success and rationalized why he or she was more successful than you? I've seen women succeed far beyond their dreams and watched others founder and give up. What distinguishes wickedly successful women from their less successful sisters?

Certainly it's easy to credit another's success to luck, money, connections or lack of children, yet famous women in a variety of pursuits prove that none of these is the essential success ingredient.

o Born the twentieth of 22 children, premature and stricken by polio, Wilma Glodean Rudolph endured to become the first American woman to win three Olympic gold medals.

o Determined to help her twice-widowed mother with the family finances, young Phoebe Ann Moses, later known as Annie Oakley, practiced with her father's old Kentucky rifle. By hunting small game and selling it to hotels and restaurants, she earned enough to pay off her mother's mortgage. She was 16 when she beat well-known marksman Frank Butler in a shooting contest.

- A year after being dragged from icy waters during her aborted first attempt to swim the English Channel, Gertrude Ederle plunged again into the water at Cape Gris-Nez in France. She was assailed by wind, rain and powerful currents in water brimming with stinging jellyfish and the occasional shark. She had already endured the humiliation of her previous defeat and ridicule from the press, which asserted that no woman could swim the Channel. But having developed her "never quit" attitude as a child, after a near-fatal drowning accident, Gertrude shattered the men's record by more than two hours. In fact, due to rough waters, she swam an extra 14 miles on top of the 21-mile crossing.

- Rosebell Kirungi's airplane, carrying nine other passengers, crashed in the Rwenzori Mountains in the Democratic Republic of Congo. The survivors broke into two groups of five and headed out separately. Despite freezing conditions, snow and thunderstorms in mountains covered by a dense jungle of brambles, wild animals and rebel soldiers, she managed to walk 100 miles in 10 days, becoming the sole survivor of the crash. After her rescue, both her legs had to be amputated to arrest the gangrene she'd developed walking to safety. Today she manages a charity for other Ugandan amputees.

- Susan Butcher moved to Alaska, drawn there by her love of animals and her dislike of cities. She began training for the Iditarod, a 1,110-plus mile dogsled race through the Alaskan wilderness, which tests the endurance of both the mushers and their dog teams. Iditarod racers must endure Arctic blizzards, sleep deprivation, wild animals and every assault Alaska can throw at them. After placing in several races, Susan lost one she was leading when a crazed moose attacked her team, killing two of her dogs and injuring 13 more. The next year she became the second woman to win the Iditarod. Then she became the first woman to win four Iditarod races, the first person ever to win three times consecutively; and she broke the finishing time record on three separate occasions. Asked her secret, she said, "I do not know the word 'quit.' Either I never did, or I have abolished it."

The wickedly impressive commonality for all of these women is endurance. They chose to keep dancing their passionate vision with full expectation of reward.

When I first knocked on attorneys' doors, I knew they had a need and would hire me, so I kept knocking until they said yes. I've seen aspiring entrepreneurs give up after one month, or three rejections or one person discouraging them. Likewise, I know a woman who used her strength of endurance to make 75 prospect calls to get her first client.

Keep dancing your passionate vision fully expecting to be rewarded.

FUEL YOUR ENDURANCE WITH PERSISTENCE

In February of the year I was to be married, I lost a six-figure client—on my birthday no less—when a law firm dissolved. It didn't make for a terrific day.

That evening, Tom and I had planned to go out with friends to celebrate my birthday, but my heart wasn't in it. We opted instead for a dinner of popcorn and saw the movie, *My Left Foot*, the story of Christy Brown, whose cerebral palsy confined him to a wheelchair. Christy overcame all odds to become a celebrated writer and painter—using only his left foot, the single part of his body he could control. What a model of persistence. I left the theater a different person, my own problems seeming minor in comparison. The following months I threw myself into reorganizing my business and came out from under that disappointment stronger than before.

I thought I personified endurance until I met Mary. I'm used to being the instructor, but in all my classes I learn at least one new thing from my students. This teacher turned serious student when Mary taught me a lesson in endurance.

She had attached a letter to her seminar registration stating that she was deaf and would require a "signer." My initial annoyance at the expense heightened when I learned that not one but two professional signers would be required, alternating every 15 minutes. The cost of meeting Mary's needs was three times more than the tuition she paid.

Besides, how could a deaf woman hope to establish her own business as a legal nurse consultant?

The first day of the seminar, Mary's signers arrived early and militantly staked out three seats in the front of the room—not in the back, where I had hoped to seat them. Unused to sharing the stage, I was already out of sorts when Mary and her seeing-eye dog arrived. It was then I learned she was not only deaf but legally blind, with thick glasses to augment her limited vision. I now had to compete for my other students' attention with a pair of sign language interpreters and a dog.

And for what? There was no way a deaf, blind nurse could analyze medical records well enough to get business from attorneys.

I started the day by trying to pretend they weren't there at all, even when the dog barked for no apparent reason and laughter rippled through the crowd. Isolated by her dog's watchful protection and oblivious to the racket, Mary paid close attention to my every word. I pasted on my best plastic smile and patted myself on the back for handling the distraction so heroically, until eventually I accepted that my inconvenience paled in comparison to hers. Swallowing my humiliation, I approached Mary during a break and asked what had attracted her to legal nurse consulting.

She said, "I was working on my own malpractice case. The attorney was so impressed with my help that he said he'd hire me if I took your course." *Gulp*. I was grateful she couldn't see the surprise, guilt and contrition parading across my face.

Mary admitted that the eyestrain of trying to follow the text and the signing sent her back to her hotel room each evening with a severe migraine, but she was determined to endure the training and pass the exam. Which she did.

Despite the overwhelming odds against her, Mary began her days with a smile and fueled her endurance with persistence, working harder than the other students and knowing that each day she endured brought her one step closer to her big goal of starting her own business. I was honored to sign her certification card.

We each have our own endurance challenges. I've met thousands of women who've had setbacks. Divorce, breast cancer, loss of a 401K or loss of a child.

Any time we feel overwhelmed or on the verge of defeat, every step can seem an enormous effort, every minor conflict a major obstacle. Yet a small change or action can make a huge difference. One toe inches forward, then another, and before long we've taken a stride past the obstacle, a stride we once thought would never happen.

Endurance enables you to stand alone or with others and accomplish whatever you choose to take on.

STOP RUNNING ON EMPTY

In business, as in marathons, you have to pace yourself. If you shoot off the starting line too fast, you'll lose steam and won't have the energy to finish the race.

The big difference between marathons and your career is that in business, there's no finish line. You must keep your pace as long as you want to keep your career alive and your business growing. This means that sometimes you jog, sometimes you sprint and sometimes you stop to catch your breath. The trick for each of us is to find our natural pace and keep it. Knowing my pace and sticking to it are two reasons I've stayed in business for 29 years, and the biggest reason I still love my business.

I've seen women who start their careers full of fire. They move at a sprinter's pace and then suddenly get tired and quit. Business can be like a Venti Peppermint Mocha Frappacino from Starbucks. Those 660 calories and 116 grams of carbs (not to mention the 55 milligrams of caffeine) fire you up and set you off at a sprint. Soon though, you're in a carb-sag and need a nap. It's hard to keep the fire burning on artificial stimulants.

For the first week of January, our gym is full of newcomers throwing weights around like Arnold, and nearly flying off the treadmills and elliptical trainers. By the second week in January, the gym's back to normal because those newcomers went at it a little too hard, got stiff and sore and lost their steam for the long term. I see this in yoga (stretched a little too vigorously the first day back) and in dieting (after a week of steamed broccoli and turkey, a hamburger and cheese fries sound really good).

Women often leave satisfying careers because they can't envision enduring one thing more. Other women plug successfully away, day after day. They've chosen to endure for their own reasons—making a difference, money, sense of accomplishment or power. But like a marathoner, they know how to train, they know how to run. They know how to endure. Don't run on empty; run on your passionate vision.

Your personal life and your business life are like marathons. The key is to manage the pace at which you run them. You need to pace yourself to maintain energy for the long run. For my business, sometimes I go fast, sometimes I go faster, and sometimes I just stop. I do take 12 weeks off each year for renewal time. That's what gives me the energy to stay in business, despite the toughest economic crunch my company's ever had to endure.

Are you running at a pace that will keep you successful in your career? Or will your pace take you out of the race before the finish line?

FUEL ENDURANCE WITH INCREMENTAL PAYOFFS

At Hawaii Volcanoes National Park, I set out to hike a 14-mile trail. Although this walk was longer than I'm used to taking, I didn't see it as an overwhelming challenge. I consider myself to be in excellent physical condition.

The combination of a long hike and an excessively hot day—made worse by the uneven, hot volcanic terrain—turned out to be more difficult than I expected. Four miles into this sauna I thought seriously about turning back.

Fortunately, my pride and stubbornness pushed me to endure. At the end of the trail, my endurance was rewarded with a breathtaking view of the active volcano, an eerie yet awesomely beautiful sight like nothing I'd ever experienced.

It wasn't this final payoff, however, but the amazing small payoffs I received along the way that helped me endure: the uniqueness of each square inch of the black lava formation I crossed; abundant plant life in this seemingly barren area; incredible red flowers superimposed on the stark background; and, in the twelfth mile, the most beautiful rainbow I've ever seen—I would have missed it all if I had quit. Although the hike was a humbling experience, I had the satisfaction of knowing I had endured to the final payoff.

Marie's story of entrepreneurial endurance reminded me of my hiking experience. She hadn't anticipated the many challenges of starting a business. Along the way she often felt overwhelmed and questioned whether she could possibly turn her part-time venture into a profitable full-time business.

But she refused to quit. Finally, after much hard work, things seemed to come together. In her fourteenth month she grossed $17,000—an amount she couldn't have imagined earning two months earlier. This promised to be only the first of many similar rewards. If she had turned back when she doubted herself, not only would she have failed to receive that first big payoff, she also would never have known what she was truly capable of accomplishing.

Many women who fail in reaching their goals simply turn back too soon. The path is long and the terrain is rough. Unforeseen obstacles crop up—a difficult assignment, a fierce new competitor.

Stop and analyze your efforts to see if adjustments should be made, but don't give up on your passionate vision and life goals. Sooner or later small payoffs will brighten your path.

When your endurance is tested and you're tempted to give up, remember this: You will miss not only the gold at the end of the rainbow, but also a wealth of amazing treats along the way. Whether you're hiking, or building a business or striving for a promotion, the ultimate reward goes to those who endure, even when the big reward is far away in the distance.

Fuel your endurance by actively planning small incremental payoffs. What incremental payoffs will fuel your endurance?

FUEL ENDURANCE WITH THE RIGHT FOCUS

Great athletes focus on making their next stroke, pitch or swing even better than the last, not on the painful stitch in their side. Watch your favorite athletes on the tennis court. They're not chatting between rounds. They're harvesting energy for endurance. When you're mindful, you're not wasting energy. Masters of endurance are very good at blocking out the world.

When I'm in a "hot yoga" class, which is 90 minutes in a 105-degree room, I endure by focusing on each posture and my breathing, not on the sweat running down my face. I know I'll feel phenomenal afterward, that's a given, but I also try to enjoy the practice itself. I do best when I visualize perfecting the posture while at the same time concentrating on the instructor's directions and my muscles that are doing the work. I also repeat to myself a mantra: "This is my time. This is my 90 minutes. This is for me."

The free diver swims hundreds of feet down and back again on one breath. Every movement, every thought, uses up precious oxygen. Can you imagine her worrying about when she'll get her next breath of air? Even worrying about beating her competitor's time is a dangerous distraction. Instead, she's mindful only of the task at hand, concentrating on performance.

Actress Jane Froman related her experience after badly injuring her leg in an airplane crash:

> For about four months, I just lay there, thinking not-too-pretty thoughts. Then, one day, I got to wondering. I wanted desperately to sing; still, I hadn't sung in so long that I wondered whether I could . . . so I just did! And it felt wonderful. People in the hospital thought I'd gone crazy—that the leg pains had worked up to my head—but that didn't matter. I could sing! Whatever else was wrong with me, the breath-bellows and the voice box were sound, and that was all that counted.

Nine months after her accident, through the right focus, Froman performed in a Broadway show.

Wilma Glodean Rudolph focused first on survival, then on getting fit, then on running, not on polio.

Annie Oakley focused on shooting straight and true, not on being poor.

Gertrude Ederle focused on swimming the English Channel, not on the naysayers and perilous water.

Rosebell Kirungi focused on survival and on seeing her family again, not on the long walk to safety.

Susan Butcher focused on the love of her dogs and the sport, not on the dangers and hard conditions of the wilderness.

Worry is a useless emotion. You can't nail a triple axel while focusing on your sick child. Dividing your focus whittles away at your endurance, and worry doesn't benefit either situation. I understand worry. In the past, every time I had a breast biopsy I worried I was going to die young, like my mom. Today, I laugh, knowing that all those hours of worry didn't help a bit. From those experiences I've learned worry is a useless emotion that accomplishes nothing and takes me off focus.

Finish It Out

Right focus also means to "finish it out." This is the mantra of my trainer Jerome. It doesn't matter what exercise I'm doing, he's always pushing me—"Finish it out, Vickie, finish it out." If I'm doing a lat pull-down or a one-arm row, he doesn't want me stopping short.

Every exercise has a full range of motion, and it's easy to quit before contracting those muscles to their full potential. For example, if you're doing one-arm chin-ups, it's easy to quit before your chin crosses the bar, and that's exactly when I'll hear Jerome chanting, "Finish it out, Vickie, finish it out." Okay, I really don't do one-arm chin-ups (yet), but you get the idea, right?

I've critiqued more entrepreneurs' work products, promotional pieces and business plans than I can keep track of, and often my feedback mimics Jerome's: "Nice start, but now it's time to finish it out." Always assess whether you have engaged or analyzed as deeply as is required. Whatever you're doing, ask yourself, "Have I finished it out?" If you don't, then plan on keeping an ear cocked for Jerome and me as we remind you to "finish it out."

Is There a Skip in Your Record or Just in the Song in Your Head?

In the world of digital meda and MP3s, we no longer have to deal with skips in the middle of a song, as we used to do when listening to CDs or LPs. Most of us, however, have our own soundtrack running in our heads. Sometimes that soundtrack has a loop in it, causing us to hear the same information, right or wrong, over and over. Other times it skips, and that skip causes us not to hear what another person is telling us over and over again, or we don't hear our own repetitions as we belabor a point that's already been rejected outright. When that happens, not only does it drain our endurance, it also annoys the heck out of other people.

Train your brain to reduce the looping and skipping. If you're offered a promotion, don't respond with, "Thank you, but before I can accept

I have to finish explaining the 10 new ideas I have for the company," then loop back into your script. You've got the job, so stop, think, skip the script, and agree on the salary increase.

In some situations, repetition can be entirely appropriate. I love listening to my brother's "true Hollywood stories" from our childhood in Louisiana. Each time he embellishes a bit more, and it's fun calling him on those embellishments.

But there's a big difference between repetition for a purpose, even entertainment, and repetition due to lack of focus.

I often mentor Amy, who can fixate on an opinion. Instead of engaging in the intelligent discourse of conversation and the back-and-forth flow of ideas, points and counterpoints, she'll simply repeat her last point, like a skipping record, figuring that if she tests my endurance long enough, I'll concede her point.

It doesn't work that way. Instead, I interrupt her and ask, "Amy, have I given you any indication that I haven't heard you? It's time for you to move on, unless you have a new and different way to express your opinion." Sometimes I have to repeat myself to stop her from repeating herself.

Recently, at a live event, I spent a considerable amount of time privately answering a woman's questions. I patiently covered all her issues, and I thought she was satisfied with my answers and recommendations. To my surprise, the next day she asked me the same questions again. I politely told her that no matter how many times she asked me, my answers wouldn't change.

I later found out that after talking to me twice, she buttonholed one of our mentors with the same questions. That woman politely told her to follow my advice. The internal loop of the woman's soundtrack and story was causing skips in her ability to listen and process information.

I challenge you to be like an MP3 in your career and personal relationships. You'll run into plenty of situations where repetition is necessary, but when it's not, before you start looping and skipping, ask yourself what you want to achieve and if you're staying on focus.

Focus is the rocket fuel of endurance. Concentrate on the right focus, the one thing that matters and shut your mental door on all the rest.

ENDURE FOR THE FUN OF IT

My parents taught me that fun was where I made it. I was their shy, quiet and serious child, and they made it their mission to help me "lighten up." They'd get up a game of touch football for the neighborhood kids, or take us all out for hot chocolate and beignets. "Have fun" was one piece of parental advice I took to heart.

It's inevitable that we'll enjoy some experiences more than others. Getting praised for your work is fantastic. Going on vacation is bliss. Making a difference is rewarding. And we savor these fun moments. But not every moment of success is rewarding or fantastic or bliss.

One of the biggest factors contributing to failure in any endeavor is the naive assumption that to be passionate and enjoy your work you have to enjoy every aspect of what you do. Countless otherwise savvy and intelligent women blithely expect success to be like a perfect picnic. Then when they come face to face with the inevitable biting ants, stinging mosquitoes and drenching rain showers, they run for shelter.

If you assume you should enjoy everything you do every day, you'll wind up massively disappointed. You'll constantly be fantasizing about something better, someplace else. Then when you arrive at that someplace else with your delusional expectations, the vicious cycle starts anew, leaving you dissatisfied again—and wondering how it happened when you were following your bliss toward the "perfect" future. If you broaden your concept of fun to include the hard stuff, life does become easier.

Broaden Your Concept of Fun

People often ask me, "Vickie, of the places you've been, what is your all-time favorite trip?" I'm not a fan of this question because every trip is a favorite in its own way. But my response has been the same for 12 years: "If I can only pick one, it would have to be Nepal." Nepal was my first expedition, so I felt daring, rugged and adventurous.

The Himalayas are the most stunning mountains I've ever seen. I hiked on trails carved by generations of use, and which felt like sacred ground. The dramatic peaks and high altitudes I reached took my breath away. With every step I marveled at wonders unfolding before me.

To this day I've seen nothing that rivals the beauty or the thrill of my first view of Mount Everest.

If there was a counterpoint to the beauty of the surroundings, it was the places we stayed. I love being in nature no matter the weather, and I don't mind getting really wet or dirty. But after a long day of hiking, I enjoy a hot shower, a good meal and nice surroundings. Such niceties were markedly absent in Nepal. Some of the places we stayed were downright dirty. The communal Western-style toilet (if there even was one) was often overflowing and covered in a combination of excrement and urine. Luckily, my hospital experience with all sorts of bodily fluids helped me to cope, and being a nurse, I knew how to use a toilet without touching anything; but I quickly started looking forward to using the Nepalese hole in the ground.

Then there were the uncomfortable beds made from two-by-fours and covered by mattresses stuffed with "local materials" shaved from a hairy zopkio. They didn't bring me joy. When Tom and I zipped into our sleeping bags at night, it was for protection from the mattress and whatever was living in it more than from the elements. It almost made me wish we were camping outside, not teahouse trekking. Next there were the four minutes of lukewarm, sun-still-heated water per person. Tom and I made the most of that one. Don't get excited though—any flames of romance were quickly extinguished when the water returned to freezing in the ninth minute.

Finally, there was the food. Being an Italian gal from New Orleans, I live to eat, so Tom was shocked to find that not only was I not eating, I had no appetite whatsoever. After three days, he watched me practically have a food-gasm upon discovering a dubious-looking jar of American peanut butter.

Despite the worst food and the worst accommodations of my life, Nepal was still my favorite trip.

Sometimes the most rewarding and enjoyable things come with some discomfort. We can be working away in a business we love, or on a challenging project, then something happens and suddenly a great day turns bad. What do we do: lose our momentum and quit?

No, we have to endure, for the fun of it. When this happens at my office, I'll joke with my staff and say, "Hey, if this business was easy, everyone would be doing it."

We often think easy or soft is what we want, but what we really want is something that will challenge us, and in the challenge we find a special reward. To be in Nepal, I needed to work to get there. Enjoying the Himalayas involved not only enduring the bad food and accommodations, it also included training for long treks of high-altitude hiking—not to mention traveling almost halfway around the world. One day we walked for 12 hours to get to the next teahouse.

At first I resisted the discomforts, but on day four of the trek, I woke up famished for even bad food, and on that day I had an epiphany: "Without the discomforts, I wouldn't be having this wondrous experience." Suddenly I was all in, truly alive, and savoring each and every moment.

Embrace the discomforts of your own expedition. Vow to do something that makes you uncomfortable. Whether you're cleaning a closet, working overtime, or struggling to complete a project, you have a choice about how you label that experience.

Dale uses fun to endure the discomfort of rejection: "The thought of showing up at a prospect's office with my marketing materials in hand terrified me at first. Then I began having fun with it, inventing new ways to get past the gatekeepers. Now, the challenge of seeing how many prospects will actually talk to me is a fun game."

Endurance is a choice. Fun is a choice. The more you broaden your concept of fun, the deeper your endurance for achieving wicked success. You may feel like you're climbing Mount Everest, but imagine the view you'll see from the top!

TAKE TO THE AIR LIKE A BUTTERFLY

My grandmother Pearl always called me her butterfly. I loved that she saw me as someone who was beautiful and special. What I didn't know is that she was also referring to the transformation I would go through to become the woman I am today.

As a butterfly emerges from its cocoon, it struggles and strains to free itself. The struggle is essential to strengthen the wings and shrink the body. Without such strain, the butterfly's wings would be weak, its distended body ungainly and it would never take to the air. Butterflies everywhere that endure this struggle are rewarded the glorious adventure of flying from blossom to blossom.

We are all constantly emerging from our cocoons, struggling and straining to become free, strong, beautiful women. Growth of any kind cannot occur without enduring some degree of discomfort. Here's your choice: You can play it safe, avoid the pain of growing and experience the narrow, earthbound existence of the lowly caterpillar. Or you can throw yourself fully into the struggle of living, pain and all, and enjoy the soaring freedom of the lofty butterfly.

Building muscle mass is another "no pain, no gain" experience. To build muscle mass, you have to hurt. And you won't just hurt the first few times you do it. If you're training correctly, it will hurt every time you work out. If you're not hurting, you're only pretending to be working out. Bear in mind that this hurt is what trainers refer to as a "good hurt," not the kind that causes injury; but it's uncomfortable all the same.

Have you ever observed a person working out halfheartedly? Be careful that you're not playing that pretend game with yourself. Real growth requires real effort and real endurance. Don't take the easy way out, telling yourself you'll reach your performance goal by a shortcut that skips the painful part of the journey. Each hurt, each struggle you endure transforms you. Shortchange yourself in the effort department and you not only deceive yourself but also deprive yourself of the opportunity to grow.

Wickedly successful women have a pain threshold way above normal. To grow your success "muscles," be willing to up the intensity and endure "hurt" on a regular basis. Eventually those muscles will turn into wings that fly you passionately onward.

FUEL YOUR ENDURANCE WITH FIRE

Endurance comes easy when we're passionately interested in what we're doing. A ballet dancer endures excruciating practice workouts to become excellent, but the pain doesn't stop when she perfects her talent. While performing, she's so intently focused that she may not feel pain, but after she pulls off her ballet slippers, her battered, bloody feet make her cringe. She endures because she's passionate about dancing.

As I've mentioned, I'm passionate about travel. I love traveling to remote places, but have you ever noticed the inconveniences travelers endure to enjoy their passion?

It starts with the preparation necessary to be gone for several weeks—as when I went to Bhutan—packing for all that time away, then enduring the body cavity search at airport security, uncomfortable seats and questionable airline food on the 14-hour overnight flight to Hong Kong, multiple connections on progressively more and more dilapidated aircraft, the frightening descent into Paro and the incoherent questioning by the overly suspicious customs agent—knowing that after you've fully relaxed you'll have to endure it all again—backward.

You start questioning, "Why am I doing this?" Finally you're in Bhutan enduring lost or damaged luggage. Part of you is miserable, while another part is muttering, "I love this, I really do." But when you finally stand amidst the flapping prayer flags at the top of the Chelela Pass, peer into Tibet and marvel at the majesty of Mount Jhomolari, it's worth every moment of your endurance. Conversely, without the passion there is no way I'd subject myself to the endurance required.

Fire and endurance, when tightly connected, can take you all the way to the top. My business is a good example. Like all true entrepreneurs, I passionately love entrepreneurship, but the employee and management issues are an endurance for me. Because I love the creative development of the business, and I enjoy the relationships that surround it, I endure the less desirable aspects.

I'm continuously amazed at the variety of businesses that people seem to be passionate about, especially those that make and sell widgets. I couldn't wrap my passion around a widget, so I would never have the endurance to make such a business successful.

I shared a podium with a woman who owns more than 60 McDonald's restaurants. She started as an employee, at the bottom of the hamburger business, and left for a different career only to later return to McDonald's as an owner. When I asked her why she left one successful career for a career in hamburgers, she replied "Because I'm passionate about hamburgers."

I'm thankful that other people can get fired up about making hamburgers, because otherwise they would never get made. Likewise, I've seen people whose spectacular idea never gets off the ground because they don't have the passion to endure what's required.

Since I started writing this book, I can't count the number of people who've told me, "I plan to write a book some day." They have a bright idea for a book, and they think that's all it takes. But even the brightest idea doesn't shed any light until it's expressed in 70,000 words, or 280 manuscript pages or more.

It means enduring days and weeks and even months of fleshing out your idea until you finally type "The End," and then enduring weeks or months of revision upon revision. You need more than a bright idea; you need a passion for writing that makes endurance possible.

To reach the end of anything—a project, a hike or 14 hours of labor—you need the Feminine Force of endurance. Fortunately, women have all the endurance they need. Merge endurance with your passion, and you can accomplish anything.

HARVEST ENERGY TO INCREASE YOUR ENDURANCE

Somewhere in your home or purse you have a device that runs on a battery. It could be a smoke detector, iPhone, digital camera or laptop computer. Like the battery in that device, endurance is there when you need it. But without occasional recharging, a battery runs out of power. So will you if your energy is not fueled by passion, focus, fun or another renewal source.

One source you can count on for harvesting more energy is positive relationships. We all know at least one person who lifts our spirits and makes us feel more alive. It might be your mother, your spouse, a good friend, your children or, if you're truly fortunate, all of them. Surround yourself with positive relationships, especially with people who support your passionate vision, and your natural endurance will be eternally rechargeable.

If positive relationships can power up your endurance battery, what do you think happens when you invest time in negative relationships? *Zap!* Why squander such a valuable resource?

Don't tolerate a relationship that returns little or nothing, despite how much you put into it. Limit any exposure to people who drain you, and sever dark, toxic relationships.

I love my employees, but I know my limitations when it comes to enduring employee issues. In my start-up days, I handled everything. I was head of production, wardrobe, marketing, shipping, transportation and cleaning, as well as running the cafeteria (I had to eat, after all).

When I expanded beyond my one-person business, I thought employees would take some of that weight off my shoulders. Instead, their burdens became mine too, and I was now head of adult psychiatry as well. Employees waited until the end of a long day to come into my office, shut the door and say, "I need to talk with you."

Add to that such issues as petty conflicts, bare midriffs, sick children, flu season, bad hair days and people crying on my desk—and that was just the men! Talk about a constant drain.

Now I have the luxury of working at home a couple of days a week. I hired five directors on whom I can rely to run the day-to-day operations, and I interact with them by phone or email. Women can find creative ways to endure, but when possible we should step away to recharge and improve performance.

Energy is life. Energy is essential for endurance. Detach from all energy-draining people who do not align with your vision. Conserve your stamina for what matters.

10 STRATEGIES FOR BUILDING YOUR ENDURANCE MUSCLES

Endurance is a strength you can build by working out. Muscling up your inner power to match your passion is no different from building larger, stronger biceps. It takes focus, dedication and discipline. If you stop going to the gym, your muscles atrophy. If you stop strengthening endurance, you lose it.

1. **Energize your endurance.** Many people energize their running or gym workout with music and claim they can work harder and longer. One woman in our office streams soft music from her iPhone while she works. Your inspiration might be classical music, an instrumental or sounds of nature. Or it might be your digital photo frame filled with photos of friends, family, renewing vacations and scenic landscapes.

2. **See the light.** Endurance comes easier when you can see the light at the end of the tunnel, when you know what you must endure and for how long. One day I had 17 TV interviews in New York City, a red-eye flight to San Diego for a morning TV show, followed by

11 radio interviews. Then I spent the next four days preparing a
conference my company sponsored and rehearsing a keynote for
950 people. I could endure this experience because I knew it would
soon end. You might not be able to run an 8-minute mile but you
can run an 8-minute-mile pace for 30 seconds. See the light and you
will endure.

3. **Power up with knowledge.** Fuel yourself with all the skills and
   information you need, and also with any peripheral knowledge that
   might give you an edge. Knowledge makes endurance less of
   a struggle.

4. **Engage assistance.** It takes a relay of runners to carry the Olympic
   torch. Who can you engage to make your burden lighter or your
   journey easier?

5. **Condition yourself.** Some things you have to experience to endure.
   When I first started teaching, I taught all day. At first it was hard;
   now it's easy. The more you condition yourself, and the more you up
   the intensity, the longer you'll endure.

6. **Take an endurance break.** When you work out with weights, you
   shouldn't exercise the same muscles two days in a row. Similarly,
   give yourself an occasional break from your ordinary world. Do
   something totally different, meet new people or go to a bookstore
   and spend an afternoon visiting a new world. Avoid answering your
   cell phone or otherwise getting drawn back into your real world.
   You'll feel stronger when you return.

7. **Break the marathon.** When you're running an endurance marathon,
   taking five-minute breaks every hour renews your energy for
   endurance. No matter how busy you are, you can always find time to
   take five or even two minutes.

8. **Acknowledge your past endurances.** Acknowledging what you've
   endured in the past strengthens your endurance for the next challenge.

9. **Take care of yourself.** A healthy body, mind and spirit fuel
   endurance. We'll talk more about this under the strength of renewal,
   in Chapter 9.

10. **Think straight.** Your thoughts control your life, and as your most intimate companions, your thoughts can help you endure. Don't dwell on the competition. Don't dwell on the problem. Don't dwell on the rude remark. Focus on the why—why you choose to endure in the first place.

Wickedly successful women take advantage of their inner strength of endurance to sustain their success. Build up your endurance muscles, and not only will you have strength to sustain commitments you make to others, you'll also have strength to meet commitments you make to yourself.

FUEL YOUR ENDURANCE WITH THE

5 PROMISES

PROMISE 1
I Will Live and Work a Passionate Life

What do you find most difficult to endure (mentally, physically, etc.) in pursuing your passionate vision?

_____

_____

_____

PROMISE 2
I Will Go for It or Reject It Outright

What meaningful sounds and sights lift your spirits and strengthen your endurance? Write them down, then revisit this collection daily.

_____

_____

_____

Do you associate with anyone who belittles you, depresses you, or otherwise zaps your energy? If so, how will you detach from this person?

_____

_____

_____

PROMISE 3
I Will Take One Action Step a Day Toward My Passionate Vision

What three action steps will you take to strengthen the area of endurance identified in Promise 1?

_____

_____

_____

PROMISE 4
I Commit to Being a Success Student for Life

Name a woman who exemplifies endurance for you. How will you model her success to fuel your endurance?

_____

_____

_____

PROMISE 5
I Believe as a Woman I Really Can Do Anything

What challenges have you met that required endurance? How will you use those successes to strengthen your endurance in the future?

_____

_____

_____

>> DOWNLOAD THE 5 PROMISES FOR ENDURANCE AT **WickedSuccess.com**.

SUSAN'S ENDURANCE

I trained for a year for the Houston marathon. Then, about a month before the marathon, I decided there wasn't any way I could do 26 miles. After a particularly hard training run at 18 miles, I did not believe I could do much more. The person helping me said, "Oh, yes you can." I kept going, kept training. The whole time I was telling myself, "You can do this, you can do this." When I got to the point in the marathon where other people hit the wall—the 20-mile mark—I kept telling myself, "Only 6 miles to go. You do more than that each day in training. It's no big deal." I did it, and it was a fabulous experience.

The endurance of running the marathon was nothing compared to the endurance of breast cancer. There's an enormous mind game you play with yourself, hearing the news that you have breast cancer and deciding what you are going to do with that information. Thinking positively, and seeing the light at the end of the tunnel, I carried on. What I learned from the experience was to trust God's plan above all and to know that we are never ever given more than we can endure. I also learned to test myself and push the envelope, to know that my mind is a powerful tool.

I wrote down a quote that has inspired me over time: "Expand what you know you can do." Certainly my experience with cancer helped me to do that.

Constantly talking to yourself, reassuring yourself—to me that's how endurance is sustained. That's what helped me

through chemo and the bad days, and reminded me I had
something to look forward to. Now I've been cancer-free for
six years, and while I'll never run another marathon,
I'm learning every day how much more I can do.

Susan, 55
INTERIOR DESIGNER

Knowing you have the Feminine Force of endurance to sustain your passion, let's explore how endurance can be less of a struggle when coupled with the next strength, enterprise.

Nothing contributes so much to tranquilize the mind as a steady purpose—a point on which the soul may fix its intellectual eye.
MARY WOLLSTONECRAFT SHELLEY

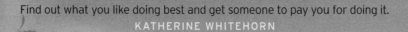

Enterprise is in a woman's DNA—just look at what we accomplish.
VICKIE L. MILAZZO

8

ENTERPRISE

Become the CEO of Your Career and Life

E very minute of the day in a woman's life presents bold
new ventures, and risks to go along with them. Women
understand enterprise. Job, education, household, spouse, lover, kids,
friendships—these are separate departments in the enterprise you call
life. Who keeps these departments rocking? You.

Let's label them differently: production, research and development,
administration, partnerships, human resources, payroll, customer relations.
Who keeps this complex enterprise humming? You.

Think about the creative, enterprising strategies you've used to manage
it all. Perhaps you didn't realize you were being enterprising. You were
simply "getting it all done." That's CEO language for keeping the lights on,
the personnel happy and quality work product churning out on time.

Now let's talk about how you can focus that brilliant enterprising
ability to become the CEO of your career and life. Enterprise is
a strength. You own it. If you are as enterprising as the CEO of a
successful business, you can use your enterprising strength to start a
business venture of your own, manage your family, build a corporate
career or any combination of achievements.

From an entrepreneurial standpoint, women own a total of 10.1 million businesses, almost 40 percent of all businesses in the United States. If you include those where women are not a majority or equal owner, you up that total to 15 million.

This is amazing when you consider that the average woman will spend 17 years of her life caring for children and an additional 18 years caring for relatives.

On trips to Thailand and Vietnam, where women aren't exactly first-class citizens, I encountered women's enterprising spirit at its rawest and liveliest. Everywhere I looked, women were running businesses. They hawked new and used clothing, lemonade in plastic baggies and everything else you can imagine—including cobras inside bottles of liquor. Women weighing 95 pounds carried wooden yokes with complete soup kitchens balanced on their shoulders: bowls, utensils and food on one side, a charcoal grill holding pots of broth and tea on the other. The grill was hot, and the pots simmered even as the women walked. In Southeast Asia, fast food comes to you.

Enterprise can be any undertaking of a venture and the reward doesn't have to appear in the form of dollars in the bank. But successful CEOs do expect a payoff for every venture.

When you invest your time and energy in a new enterprise, always ask: What's my payoff? Is it monetary? Is it good for my spirit? Will it advance my career? Will it enrich my life or benefit my family?

If you say no to this opportunity, is there a bigger payoff available to you? The profit need not always be in cash, but there needs to be a payoff. Even Mother Theresa enjoyed a payoff from her devotion. Passion for your life and work is the best profit of all.

What payoffs do you receive from your business or career and your relationships? What ultimate reward will come from living your passionate vision? Whether you want to own a Mercedes, stop global warming or both, get emotionally in touch with that payoff.

BE FIRST AT THE RIVER TO GET A DRINK

During a photo safari on Tanzania's Serengeti Plain, I encountered the least enterprising animal on earth, the wildebeest. For three hours I sat on a riverbank watching a herd of thousands build up the courage to drink from the water.

This herd was part of the Great Migration that happens like clockwork every summer. More than a million wildebeests travel northward from the arid Serengeti into the wetlands of Kenya's Masai Mara, a long, dry and arduous journey. Frequently, the only available water is the Grumeti River, which represents both life and death. Unlike some creatures that can take moisture from the grass they eat, wildebeests must drink from the river to live.

The river supports other wildlife, including predators. Crocodiles may lurk just beneath the surface. One day I watched more than a dozen crocodiles feast on an unlucky wildebeest.

Though thirsty from traveling, the wildebeests stand back from the water, sensing potential danger. Inching toward the bank can take hours, as an individual wildebeest steps forward tentatively, sniffs the air, makes the plaintive "gnu" sound, steps back and then cautiously steps forward again. Bunching together, the herd advances gradually, nudging the leaders to the river, whether they want to go or not. It's been a long time since they last drank, and you feel their desperation.

Lions, lazy creatures, but possibly the most enterprising of all, are on watch, conserving energy as they await an opportunity for lunch. Once the herd is stretched thin, they charge and the wildebeest stampede, raising a dust cloud that obscures the view of those closest to the lions. A kill is almost guaranteed.

The day I sat on that riverbank, a young wildebeest finally stepped ahead of the herd and drank while the fearful adults held back. Soon, others began drinking. But instead of lining up along the bank, taking turns, they bunched together fearfully and pushed until the surging masses shoved the young wildebeest farther into the water than it was willing to go. It panicked and in turn panicked the others. They all retreated hastily and returned to the migration. Only the few brave enough to test the leading edge got a drink. The others went thirsty.

There was no danger from predators that day. Only the wildebeests' fear and lack of enterprise kept them from drinking.

The wildebeests reminded me of my fellow nurses at the hospital. We would bunch up at the water cooler gnuing away and generally airing our dissatisfaction with our jobs, but never acting to end the desperation. Complaining was easier.

I decided I would no longer stand at the water cooler waiting for a drink. From the beginning, I treated my venture not as a part-time hobby but as an opportunity to quench my thirst for a more exciting and rewarding career. Refusing to hang out with the wildebeests and get eaten by the lions, I staged a friendly corporate takeover and became the CEO of my career and life. That was my payoff.

The lions' enterprising nature enables them to take on a herd of thousands of wildebeests. Their payoff is lunch. No doubt you've successfully managed many tough situations and, like the lion, have enterprise already inside you. Engage that strength to drink deeply of your passionate vision.

SATISFY YOUR THIRST AT THE RIVER OF CHOICE

While every woman is enterprising, not every woman is entrepreneurial, and there's nothing wrong with that. As an entrepreneur, I'm grateful for those enterprising women who work for me. They share many of my strengths, and possess unique strengths of their own, yet have no desire to start their own businesses. They prefer working as a team, possibly taking on leadership roles or interfacing at the front line with customers.

Only you know which river of success is the one for you. As the CEO of your life you must also be the CEO of your career. No matter where you are in life or career, whether you are an employee of a large or midsize company striving to climb the corporate ladder, a budding entrepreneur aspiring to break out on your own and create the next Facebook or a woman who wants to head up a team of volunteers at your child's school, approach your venture with the attitude of an enterprising and entrepreneurial CEO, and your vision will become your reality.

The Corporate Formula

Do you like working with a team? Is your idea of security a steady paycheck with guaranteed benefits? Do you like to put your work aside at the end of the day? If so, the corporate route is for you.

To forge your corporate path, act like a CEO who is plotting the purchase of another company. First, research the top levels of your division to identify positions that match your passionate vision and explore other divisions for jobs of interest. Next, plot a course from that lofty position you aspire to attain back to where you are now, pinpointing one or more positions at every level that will lead to your ideal career. Keep your vision bold, without concern for obstacles.

Study the people who currently hold those positions. How did they get where they are? If possible, get to know them personally. People advance because of relationships, so build relationships at all levels. Be friendly with everyone, but remember that advancement comes from the top down, and a little appropriate sucking up never hurts. Never sabotage managers or coworkers. You'll need them.

When I was working at the hospital as an ICU nurse, Dilbert (from the cartoon of the same name) would have been my best friend. I was young, in my 20s and too smart for my own good. With the exception of one supervisor, who would stand with us at the bedside when we were understaffed, I thought all hospital supervisors were stupid. What did they know about the real world and the front lines of patient care?

I now understand how wrong and immature I was and that even if you really are smarter than your manager, it's just common sense to align yourself with the company and the company's goals.

Engage 100 percent. Clock-watchers who go home exactly at quitting time are never around for promotions. Work as hard as or harder than your boss. If you're the supervisor, work as hard as your employees and as smart as upper management.

Rather than looking only at your advancement, look for ways in which your knowledge and expertise can grow and benefit the company. As a business owner, I appreciate employees who apply enterprise and ingenuity to their jobs. They generally enjoy their jobs more and receive more advancements and pay raises. If your company clearly has no place for you to advance, move on. Don't make yourself and everyone around you miserable.

Investigate the new skills you'll need and learn them. Some skills are developed through education, others through experience. Many of the skills I have now, including the ability to manage downturns in the economy, publish books and apply new technology to our online products came through experience. Business is a big laboratory, and every day is an experiment. On some days we invent new creations; on others we're sweeping up shards of broken beakers. Open up, experiment and learn.

The Entrepreneurial Formula

Are you the rebel—mouthy and opinionated? Do you like the thrill of change? Are you always eager for the next new venture? Is your idea of security to never be the victim of a corporation's downsizing or reengineering? Do you want to find a way to earn a living while having more control over your life? Are you willing to put in fast-paced, 12-hour days, if necessary, to reap those rewards? Are you a fiercely independent risk taker who can handle the uncertainty of being responsible for your own paycheck, even in a recession? If you answered yes, then the entrepreneurial route is right for you.

If you choose the entrepreneurial route, research your industry to identify types of businesses that match your passionate vision. Explore areas that show growth potential and look for a need not presently being filled. Then find a successful company similar to the one you envision owning, study how it started and how it grew, and learn as much as possible about the entrepreneur behind it.

Devour books, publications and online resources related to your business concept. Talk to other entrepreneurs to discover their best practices. Look to successful businesses that are different from your idea. Study strategies that transcend industries and apply them to your business.

A successful entrepreneur is a bold visionary, seeing what others cannot and willing to follow that vision despite naysayers. Many entrepreneurs never finished college, but that hasn't stopped them from owning companies like Facebook or Apple. They relied heavily on their vision, not on MBA programs.

As an entrepreneur-in-training, you'll need to build both basic and advanced leadership skills. Entrepreneurs handle ambiguity with ease, get a thrill out of leading the way into unfamiliar territory and thumb their noses at failure. Fearless pacesetters, they're usually mystified to find themselves weak at or disinterested in operations and management. That's okay. Other people can manage for you, but you must be the guiding force that inspires your managers and staff to follow your vision. As a leader, you focus on the big picture and trust others to focus on the details. People who do it all are self-employed, not entrepreneurial.

Above all, you must grow your enterprise and make a profit. People who say, "I love it so much I'd do it for free," have never owned a business. Most entrepreneurs are willing to sacrifice and do what it takes to succeed, but they fully expect to make money. There is nothing noble about being poor or failing financially.

Whichever route you choose—the corporate ladder, your own ladder or simply applying enterprise to your life—my strategies for acting like a CEO guarantee wicked success.

VENTURE OUT FROM A SOLID FOUNDATION

I started my business in my small condo. Every morning I hauled out my files and modest equipment and turned my home into a workspace. Every evening I packed it all away again to make room for eating, sleeping, and living. Within those modest surroundings I was constructing a foundation for my enterprise.

Today the Institute's foundation is not a room in my condo, but 8,200 square feet of office space supported by a team of 23 enterprising staffers. To grow my company I had to build a team that was as good as, or better than, me.

The foundation you build today will support your corporate career or entrepreneurial enterprise as you drive onward and upward. How do you make your foundation solid—indestructible, unshakable and enduring? With a Strategic Life Plan.

Fortify Your Enterprise with a Strategic Life Plan

Consider the Golden Gate Bridge, the Brooklyn Bridge or London's Tower Bridge. How did the architects dare to create such astonishing visions? They didn't just look out at the future location, point a finger and say, "Pour the concrete right about there." Of course not.

Yet how often do we look out at the perilous waters of life, point a finger and say, "I'll just pour some concrete right there?" An architect knows that failing to plan is planning to fail.

As CEO, you need a Strategic Life Plan that projects your passionate vision. Include the goals, or Big Things, you defined in Chapter 3, plus strategies and target dates. This is your blueprint for building your bridge to astonishing success.

My first strategic plan was conceived in my mind, but only came fully to life when I committed it to paper. That single page included my goals and the strategies to achieve them, with a target date attached. Every time I made a business decision, I consulted my plan. I reviewed and updated it frequently. It became my friendly nudge, my board of directors and my business manager.

Today my company's strategic plan is 65 pages, because this level of planning is necessary to run my company, but it started with a simple plan.

One woman entrepreneur shares:

> The best advice I never took was to write a strategic plan. I thought I knew better, that I could grow my business without it. Eight months into starting my part-time business, I was floundering. I finally sat down and wrote a strategic plan and posted it where I could see it every day. My business began to flourish and within a month I was wondering why I had not done this sooner. Within four months of writing that strategic plan, I quit my regular job and focused on my business. I was amazed by my success and now know that I should have followed that advice from day one.

Envision a Bold Enterprise

If anyone had asked me 29 years ago whether I could manage a multimillion-dollar company, I would have laughed. My vision was smaller then. But that smaller vision got me to the bigger vision today.

Don't hesitate to commit a plan to paper because it seems daunting; just start small. Starting small is better than not starting at all. Begin your plan by focusing on the passionate vision you developed in Chapters 1 and 2.

Describe the corporate, entrepreneurial or personal enterprise you will undertake to live your vision, and then answer the question: What will this venture do for me?

_____

_____

_____

_____

_____

Anchor Your Enterprise

The stability of your foundation comes from three cornerstones of balance: your values, your strengths and the way you handle challenges. How will yours anchor your enterprise?

1. **Define your core values.** This is not difficult, but it's somewhat magical, because your values will guide your decisions like a sage whispering in your ear.

   One of my company's core values is building lifelong relationships with our clients. Clients include our internal staff. If we don't serve each other, we can't possibly serve our external clients. This core value is the reason downsizing could not be my first reaction to the economic recession.

   Your values will shape your future as they have previously influenced your past, and will help keep your Strategic Life Plan on target. *Write them down.*

   _____

   _____

   _____

   _____

   _____

2. **Assess your strengths.** Think about the knowledge, skills and experience your enterprise will draw on. *List all your strengths that you will apply to your enterprise.*

   _____

   _____

   _____

   _____

3. **Appraise your challenges.** Whatever your enterprise, you'll have challenges. These may involve market penetration, profitability, expertise, competition or getting along with your supervisor.

   Challenges change as your enterprise changes. My first challenge was getting clients to recognize the need for a new type of consulting service. As my company grew, a new challenge surfaced: my lack of experience as a manager. That challenge led me to seek the right executives to support my vision. Without addressing that weakness, I might never have achieved big.

What challenges will you face in pursuing your enterprise? How will they impact your goals and strategies?

_____

_____

_____

_____

_____

Shape Your Enterprise

Imagine your enterprise as it exists in your ideal future. Think large as you review the Big Things and action steps you wrote in Chapter 3.

1. Does your Big Thing match your enterprise or some part of your enterprise? If not, choose a Big Thing that does match your enterprise. Write this Big Thing on the "Goal/Big Thing" line on the Strategic Life Plan form on the next page.

2. What strategies will you use to accomplish your Big Thing? Do these match the action steps you wrote in Chapter 3? Develop your strategies and write them on your plan.

3. Add target dates for completion.

4. Constantly assess where you are in your plan and how the plan is measuring up to your passionate vision. Update it regularly.

5. Repeat this process for all the Big Things you'll do to make your enterprise a reality.

STRATEGIC LIFE PLAN

VISION

_____

GOAL/BIG THING

_____

_____

STRATEGIES   **TARGET DATES**

1. _____   _____
   _____

2. _____   _____
   _____

3. _____   _____
   _____

4. _____   _____
   _____

5. _____   _____
   _____

>> DOWNLOAD A COPY OF THIS FORM AT **WickedSuccess.com**
FOR EACH BIG THING.

Expect Icebergs

No enterprise is unsinkable; the *Titanic* sank its first time out. Businesses fail. Employees get downsized. But when your enterprise has a solid foundation and when you act like a CEO, only an enormous iceberg can knock you off course.

In 1990, I hit an iceberg when my largest clients dissolved their law firm. I hit another huge iceberg when the recent recession struck. Thankfully, I had the necessary lifeboats in place, and my business stayed afloat both times.

The first iceberg took me on a new course, which changed my business and the nursing profession forever. If I'd missed the iceberg, I might have continued in my original direction, satisfied with a much smaller business. And you'd be reading someone else's book. The recession iceberg caused me to power and fund my business in new and innovative ways.

Stay on the lookout for icebergs. Don't get lost in the details or in creating the glitz and glitter. You can easily lose sight of what's ahead and forget to watch where you're going.

Unfortunately, you don't have to hit an iceberg head-on to sink your enterprise. The *Titanic's* collision wasn't head-on. Instead the iceberg glanced along the side, tearing a gash no wider than three inches in six purportedly watertight compartments; but that minimal damage still sank an "unsinkable" ship. As with the *Titanic*, even a small amount of damage can have catastrophic effects.

You do have to sail before you can fail. You can maneuver around icebergs. But if you never leave the dock, you'll never have an enterprise to keep afloat. Will your enterprise be a *Titanic*-sized failure or a *Titanic*-sized success?

COMMAND FINANCIAL CONTROL IN YOUR ENTERPRISE

A competitor once commented sarcastically that my clients pay for my big house, my big vacations and my big smile. Of course they do. That's what a business is supposed to do. An enterprise is profitable or it isn't an enterprise—it's a charity.

The word *profit* stems from the Latin word *profectus*, which means "advancement or improvement." Women should profit from their advancement.

As CEO of your life, you deserve to achieve your desired level of financial growth. When I researched my first business idea for a patient education company, I was naively ready to go for it until I realized the enterprise wouldn't even support my modest lifestyle, which at that time amounted to $28,000 a year. I had to refocus my vision on an enterprise that could feed and shelter me.

Money to start, maintain and advance your enterprise is part of any sensible plan. Even carving your niche within a corporate structure may require an investment in education or training. But that doesn't mean you have to rush to the bank for a loan.

I started my business without one scrap of outside financial support and only $100 in my savings account. I started with one client, then gained a second and a third. I continued to work full-time for 15 months while I built my business. It was a challenge running the business at night and on days off, but I knew that if I was willing to bust my butt for a short time, I wouldn't be busting it for the next 40 years in the hospital.

Statistically, fast-growing women-owned businesses rely on earnings as their primary funding source, and women-owned businesses whose revenues are below $1 million are less likely to access commercial credit than those whose revenues exceed $1 million. That can be a good or bad thing, depending upon how much you want your business to grow and whether or not you need outside money to finance expansion or improvements. My recommendation: Call on outside financing only when it's absolutely critical to fund the next bold step.

In my years of owning a business, I've never taken out a loan. Growing from $100 to $16 million at my peak, without outside capital, took time and effort, but not other people's investments. Outside investors, be they angels, venture capitalists or family, will often want a say in the business.

This is what happened to Laura:

My mother wanted to come in as a full partner. I had the idea and the skills. She had the money. So against my better judgment I agreed to the deal. Now we have competing interests and have to balance each business decision against her desire to take cash rather than grow the business, which is my desire. My advice, don't take money from family. Ever.

Needing less is also a financial asset. Do you know people who can't finance a vacation, much less their passionate vision, because they want, want, want? Nothing will sabotage your enterprise more than financial worries. Freedom from such worries enables you to make bold decisions. While I encourage stretching way out when choosing goals, I never encourage living above your income.

Operating from my 1,100-square-foot condo until my business was extremely profitable freed me to grow my business without the stress of high overhead. It also allowed me to set aside substantial savings for the future. I didn't splurge on overly extravagant vacations or buy new cars or redecorate my home.

Distinguish ambition from greed. How much money is enough? A 12-hour day of passion—that's fun. A 12-hour day of hating what we do and being driven by a wrong motive, such as money—that's torment. Don't get me wrong. I'm ambitious and competitive, but I've literally left millions of dollars on the table because the opportunity was not something I was passionate about. I make distinctions between what I love, what I need and what I don't.

Apply CEO financial management tools to your enterprise:

- Make a budget and stick to it. Keep the cash flow positive. That means taking in more money than you pay out, plain and simple. Question every expenditure.

- Create a monthly income statement and a balance sheet to monitor the financial health of your enterprise.

- Keep your new enterprise money separate from family money. This is a business, not a hobby.

When you're confident that your enterprise can support itself and eventually become profitable, focus on the next part of the enterprise model—the framework.

ASSEMBLE AN EXTRAORDINARY FRAMEWORK

I could not imagine running the company I have now without the extraordinary framework of staff, subcontractors, vendors and consultants who support it. In the early days, I didn't need that, nor would I have known what to do with it.

Even if you work solo, you can benefit from talented consultants, vendors and subcontractors. From day one I hired subcontractors to assist me with projects. This worked so well that I put off hiring my first employee for 10 years. Eventually I recognized that to stretch toward a bigger vision, I had to add employees to the framework. Expect your framework to change as your vision changes.

If you've chosen the corporate route, create as many connections as you can with vendors, clients and professional peers. They will be your framework, an invisible but substantial scaffold to support your climb up the corporate ladder.

Don't Run Over People on Your Way to Wicked Success

I live in what could almost be described as a pastoral setting. Although I live in Houston, the fourth largest city in the United States, I actually reside in a city within the city of Houston, a small neighborhood with its own fire and police departments. On Saturday mornings, I can watch the hunky firemen wash and wax their fire trucks. We have soccer and little league fields and when the weather's nice, the air is filled with the sounds of children engaging in organized chaos.

Except for one small thing, it's like living in a Norman Rockwell painting: Right in the middle of these fields of fun is an elementary school. On my morning drive to the office I have the misfortune to pass through a school zone full of frenzied, caffeine-deprived soccer moms jockeying for position to drop off their little ones.

Suddenly a quiet street turns into a heavy-metal demolition derby, death race, Indy 500 and bumper-car ride teeming with median-strip-hopping SUVs the size of small aircraft. Dropping off children is a competitive sport, likely to become the next bad reality TV show.

Like a pool of armored piranhas, they come at you from all directions—U-turning, 16-point-turning, stopping and waiting, turn signal on, for a parking spot that won't be available until that other driver gets off her cell phone, walks her child to the school, has a conference and cookie with the teacher, walks back, adjusts her makeup in the rearview mirror, punches up her favorite song and heads off to Starbucks for a scone and Skinny Latte before yoga class.

The relentlessness makes me a little crazy. At the center of this race for the door stand the gatekeepers who patiently wave the cars in, one after the other. These wizards have the power to banish an unruly mom to a second lap around the loop before discharging her precious cargo. The person who, two seconds ago, was threatening to pull your intestines out through your teeth suddenly becomes as docile as a lamb when faced with the power of the gatekeepers.

Do you act like these soccer moms in your business world—only being nice to the people who can help you, and sometimes not even them? Be careful, or you may get banished to a few more laps, delaying your wicked success.

In the corporate world, it never pays to alienate a person who holds the cards. Do you ever wonder why some employees get 10 percent pay raises while others get the standard 3 percent? Most people think it's their boss's decision, but often it's not—it's theirs.

Be nice to everyone, not just the gatekeepers, on your way to wicked success. Think of your enterprise as a relationship business. Treat everyone as an ally, even those who can't advance you. The world is becoming flatter and smaller. It pays to play nice with others and to fly lightly.

I have a paperweight that reads, "Angels fly because they take themselves lightly." Any enterprise requires involvement with another person. Take what you do seriously, and yourself lightly. Have fun and make the people around you happy you're there. Make everyone in your enterprise (small and large) feel heard, valued and important.

Get Your Hands Dirty

I always joke that I'm a working CEO, a style that makes things happen. Successful CEOs get their hands dirty. All great chefs work in the kitchen. You can't cook from behind your desk. The best leaders lead by example. Get out from behind your desk and chop some onions. If you're down in the trenches, instead of always standing on the sidelines giving orders, it's easier to convince others to fall in with you. And you'll consistently demonstrate the standards you expect.

This doesn't mean you're doing someone else's job; it means your team sees you as working as hard as they do.

Vote Them Off Your Island

Satisfying relationships are a joy to have in your enterprise. We all prefer working with people we like, who deliver what they promise. It could be a boss who mentored you into a promotion, a business advisor who helped you through a tough period or an employee who's always the first to show up and get the day started.

My marketing director, Megan, jumps on each and every project on her to-do list like a serial killer. She attacks, delegates, completes and moves on to the next item without pause. I know I can trust her with an assignment, and once I do, it's as good as done.

Certain individuals, however, no matter how positive you are about your enterprise, can wreck your framework. It might be a subcontractor who's always late with work product, a Debbie Downer dragging at you and sucking the fun out of the room or a drama queen who makes mountains out of the tiniest molehills.

If a client, vendor, boss or employee isn't meeting your vision's criteria, vote them off your island! You have the sole power to hire and fire. No, you can't fire your boss, but you can look for another job or a transfer to another department.

This is America. Be enterprising and exercise your freedom of choice. Is there someone you need to vote off your island to ensure your foundation and framework stay strong? How long have you been putting it off? Just do it.

EVERYTHING IS MARKETING

The old saying among entrepreneurs, that nothing happens in business until "somebody sells something," is equally true in life. From the moment you were old enough to realize that a smile could "sell" your parents on giving you another cookie, you've been marketing your ideas.

- Getting a pay raise means selling your supervisor on your abilities, attitude and experience. That's marketing.

- Convincing your spouse it's okay to turn off the ballgame and cuddle up for some intimacy may require charm and persuasion. That's marketing.

- Convincing your property owners' association to resurface the tennis courts might require a benefit analysis and presentation. That's marketing.

When I earned my master's degree, I learned the hard way that this valuable asset had no value unless I marketed it. No one at the hospital said, "Thank you for pursuing higher education. Here's the pay raise you deserve." I attempted to market that idea to my manager, but she didn't buy in (not even 25 cents/hour), so I marched my asset out the door. I marketed that same concept to a different hospital and got the raise I deserved.

Perhaps your passionate vision doesn't include career or financial goals. Perhaps your vision is to bring together a widely separated extended family for a big reunion.

Note that for the remainder of this chapter I will be using the terms "clients" and "prospects" in a broad way, not just for selling in the business world. Your supervisor is a client. Your spouse is a client. For purposes of the family reunion, family members are prospects. The concepts of marketing apply to the family reunion—you'll have to sell your reunion idea, including the date and place, to all family members.

Here's the question you must answer for any enterprise you pursue: Why should a prospect choose you and your enterprise?

Find a Need, Fill It and Get People to Buy In

What Need Will You Fill?

A woman seeking promotion spots an opportunity to use her skills and experience in an area that will benefit the company or department she works for. An entrepreneur spots a need for products or services in her industry that's not being adequately met. What do they have in common? They both have insight into a need that will potentially spark a successful enterprise.

Purchasing any service or product is an emotional event. The primary reason a customer buys is not to own the item or have the service, but to meet emotional needs: to seek comfort, reduce stress, fulfill social needs, achieve something significant, change status or lifestyle or even invest in the future.

For example, a woman shopping for lipstick at a makeup counter is satisfying the emotional need to feel good, look pretty or indulge herself after a hard week at her job. An employer or supervisor who hires or promotes you may be satisfying high-stake emotional needs, such as winning at the corporate game, attaining status and gaining a promotion.

Understanding that people use emotion to make buying decisions gives you an edge in marketing to them. There's probably no purchase more emotional than buying a wedding dress. Emotion is the very reason I accidentally purchased a very expensive one (not in my budget) on Rodeo Drive in Beverly Hills. I was just out browsing that day. Within seconds after I entered Fred Hayman, an enterprising saleswoman approached and asked if I was looking for anything special. I joked, "Just a wedding dress."

Without taking her eyes from mine, she reached into the rack with her left hand, pulled out a dress, held it up against me and commandingly snapped the fingers of her free hand. I was swept into a dressing room by winged monkeys and before I knew it, not only was I wearing the dress, but also shoes, purse, earrings and necklace—fully accessorized and ready to walk down the aisle. Sipping champagne, I was living my wedding in full-blown color. I didn't just want that dress; emotionally, I *needed* it (accessories too). No other dress would do. My American Express card was distressed, but I was an ecstatic bride-to-be.

How Will You Fill the Need?

The corporate woman must have experience and knowledge that benefit her company. The entrepreneur must provide products or services that fulfill a need or perceived need, in the marketplace. Likewise, your prospects need to believe they're making a wise choice when they buy your product, purchase your services or hire you into their corporate world. Credentials and qualifications are nice, but that's not why people buy.

The most common mistake I see people making, whether job searching or advertising a business, is stating generic qualities that anyone can claim, such as, "organized and analytical" or "on time and dependable." Who among us would say we're not organized, analytical, on time or dependable? If you have a unique quality, sell it.

A second common mistake I see is stating expertise or credentials without a benefit statement; for example, "I have 10 years of experience." The prospect might not instantly understand all the benefits these 10 years of experience offer.

Instead, entrepreneurs or aspiring employees should research the prospect or company before entering the market or interview. From that research they should not only demonstrate that they understand the prospect's needs but also offer concrete examples of how they can fill those needs.

No one demonstrates how they're going to fill a need better than Abercrombie & Fitch. They cordon off the entrance of their New York City flagship store with a velvet rope, like a nightclub, forcing shoppers to stand in a long line on Fifth Avenue. Add heavy clouds of fragrance, loud music and a live model posing just inside the entrance, seducing you to step in for a photo. All this buzz entices more people to get in line to be part of this happening experience.

This not-so-subtle practice is a shout out that A&F understands their prospects need to be hip; and this is only the beginning of how they will fill that need. If you stand in line, you're already wicked cool and certain to be more so when you've surrendered your hard-earned cash to walk out with their hip, loaded shopping bag and that photo of you with the young stud-muffin flaunting his six-pack abs.

Who Will Buy It?

The corporate woman must sell her promotion to her supervisor, who must then sell it to management. The entrepreneur must identify and understand her market to sell her products or services.

Walking through the Houston Galleria one evening with no particular destination in mind, no goal or focus, I found myself taking in the shops from a different perspective. Normally, I'm what Tom refers to as an F&F shopper—fire and forget. I usually enter the mall with laserlike focus, make my purchases and come right back out, paying little attention to the in between.

This night, I strolled past one window after another featuring mind-numbing displays of solids, stripes, plaids and every color under the sun. I started to wonder, "With such intense competition, how does a store persuade a prospect to buy?" The answer: by understanding who will buy their product and catering to that knowledge.

For example, when you walk into Neiman-Marcus, everything about that store, from displays to customer service, suggests you've already arrived, and you probably have. When you walk into bebe, everything about that store suggests you're 18 years old, size 2 and just discovering sex for real; and you probably are.

Are you trying to be all things to all people, or is it clear you understand your buyer?

Finally, the most effective marketing strategy is the work product itself. Quality work product (or lack of it) has the last word in determining who will return to buy again. The quality of your work product precedes you, and, good or bad, hangs around long after the sale.

Add Pillars to Your Marketing Foundation

There's no single magic bullet for effective marketing. Marketing is most successful when based on a foundation with multiple pillars. If your whole enterprise depends on one marketing strategy (one pillar), your business or career could easily fall, knocked off its lone marketing prop by unforeseen circumstances.

Add one pillar at a time, systemize that strategy, then repeat the process, adding pillars and systemizing each one, with the goal of adding as many effective strategies as possible. For example, if you choose to focus on word-of-mouth referrals, first systemize how you request and obtain referrals. Once you're satisfied that you've mastered the art of winning referrals, add the next pillar (e.g., social media), then the next (e.g., advertising).

Free and inexpensive strategies, such as networking, can be equally as effective as marketing strategies that require an extensive budget. Market smart by first creating as many free marketing pillars as you can.

A single additional pillar could increase the growth of your enterprise 5 percent, 20 percent, even 100 percent or more. As you add solid pillars, each one effectively attracting customers, you'll become a true marketing pro.

Women Aren't the Only Ones Who Love a GWP

Like most women, I'm a sucker for a gift with purchase (GWP) at a makeup counter. I never met a GWP offer I could refuse, so I try to steer clear of the mall when I know they're being offered.

I have a favorite sales rep, Lisa, who tried to sell me a new product, but I didn't bite. To my surprise, when I got home, that very product was in my bag! That's right, the actual product, not the sample size. That free gift turned out not to be free at all because I love this product so much I'll probably be buying it for the rest of my life, or its life.

"Free" is the single enterprising strategy that keeps going and going and going. It has gathered so much momentum that today it's expected. If there's no GWP, we'll pass.

My first attorney-client was interested in one service from me: research. So what did I do? I completed the research and, additionally, wrote him a report. On the second case, he said "Vickie, write me one of those reports."

If you're seeking a promotion, don't just do your job well. Get in the middle of something that's not your job. That's how you'll get noticed and recognized. I rarely promote someone who only does what his or her job description requires. Why would I? If I have to tell you what to do, you're not going to be on my promotion list.

One woman in my company almost single-handedly took over the automation of our online program—not a small task. She steeped herself in the details and built rapport with the vendor. She created meticulous policies and procedures to capture the processes so anyone in the company could work comfortably with the system. Today Brandy is a manager in her department because of the enterprising way she "owned" that project.

If you believe strongly in what you have to offer, you'll find a way to get a GWP into the hands of your prospects. Warning: If your prospects like it too much, you may not have time for your own shopping anymore.

Don't Market Up the Wrong Tree

Sometimes entrepreneurs get so caught up in marketing to prospects that we forget one of the most lucrative marketing sources—our existing clients. In the corporate setting, sometimes employees are so busy seeking out their next job that they miss the opportunity right in front of them.

Focusing your marketing efforts on existing and prior clients will often yield a much higher return on your efforts than prospecting for new ones. A satisfied client is your hottest prospect because she already appreciates the benefits of using—and is willing to pay for—your product or services. The relationship dramatically increases the odds of successfully selling yourself again.

It takes time and effort to create a business relationship with a stranger. Creating and distributing your marketing packets or resumes, making phone calls, scheduling and attending interviews, then following up, can swallow precious time you could devote to working on your enterprise.

Even experienced entrepreneurs sometimes forget to go back to existing clients for new business. I mentored an entrepreneur who was providing one or two services to approximately 30 clients. We focused on growing her business by providing just one more service, then one more after that, to each of her clients. By concentrating her marketing efforts on existing clients, she made better use of her time and has tripled her revenues.

We're all in a relationship business, and I like to think of client relationships as long term. Once you've invested the marketing time and money to establish a relationship, it's nothing short of criminal to abandon it.

DON'T JUST CREATE AN EXPERIENCE—CREATE AN UNFORGETTABLE MEMORY

Why do we pay big bucks to Disney to stand in long lines, for long periods of time that challenge any woman's bladder? And why do we laugh and smile while we're doing it? Why do we pay 30 times more for that 12-ounce cup of Starbucks coffee than it costs us to brew it at home? The product? No. The experience? No. It's the unforgettable memories of the experience.

Fifty-year-olds vividly remember the experience of their first trip to Disney, but what they cherish most are those unforgettable memories and the feelings wrapped around them. Starbucks lovers remember the experience of the coffee, but cherish the unforgettable memories that go with the cozy coffee shop atmosphere. Creating an unforgettable memory is what enterprising women exploit in all ventures they undertake.

Every New Year's holiday, Tom and I head to one of our favorite places in the world, Napa Valley. This is a secret I shouldn't tell you, but New Year's is one of the best times to visit Napa—few tourists, no traffic, a stark beauty to the empty vines and, my favorite reason to go, the wine.

Wineries offer two types of tastings. The first is the generic over-the-counter tasting available in the winery's public space. You walk in, plop your money on the counter and, depending on the winery, toss back either some decent wine or a glass of grape juice. If you like it, you buy it and move on to the next tasting.

Less common is the "estate" tasting. Usually by appointment only, some estate tastings are so exclusive you need the right networking contact to get in. Once you're there, it's free. But better than free, you get to taste the best wines offered by that winery; and the event often ends with the winemaker making referrals and inviting you to the next estate tasting.

Over the years Tom and I have done many tastings of both types, but nothing compares to sitting in a wine cave exploring the complexities of a great wine with the actual winemaker. Tasting in the cloistered ambience of the cellar is an unforgettable experience. I know intellectually that I should never buy wine after drinking in the cellar, but I'm the sucker who always does. Spending a glorious afternoon chatting and sipping Continuum with Robert Mondavi's granddaughter, Carissa, in the sunroom of her family's hilltop winery created an unforgettable memory that will enhance every bottle of Continuum I drink. Have I tasted a better wine? Sure, but not every bottle in my wine cellar is infused with that tasting memory.

Now, I'm not recommending that you serve wine to your clients or colleagues (unless it's after noon). But I recommend that you go above and beyond the same old wine tasting experience that less enterprising people offer in similar ventures. Don't create a pedestrian, over-the-counter offering when you have the ability to create something spectacular that will capture more business, more job promotions or more lucrative deals.

Customer Service Rants and Raves

David's Folly

Tom and I were having dinner in a fairly chic restaurant. Our waiter, David, asked what we wanted to drink. Having already reviewed the menu while waiting at the bar, we proceeded to order wine and appetizers.

He came back with our wine and proceeded to tell us about the appetizers. He had his script down and launched into it as if he'd never seen us before.

I politely interrupted his litany to remind him that we'd already ordered appetizers and wanted to learn the daily specials. That seemed to jog David's memory somewhat, but a little disconcerted by our preempting him, he skipped over the specials and told us he'd be right back with our starters.

I heard the woman at the next table say she "would have loved the fried soft-shell crabs, but fried foods are so bad for you." My ears were on it and I was all in. Being from New Orleans, the idea of sentencing a soft-shell crab or two to a quick, cornmeal-battered, deep-fat-fried death doesn't bother me.

I wondered why David hadn't mentioned the crab, or any entrée specials, and then I realized—it was because he couldn't handle the script change. I asked him about the soft-shell crab special when he returned with the appetizers, and he compounded his errors by denying they were offering such a dish. My guess: he'd already put in our dinner order and was unwilling to retract it from the computer.

Throughout dinner, this waiter's service was distracted, snooty and too serious for what was supposed to be a fun night out. David cost the restaurant future business. We never went back.

Tiffany's Enterprise

Tom and I went to purchase a new mattress. Immediately a young salesperson named Tiffany walked up and introduced herself. She asked what we were looking for, and actually listened to our answer. After helping us with the mattress set, she pointed out other products we might love, without exerting any pressure tactics. She was so good at marketing, I thought I'd just met a new best friend.

We went in shopping for a mattress, but on her recommendation, we tried out all the recliners and added two of them to our growing list of purchases. I had to draw the line when I heard her telling Tom about cup and snack holders for his recliner.

When she rang up our purchases, she noticed the store's inventory indicated it would be a week before the mattress set could be delivered. She offered to send over the floor model, along with a complimentary set of sheets, to let us sleep on as a test until ours arrived. We walked out of the store the proud new owners of not only a mattress but also two new recliners, two reading lamps and other accessories—a not inconsiderable sale for a couple of hours work.

On the day of delivery, Tiffany arrived at our house with the delivery truck. She supervised the load-in and helped set up everything. After the crew left, Tiffany stayed to orient us to our purchases and to go over our invoice. The next day she called to see how we'd slept and asked if we had any questions or needed any adjustments. She also updated us on the delivery date for our mattress.

Who was this woman? And why aren't there more Tiffanys in the world? Tiffany not only took charge of the sale from the minute we walked into the store but also did everything she could to make our experience memorable. To this day, I'm in awe.

The Airline Industry's Idiocy

Christmas and the holidays are supposed to be the merriest time of year, so why is airline customer service at that time of year the gloomiest? It starts with the smiling (not) faces of the check-in staff. They're the first impression you get of the service you're about to receive (or not).

I'm sure everyone dislikes some part of their job, but excuse me, sir, you're there to help me check in, tag my bags, get them on the belt and tell me my gate number. If you don't like your job, rotate to something else. Don't make a face because my bag looks heavy or because I have three. Yes, I know you're going to charge me to check them, but you don't have to be so stern about it. I'm a customer, not a prisoner—at least not until I board.

Once onboard, being a nurse makes it impossible to sympathize with a flight attendant who's upset that I asked for a second glass of lukewarm water. Here's what nurses do every day: change catheters, clean suppurating wounds and get sprayed by bodily fluids we shouldn't discuss in mixed company, but still do.

Some flight attendants make me want to stick them with an oversized needle in their most tender body part while saying, "Look lady, I asked you for a napkin, not to wipe my ass. Yes, I know there are other passengers, but right now the three of you are standing in the back of the plane kvetching about your upcoming layover in Poughkeepsie."

Remember, your client isn't always right, but he's still your client. Just be grateful he didn't ask you to wipe his butt. If he's paying you to do a job, it's your job to do it with a smile on your face, if not in your soul.

Apple's Awesomeness

The Apple store on Fifth Avenue in New York City is the mecca of customer service. Like an airline, this store is open 24 hours a day, and there's usually a line to get inside. Unlike an airline, people wait patiently, even expectantly, because they know that once they're inside, the experience will be extraordinary. When's the last time you heard someone say their flight or shopping experience was extraordinary—unless they were talking about extraordinary prices?

Apple sets the highest bar for customer service, plus the store is wicked cool inside. The staff helps you with your purchase and stays with you until you're finished shopping. They accompany you to the checkout line or point out one of the roaming checkout staffers, who come conveniently equipped with a wireless credit card machine. You walk up to any of them with your purchase, joyfully swipe your credit card and get on your way without a hassle. My receipt is emailed to my iPhone before I'm out the door.

Even if you don't buy anything, staffers will patiently answer any question about all the cool stuff on display. And you get to play with it as long as you want, without the stare-downs aimed at making you feel guilty for not buying. You can even make an appointment to bring in your computer, iPad, or iPhone to get whatever service or training you need, including how to turn it on. The entire experience is exhilarating. It makes me want to turn my whole office into Mac users.

And when you purchase an Apple product, you're getting not only the glitz and most amazing sensory experience, you're getting products of real substance. You feel special and cooler for owning them, as if you've received the most wonderful gift, even though you probably forfeited your entire paycheck to buy it.

Like Disney, give your clients, customers, boss, spouse, or significant other a reason to stand in line and pay big bucks for you.

Like Tiffany, offer a seamless experience from beginning to end. Offer lagniappe, something extra.

Like Apple, make your client feel cooler for using you or your product.

Whether you own a business or work for someone else, know this—we exist because of the people we service. Aim to be like Tiffany, Disney, Starbucks and Apple, not like David and the airline industry.

BE YOUR OWN NUMBER ONE FAN

CEOs promote their companies and their achievements. They know that buyers don't want to purchase from losers. Announce your achievements. This is hard for many women, but if you don't do it, who will?

With humility, let people know when you've won an award, finished a big project or expanded your services. Studies show that women will underestimate their own abilities, judging themselves lower than their skills prove, while men overestimate their abilities, judging themselves more competent.

Men are bold about taking credit for everything they do at work. They do it at home too. "Honey, I took out the trash!" And you say, "Thanks honey, that was sweet to help out since I just worked a full day, bought groceries, cooked dinner, helped the kids with homework and cleaned the house. Would you like another beer?"

Who you know is important, but even more important is who knows you. Achievements spotlight your resume and expand your credibility. Keep your name in front of everyone—your supervisor, your banker, your grocer, your Facebook friends. You never know where opportunity will strike.

Announcing your achievements also validates the choices people have made on your behalf. The boss who promoted you, or the buyer who purchased from you, wants to know they bet on a winner.

DON'T BE A COMMODITY

Top CEOs build businesses that are not easily duplicated. Ease of duplication creates commodities, and a commodity business is the kiss of death.

Water used to be a commodity, until companies like Fiji and Perrier changed our perception. Today, water, available just about everywhere for free, outsells almost every other bottled drink, at a high price and high profit margin.

When you build relationships, you can never be duplicated. Our company doesn't sell seminars, online education or DVDs, although those are the media we employ. Instead, we sell a relationship, which includes mentoring. Our ideas might be duplicated, but our relationships with our customers cannot be. After the purchase, our relationship doesn't end, it intensifies.

We also have a six-month guarantee, unprecedented in the education industry. Our guarantee earns the trust of our prospects when they see the $13,000 sticker price. When you choose to not be a commodity, and price yourself accordingly, a guarantee helps to take some of the risk off the shoulders of your prospects.

If you're advancing through the corporate route, don't be a commodity. Don't shrink into your chair and become the invisible employee. Get in the middle of everything. Bring new ideas to the table. Make yourself invaluable and hard to replace by building relationships throughout the company.

Don't Underprice Yourself

Top CEOs reject the common thinking that "if you drop your price, you'll get the job" or "lower price equals higher sales." For 29 years people have said my products are expensive—until they purchase and use them. Smart buyers understand that anything cheap can be expensive in the long run; they will buy in to your enterprise as long as you provide value for the dollar. You actually lose credibility when you underprice yourself.

When recruiting, I weed out the candidates who underprice themselves, assuming they wouldn't work at the level I expect. In my office I've had to give women pay raises because they underprice themselves, but don't expect your boss to do the same for you.

Don't underprice yourself in relationships. Surveys reveal that one of the least happy groups of people are married women. I suggest that these unhappy married women are underpricing themselves in the marriage enterprise.

Don't underprice yourself by exhibiting unprofessional behavior. What your boss really wants is a personal clone in terms of work ethic and loyalty to the company. Model your boss. Know what your boss needs and wants, and deliver it. Become indispensable.

Most people socialize with coworkers at their same level while considering executives unapproachable or, worse, the enemy. The real secret to advancement is to spend time with coworkers at all levels, especially the one who decides your next raise.

To ensure you never become a commodity, set your own standards. Someone else's may not be high enough. Mushing a dog sled across an Alaskan glacier, I learned firsthand that if you're not the lead dog, the view from the rear never changes. And the rear is exactly where you'll be if you compete only with others.

To excel in enterprise, be the lead dog. Be aware of competition, but don't allow that awareness to veer you off course. If you focus on your competition (someone richer, more successful or better looking), you'll always be one step behind them. If you focus on your own enterprise and compete with your own best performance, you'll be the lead dog your competitors imitate, leaving them in the rear. Be an innovator, not an imitator.

NEGOTIATE LIKE YOU MEAN IT

As a woman, you already negotiate every personal enterprise you're involved in. You negotiate with your spouse about family finance. You negotiate with your children to get them to eat their dinners. You negotiate with your in-laws to spend a holiday with your own family.

You are constantly negotiating, so add the following strategies to your already existing arsenal when you negotiate for any enterprise.

Ask for Everything at the Beginning of the Negotiation

Don't add on as you go along. It makes you appear unfair. For example, if you tell a prospect your consulting fee is $150/hour and his reply is, "That's very reasonable," you can't jump in and say, "I really want $175/hour."

Think through what you really want before you sit down to negotiate. Prepare the list of points you must have and the points you're willing to give up. Some people do keep score. Being able to track what you really need helps you let the other party win points as you score big.

Ask for More Than You Think You Can Get

Don't jump too fast to say yes to the first offer, even if you think it's fair. Assess the situation, the person making the offer and how far you can go. This is not being greedy; this is being a strong negotiator. You might be surprised at what's yours for the taking if you only ask for it.

I mentored an entrepreneur whose client firmly told her that instead of her hourly fee, he would pay her a flat rate for a project. The problem: The project involved too many moving parts. Locking herself into a flat fee could cost her. She was concerned that she would lose this project unless she agreed to those unfavorable terms.

My advice was to stand firm on her hourly fee. She did, and as I predicted, the client agreed to her hourly rate.

You must be willing to ask for more than you think you can get, especially when the offer is not favorable to you.

Appear Detached Even When You're Not

The most pivotal day in the early years of my business was recognizing that my success did not rely on any one attorney-prospect. If one said no, there were a million more out there. This insight gave me the ability to detach when negotiating. One attorney wouldn't make or break my business, but entering into bad deals because I was too caught up in making a deal certainly would.

If you don't like the deal with one person, remember there are plenty of others waiting for you to call.

Negotiate with the Person, Not the Billion-Dollar Company

Don't assume your bargaining power is weak just because your business is smaller or you need the deal more than the other party. Negotiating can be challenging when you're faced with the perception of uneven power positions, but weakness is one thing you can't allow the other side to see.

I have rewritten entire contracts sent to me from companies much bigger than mine that claimed I must sign their contract "as is." Everything is negotiable, so if you have something to offer, go ahead, negotiate.

I successfully negotiated a contract with a company that exceeds $1 billion in revenue, simply by remembering it was the person, not the company, I was negotiating with. Eight contract drafts and numerous negotiations later, we reached an agreement beneficial to both of us. That's negotiation.

Go in knowing and believing in what you have to bring to the business relationship. Even if you believe the other party holds the power card, don't underestimate what you have to offer and how it benefits that party.

Never Talk Off the Record

Never tip your hand. "Just between you and me, I want X but I'll settle for Y." In negotiations everything is on the record, and if you say you'll settle for Y, that's what you'll end up with—or worse, even less.

Never Let the Other Party Bully You

I've worked with plenty of attorneys, met some tough negotiators, and seen many different negotiation styles at work. When I'm up against a pit bull, I'll take a walk and role-play with Tom, who can be a pit bull himself. I anticipate every possible objection and get myself into a Zen-like state. When it comes time to negotiate for real, I am centered and ready. If I go head-to-head like two pit bulls, instead of remaining calm and professional, the negotiations are destined to fail.

RETIE THE CONNECTION OVER FRIED OYSTERS

Enterprising women understand the importance of nurturing meaningful connections. Connections deepen relationships and foster loyalty for that day when a competitor knocks on your client's door, or that new talent sucks up to your boss.

Connections are also important with people who can influence your business or career. And one of my favorite benefits of connecting is referral to new clients or new opportunities.

I recently got together with one of my oldest attorney-clients over some fried oysters. I'm crazy busy, but I always make time for important relationships and fried oysters, especially with well-respected clients.

When was the last time you retied a connection with a client? If someone is important to you, get out and get them out. Even if he or she doesn't have something to give you that day, you're strengthening the relationship for future opportunities.

Ask for Referrals While You're Connecting

Referral is my favorite enterprising strategy, not just because it's free, but because it works more effectively than any other strategy I've ever used. Referral works so well because people prefer to avoid unnecessary risk. When the right person refers you, that's instant credibility. You're risk-free in the prospect's mind.

Referral, however, is not a gift. Referral business is something you have to earn. It's the result of consistently providing an excellent product or service. Put these referral strategies into action:

- To get referrals, you have to ask and women don't always ask. How many times have you said to your spouse or significant other something like, "Honey, are you hungry?" or "Is it cool in here?" when what you really mean is, "Honey, pull the darn car into the next McDonald's, I'm starving," or "Turn up that air conditioner; it's cold enough to hang meat in here!" Ask and be specific in your request for referrals.

- Request letters of recommendation from your client or referral connection. I've had busy clients ask me to write the letter for their signature, and I was happy to oblige. If you do write the letter of recommendation, interview the connection to capture their words, so it sounds like them.

o   Ask for referrals when the timing is right—that is, when a client or connection is raving about you. Assure clients of your commitment to them. Express appreciation for referrals. Say thank you often in a variety of ways.

o   Follow through on the names provided and contact each referral. When you follow up, mention specifically how the connection suggested you could benefit them. Invoke the referring connection's name at every opportunity. Use information learned about the referral in all communications.

o   Always try to get your foot in the door. The odds of advancing your enterprise are much stronger if you meet in person. Where possible, avoid selling yourself over the telephone or with an email—a meeting or interview is your goal.

o   Systemize the referral process, and soon you'll be begging your connections to keep your name to themselves.

Retie connections often, and when you do, remember to pick up the tab. Stay connected on Facebook or through email. The connection is what's important—although I'll take fried oysters over Facebook any day.

NETWORKING IS NOT WORKING

People often say to me, "You must have known a lot of attorneys when you started your business," suggesting that the adage "It's not what you know, it's who you know" is the guaranteed path to success. Actually, I didn't know any attorneys. I didn't live in their neighborhoods or get invited to their parties.

Networking did lead me to my first client, but it works best when you're selective. Unless you're selective, networking events become nothing more than a waste of your time, and that's when networking is *not* working.

Successful people are selective about where and with whom they network. You won't find them at your typical breakfast club meeting. They research what they need, locate the source and ask. They create a network of colleagues, clients, consultants, vendors and acquaintances they can depend on to deliver anything from information to referrals.

One woman entrepreneur shares:

> The worst advice I followed had to do with a networking group a friend recommended. She received a lot of business from this group, so I joined too. The group consisted of manicurists, massage therapists, hairdressers and electricians. There were no prospects, and no one seemed to know any prospects that applied to my business. I stuck with it for a year and got zero business from it. I later joined a high-powered business group for attorneys, CPAs, bankers and executives. My business grew from these connections. I wish I'd not wasted that first year. It pays to really check out the makeup of a group and its main focus prior to joining.

That year she spent in the wrong networking group is an example of networking not working. Ultimately she wisely sought out and found the appropriate group to network with, but at what cost?

Be cautious also with how much power you give established networking groups, such as associations. Such groups can absorb time while distracting you from engaging big. And you could be taking advice from people who mean well, but are not qualified. Always assess the validity of advice offered.

Cast your net selectively. Don't confuse networking with socializing. Choose opportunities that put you in the middle of people who are even more successful than you are. Cultivate your network using your relationship skills to include successful people outside your industry.

Expect to give as much as you get. I receive requests daily from people I don't know or know marginally. If I said yes to them all, I wouldn't get my own work done or I'd be in a psychiatric unit. Most successful people get bombarded. That's why networking is often not working, and that's where the relationship makes a difference.

An ex-employee I respect and like asked me to speak to a group of 50 college students. I said yes. This is time I wouldn't have donated if we had just met casually through networking. The power of networking comes in the strength of the relationships you build, not just showing up and asking people to do something for you.

Engage in powerful and meaningful networking, not just a pocket full of business cards and a glass of cheap white zinfandel. Expect high performance from your network. If it's not productive, move on.

KEEP THE WIND IN YOUR SAILS

Every business is made up of thousands of details. Entrepreneurs like to spend their time creating, so the smartest are adept at systemizing routine tasks. Don't reinvent the wheel every day.

Someone once commented that processes take the wind out of his sails. For me, it's just the opposite. When I or my staff try to manage complex details without processes and systems, the wind goes right out of our sails.

I want as many practices as possible to be automatic. I don't want to be distracted by incidentals when I can be concentrating on something big. I don't want to be searching for a lost file because someone misfiled it; I want to focus on important projects.

In the early years of my business, I woke up one morning and had a reality check: My lack of systems and processes were kicking my butt. My office looked like a shipwreck with the debris and detritus strewn about by the tide of day-to-day business. I was so busy working projects I had completely ignored my business and the systems necessary to manage it properly. I could no longer afford to take 10 minutes to locate this file or that file.

I needed to act fast to avoid drifting out to sea, so I tackled the problem with a vengeance and determination equal to Captain Ahab's in his pursuit of the great white whale.

Systems and processes not only help you, they are essential, as you grow by leveraging others' time and talents. If you can systemize a task so that it's reproducible, you can delegate it, which means you create time to do more important things.

Systems help to ensure quality and continuity:

- Create templates for emails, letters, forms and other documents that must be re-created or used frequently.

- For any new document, first review what already exists. Then copy, adapt and pull from previous efforts.

- Finally, automate any and every process possible, whether online, computerized or physical.

Make Perpetual Lists

CEOs have assistants to remind them what to do. Like executive assistants, lists can save you hours of fumbling and head-scratching. When you're managing a lot of moving parts, lists can keep you organized and prevent the tragedy and panic of forgetfulness. Our conference timeline has 708 tasks that 23 people must accomplish. There is no way we could successfully execute a conference without it.

For home, I keep a perpetual grocery list on my computer, which I simply update and print out when it's time to shop. I keep a list of travel items to pack, no matter where I'm going. Of course that hasn't prevented me from forgetting my underwear and having to take an "emergency" shopping trip to Victoria's Secret.

Which of your routines would benefit from being perpetualized on a grab-it-and-go list?

Move Like a Maverick to Solve Problems Quickly and Decisively

Top CEOs move so quickly they sometimes exhaust the people working with them, but speed is one of their success secrets. Not haphazard, as some might believe, fast-moving CEOs use a process even to guide their rapid decisions as they strengthen their enterprise.

To become an enterprising problem solver, use the genius strategies in Chapter 5. Then apply the following eight-step problem solving system. You'll never be daunted by problems again.

8 STEPS
TO FAST PROBLEM SOLVING

1. My problem is:

_____

2. It is important to me because:

_____

3. Current factors impacting and relevant to the problem include:

_____

4. My overall goal in solving this problem is:

_____

5. The strategies I've already implemented to resolve this problem include:

_____

6. People (family, consultants, housekeeper, nanny) who can help me resolve this problem are:

_____

7. Actions I will personally take in the future include:

_____

8. Actions I will delegate include:

_____

>> DOWNLOAD THIS PROBLEM-SOLVING TOOL AT **WickedSuccess.com**.

BECOME THE CEO OF YOUR
CARE ER AND LIFE WITH THE
5 PROMISES

PROMISE 1
I Will Live and Work a Passionate Life

Write down all the reasons you want to engage in your new enterprise.
What's your payoff?

_____

_____

_____

PROMISE 2
I Will Go for It or Reject It Outright

What risk must you take to pursue your bold new venture? Identify two
potential icebergs and how you will maneuver around these obstacles.

_____

_____

_____

PROMISE 3
I Will Take One Action Step a Day Toward My Passionate Vision

Assess the effectiveness of your Strategic Life Plan. Write down the first
action step you will take to make your enterprise a reality.

_____

_____

_____

PROMISE 4
I Commit to Being a Success Student for Life

What is the most enterprising thing you've ever done? What can you learn from that experience and apply to your new enterprise?

_____

_____

_____

PROMISE 5
I Believe as a Woman I Really Can Do Anything

Identify two achievements and explore how you can communicate them to promote your enterprise.

_____

_____

_____

▸▸ DOWNLOAD THE 5 PROMISES FOR ENTERPRISE AT WickedSuccess.com.

MARTHA'S ENTERPRISE

In 1961 I came to the United States planning to stay for only one or two years, then go back to Switzerland. I met Helmut, my husband, and the United States became my home. Financially, times were not easy back then, and we had children right away. As a stay-at-home mom I always worked. I sold Avon, Tupperware, Amway. I sewed for some of my friends and word got around. I became the seamstress for a boutique. When the children were older I went into the corporate world for a while, and I didn't like it.

Following my passion for healthcare, I signed up for a yoga workshop, but it was already full and I ended up in another class. Before I left Texas to go to Montana for the workshop, the coordinator inquired whether I would need a wheelchair. I hadn't realized I had signed up for a multiple sclerosis (MS) workshop. I didn't want to tell my husband I had registered by mistake, so I took a chance and went to it. The speaker, who was also an MS patient, needed a massage every day on his shoulders and neck. I pitched in, and he told me I was very good, that I should do massage professionally.

I came back from the workshop, gave my notice, and told my husband I wanted to be a massage therapist. He thought I was crazy, but I did it anyway. Ultimately I followed my calling, first as a therapist for about five years, then as a teacher specializing in a very technical form of massage therapy, manual lymph drainage. I travel nationwide and am well

known and respected in an industry I entered by accident.
Amazing what a little enterprise and
massage oil can accomplish.

Martha, 66
MLD THERAPIST AND INSTRUCTOR

Your life is the most important enterprise of all, and you'll need one precious resource to fully enjoy your enterprise. We'll explore energy renewal next.

If [women] understood and exercised their power,
they could remake the world.
EMILY TAFT DOUGLAS

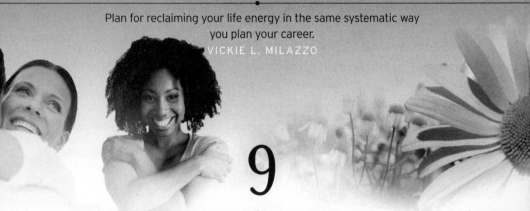

9

RENEWAL

Reclaim Your Life Energy Through Frequent Renewal

W hen it's your first time, everything is exciting. Sure you're
nervous, but that's a good thing, like the way you feel waiting
in line for a gigantic roller coaster, the one with the 418-foot drop that
reaches 128 miles per hour. "Oh, I don't know if I can do this." Then
you go on the ride and squeal, "Whoa! That was fun! Let's do it again."
When you first start a new job, a new quilt, a new marriage, even the
little things are exciting.

Imagine with me your first day on the job. It's 5:00 a.m. on a Monday
morning. You spring out of bed, no alarm necessary. You hardly slept the
night before, but you're somehow refreshed. You're looking forward to your
first official meeting, the stimulating interplay of ideas and collegiality.

You stroll into your kitchen and make a cup of healthy green tea.
Your spouse comes in and flirtatiously tells you, "You're glowing." You
flirt back, your eyes holding promises of something fun to come later.
Yum! Mysteriously, your new career has even improved your sex life.

Fast forward a few years. You have yet another early-morning meeting,
a product launch discussion—two hours of bad coffee, boredom and email
withdrawal. You didn't sleep the night before. Not because you were excited,

but because you never made it to bed. You were up all night working. You rush to the kitchen, chug down your tenth cup of coffee and mentally count the Starbucks drive-thrus between your house and the office.

Then, "Oh my gosh, who is that strange man in my kitchen? He sort of looks like my husband—but he's balding. The man I married had a full head of hair, and *what* is with that beer gut?"

Then, "Ahhhh! Who do those two teenagers belong to? They couldn't be *my* kids. My kids don't have tattoos." But they must be your kids, because one of them says, "Mom, are you okay? You look like crap." Actually, "crap" is a compliment considering how you're really feeling today.

As years roll by, it's easy to forget the excitement we felt the first day of a new career, or just after the wedding vows or when we held our first newborn. Along the way, successful living came to mean more stress, less time and less fun.

Today's woman has taken on a wondrous carnival of life crammed to overflowing with options. We want to sample every possibility. No wonder we feel depleted. We give our all on so many levels—family, friends, career—then expect to have energy left over to help the kids with complicated homework assignments *and* still enjoy great sex. Your life is energy. Every moment of every day you're burning energy, energy you might otherwise use to pursue your passionate vision.

But it doesn't have to be that way.

You wouldn't expect a battery to keep going forever without recharging. Don't expect it of yourself. Revitalize your mind, body, emotions and spirit frequently and you'll find the energy abundantly available when you need it. Depletion of one energy pool negatively impacts the others. If you're 50 pounds overweight, that not only affects your physical energy, it's probably affecting your emotional energy too.

Symbolically, the circle of life starts and stops with us, and women who invest in renewal have the energy to enjoy the ride long after the carnival has left town.

RENEW YOUR RELATIONSHIP WITH YOURSELF

If you stepped back and looked at your daily routine objectively, as if it were happening to your best friend, what would be your advice? Slow down?

Take a few deep breaths? Spend a few moments enjoying one day before another day crashes in with new demands?

We need to give ourselves such loving advice—and listen to it. We need to thrive, not just survive. To have healthy, exciting and fulfilling relationships with others, we must first have a healthy, exciting and fulfilling relationship with ourselves.

When you're your own best friend, this is easy, but too often our practices sabotage what we need, and we act instead as our own worst enemy—repeating behaviors we know are bad for us and not taking renewal steps to restore ourselves. If we don't renew on a regular basis, we'll slip further and further into the state we're seeking to escape.

When you renew, you recharge your batteries to gain the energy for your big goals while still juggling the daily challenges of your career and life. It's okay to take care of yourself. If you don't, the odds are nobody else will.

Your body, feelings, mind and spirit are passengers on your journey through life. Renewal is the process of refueling these passengers. Renewed, you have the energy to accomplish your Big Things and juggle the daily demands yet feel centered, even in the unrest. Renewal lightens your load, and while the world around you may be chaos, you can remain solid in the midst of it.

Plan for Your Renewal

When you're young, you can spontaneously dash off and play for a day—remember how instantly renewed you felt? But as you add layers of responsibility to your life, the only way to reclaim the energy you burn is to do it with consciousness.

Starting my business while still employed as a hospital nurse meant working extra hours. There wasn't enough time in a day to honor my commitments and also take time for renewal. At least, that's what I believed. When my energy became depleted, I drank another cup of coffee to keep going. After a few months of becoming progressively more exhausted and less productive, I had to make some changes. I wrote myself a simple but effective rejuvenation prescription: exercise, good food, quiet time and daily doses of fun.

I now plan for renewing my energy in the same systematic way I plan to manage and grow my company. I set renewal goals and strategies and formulate action steps. I schedule vacations and other Vickie-enhancing activities far in advance, to guarantee that no one (including me) overbooks my calendar. Unless something urgent arises, I say no to anyone attempting to disrupt this schedule. For example, Monday is massage night. Even Tom knows to back off on Mondays.

Dealing with the recent recession for years, not just a day or week or month, required the stamina of a teenager. Fortunately, my renewal practices sustained me along the way.

After 29 years in business, people continue to ask me where I get my energy, as if I'm mixing up a secret potion in my kitchen and refusing to share it. Yet when I share it, they refuse to believe my "secret" formula can be as simple today as it was 29 years ago.

1. Exercise daily.

2. Eat good food daily.

3. Stop for a few minutes of honest quiet time daily.

4. Have fun daily.

More details lie ahead, but those are the basics.

Life is meant to be lived to its fullest, and for women who live passionately, sometimes that means spinning out of control. For passionate women, a totally balanced day is not only unachievable, it's undesirable, boring. As much as I strive for a balanced life, sometimes that balance can take extremes. You can't always measure it on a day-to-day basis.

While writing this book I have been working 16-hour days, between the office and writing, so that I can leave for Provence to celebrate my wedding anniversary right after turning in the manuscript. And I am loving it. But even for passionate, unbalanced women, renewal is necessary.

When I'm in Provence, I'll be off—completely disconnected. My office knows they can reach me if the office is on fire, but they also know I'm not calling in unless I need a ride from the airport. When I return home, my fire for my business will blaze, just as it did 29 years ago.

Only you know when your life feels off balance. Your personal and professional lives are clashing and you feel little satisfaction in anything you do. Your inner fire has died to a pile of cinders. Your intuitive vision is a hazy memory.

Because women are good at masking it, your boss or family may not notice you're overwhelmed when they ask you to do one more thing. It's only when the volcano finally blows that people look back and see the warning signs.

RENEW YOUR PHYSICAL ENERGY DAILY

Growing up in New Orleans, I never gave a thought to the food I was ingesting. In Louisiana, if it fits in a skillet—with or without a fight—we fry it and eat it. I also thought nothing of emptying three bowls of my grandma's spaghetti or spicy seafood gumbo.

As I grew older those eating habits left me fatigued, and my bathroom scale showed a weight gain. The habits that had worked fine when I was young no longer worked for me. I had to change my habits to reclaim my physical energy and maintain my weight. Thank God for vanity. It really does have an upside.

Physical energy is essential, not only for a healthy life but for any success. It requires exercise, nutrition, sleep and a health maintenance plan. My travel schedule means exposure to lots of different types of food, over which the quality is often out of my control (sort of). No matter how hard I try, I can't control the amounts of sodium and trans-fats in it, or even get real extra-virgin olive oil for a salad. I have my own vices and do occasionally wrap myself around movie popcorn, fried chicken or a good bowl of spaghetti and meatballs.

To compensate for my precarious road diet, plus my personal vices, Tom and I eat organic when we're at home. Healthy and clean—one friend says I'm practically fascist about it. We consume lots of veggies (what Tom lovingly refers to as "weeds"). We try to avoid pastas (heartbreaking cold-turkey withdrawal for an Italian girl) and empty calories. Red wine stays. Tom's come up with all sorts of medical reasons—improves eyesight, decreases heart disease, relaxes muscles. My favorite Tomisms are: "Tastes good to me." and "Are you going to finish that?"

The more empty calories we eat, the more we crave and the unhealthier our bodies become. The fewer empty calories we eat, the less we crave and the easier it is for us to stay healthy.

I've always been a hearty eater. One of my friends calls me the "eating machine." Self-deprivation diets are demoralizing. I'd much rather exercise so that I don't gain weight every time I look at a bag of movie popcorn. I exercise six times a week, first thing in the morning. My workday starts early and it ends when it ends, whenever that may be. If I don't work out at the beginning of the day, chances are I won't get to at the end of the day.

I once naively scheduled Pilates lessons at the end of the day. Paying for more no-show classes than those I attended persuaded me to face facts: I'm more energized for exercise in the mornings and if I don't jump in and get it done early, life gets in the way. I learned to put exercise at the beginning, not end, of my day.

10 Strategies for Renewing Your Physical Energy

1. **Gas up!** Without being fanatical, give your body the fuel it needs. Boost your energy and immune system with vitamins, antioxidants, green tea and ground flaxseed mixed with natural Greek yogurt. Refined carbs and sugars deplete energy; replace them with fruits and vegetables. Eat small amounts every three or four hours. Maintain your weight at the optimal level. Think of the excess weight as a bag of groceries you have to carry all day long.

   A big mistake is skipping breakfast or lunch. Your body will compensate and you'll lose steam later in the day. Another big mistake women make is avoiding fat altogether. Healthy fats such as omega 3s are essential for physical energy and a strong immune system.

2. **Move it.** Find a type of exercise that sparks your fire. You need to enjoy what you're doing in order to keep doing it. Create a plan that includes variety. Start with aerobics, such as walking, jogging or biking; add weight training three times a week to increase lean body mass and boost metabolism. Build core strength and flexibility.

   Try working out with a trainer. It's mental of course, but I always hold that plank longer when my trainer Jerome is watching.

3. **Sleep it off.** Eight hours every night is a restorative elixir. When you're sleep deprived, you'll notice a big difference in your physical condition, mental attitude and ability to cope with stress. Sleep research has shown that with less than eight hours sleep you are working at increasing levels of cognitive deficits. Less than six hours

of sleep and you're considered tantamount to DUI—driving under the influence. Skip that late-night TV show and regulate your sleep schedule, which will help you avoid energy imbalances.

4. **Clean up.** When you're as addicted to coffee as I was, good strong New Orleans coffee, you don't quit cold turkey. First I replaced one scoop of regular coffee in my coffee pot with decaf, then two scoops and so on. Then I started drinking green and white tea. Now my energy doesn't sag in the afternoon. I still have one cup of coffee in the morning, but enjoy tea all day long, without all of the highs and lows.

5. **Rub it out.** Get a massage weekly. If that's not realistic for you, start with once a month. My favorite is deep tissue massage. Manage cost by getting discounts at a massage school or by trading massages with a friend. For me massage is maintenance, not a luxury.

6. **Indulge.** Treat your body like the temple it is. Carve out a time when you can pamper yourself with a facial, pedicure or soak in the tub. Even if it means skipping a TV show, you'll find the extra time spent on yourself well worth the investment.

7. **Breathe.** Breathe consciously at least once an hour. Expand your lungs. Practice diaphragmatic breathing, consciously taking that diaphragmatic breath all the way into your lower back. Oxygen is energy.

8. **Shed your skin.** Your largest organ, your skin, is responsible for much of your body's elimination and detoxification. Give yourself a dry brush massage before showering. In minutes you'll feel wonderful. Start at your toes and work upward, brushing in small circles.

9. **Just say no.** Avoid depending on drugs for a quick fix or cure for what ails you. Drugs (even herbal remedies) have side effects and often divert you from making changes toward healthy living habits. Before getting on the drug bandwagon, seek healthier, safer alternatives. Better yet, be your own doctor and prescribe for yourself a no-drug lifestyle.

10. **Aim for attainable fitness.** Having a healthy, energetic, trim body at 50 is a perfectly realistic goal. Looking like a hot 20-year-old in those low-riders won't happen, and aiming for that latter goal will rob you of the enjoyment of your healthy body.

Susan's story is a testament to how powerful replenishing your physical energy can be.

Facing my forties, I was dragging through each day. The mirror reflected an overweight, overstressed mass of sagging cellulite. I was working 60 hours a week, on my feet. Even when I had time off, I felt exhausted and sluggish. My diet consisted of a high-sugar breakfast in the car on the way to work, bad food for lunch and fast food on the way home. Caffeine—10 to 12 diet colas a day—fueled my existence.

These harmful habits caused my weight to balloon above 200 pounds. My legs and back ached constantly, further limiting my physical activity. My irritability increased; I snapped at everyone, and I sank into depression and self-loathing.

If I was ever going to turn my life around, I obviously had to change my lifestyle. After much research, I began a weight-loss program, and the weight began to come off. As I lost the excess pounds, I gained enough energy to start walking with a support group of women in my neighborhood. We started slowly, but now I walk three miles at a brisk pace three days a week, and six miles on weekends. I also fit in weight training four times a week. These workouts charge me with energy that propels me through each day.

Today, the processed foods that used to sustain me no longer hold any appeal. Green tea and water have replaced the diet soft drinks. I now crave fruits and vegetables instead of sugary sweets.

Here's the most astonishing part of my story: Once I began to value myself and focus on energizing my body, the other areas of my life began coming into focus as well. My increased energy has opened doors I never knew were available. I became more confident and productive at work.

Today, I own my own consulting company and travel frequently. Yet I'm still able to keep up with my husband and four children, everywhere from the ski slopes to the soccer field.

Like Susan, get healthy and stay healthy. Your life and love of life depend on it.

REPLENISH YOUR EMOTIONAL ENERGY

When my mom died from breast cancer, I knew I was at risk, but at only 35, after my first biopsy, I was stunned to find myself facing my own mortality. Three benign biopsies followed. I lived in an emotional battlefield, with fear impacting every moment.

Along the way, I collected the battle scars on my breasts, physical reminders of a possible outcome I could not control through vision, passion or engagement. This experience put life in sharper perspective—for a while.

Then, as my business began to prosper in a big way, I found I wasn't enjoying my success as I had imagined. I was showing up edgy and grumpy. It made no sense to me. Attaining my goals was supposed to equal happiness. What had I worked for so long and so hard?

Managing my business and the 23 employees that go with it is challenging and potentially exhausting. There's one of me and 23 of them. I'll readily admit there are days I might prefer to just zap them with an Epi-Kit, defibrillate them back to life or just holler "Off with their heads!" from the throne in my office. I know when they have problems they naturally think they're worse than anyone else's, but when you're the boss, their problems are magnified 23 times—plus I've got my own! I need emotional renewal to joyfully come back for more of this punishment day after day after day.

Applying my nursing assessment skills to myself as I would to a patient, I saw that I was always pushing. I had an unhealthy sense of urgency that prevented me from enjoying my life or my success. I needed time for emotional renewal.

I've learned to temper the unhealthy sense of urgency so I don't have to be in a frantic state to be productive. I've learned to temper my whirlwind pace with occasional pauses. Calm and achievement are partners.

To be wickedly successful and emotionally intact, we have to be kind to ourselves. Because my busy schedule may not grant me a break later, I wake up 30 minutes early to a quiet cup of tea. In Nepal, Tom and I picked up a renewal habit called "bed tea." Every morning of our trek, a Sherpa came by at dawn and thrust a cup of steaming hot tea into the hand extending from our sleeping bag. It eased the transition from our warm cocoons into the cold, thin mountain air. Today, wherever I am, and no matter what time my busy day starts, I have a cup of bed tea. Starting my day with a break eases the transition from bed to boardroom. That cup of tea helps me to step into my office with a "Come on, bring on the madness" attitude.

I also end each evening with a break, reading in bed or my favorite chair, with a glass of healthy red wine in hand. My bedroom is my sanctuary, free of clutter, food and television. No matter what I've experienced that day, these quiet minutes anchor me deep in relaxation and guarantee a good night's sleep.

Being kind to ourselves emotionally includes getting away from it all. It's a challenge for me to take even a week off and not connect with my office, but I have to create an environment that allows me to escape my business, my responsibilities and even myself. I love my business, but I love it more because I squeeze out 12 weeks of vacation per year for myself. Every time I leave, I come home new and different.

And I've stopped making vacation a competitive sport. While biking in Puglia, Italy, a realization about myself and my emotional state unfolded. Picture this: Breathtakingly beautiful bougainvillea covering a 15-foot wall. Brilliant sprays of orange, red and fuchsia against a background of deepest green. Only I scarcely saw them from the corner of my eye as I sped by at 20 mph, pedaling as fast as I could to keep up with the peloton of riders ahead of me.

They were all faster riders than I, which meant I had to work hard just to keep the last rider in sight. I had to move fast, catch up, keep up and get ahead. And to think I'd come here to play, see the countryside and relax my usually rapid pace.

Acknowledging to myself that this pace was no fun, I braked to a stop. When Tom came pedaling back, I was easy to find—sitting under an olive tree, staring at that wall of bougainvillea and breathing its heady bouquet. He parked his bicycle and sat down beside me. For the rest of the trip we never rode faster than 12 mph. We reveled in my discovery— not only the flowers but the peace and the emotional peace. That Puglia lesson was the best souvenir we've ever brought home.

19 Strategies for Replenishing Your Emotional Energy

1. **Get away.** Take one day off with no responsibilities, like Melissa, who assigns Saturday child-care duty to her husband, sends them to the zoo or park and enjoys a renewal day.

2. Take a virtual vacation. My second mom, Blanche, vacations in her bathtub with candles, bath oil, a glass of wine and her favorite CD. Maybe you'd prefer to lounge in your backyard or hammock with a favorite beverage or curl up in bed with a deliciously light book.

Women are sensual creatures. We enjoy rich fabrics, exotic fragrances, music, dance and art. Yet, as we reach for wicked success and attainment, sometimes we leave these restorative sensory pleasures behind. Indulging in the occasional sensory banquet is second only to an actual getaway.

3. Hug a tree or an iceberg. Getting off the grid is not always an easy thing to do. (You don't just hop onto the 5:15 train to Bhutan.) But I make it my goal at least once a year to get far away, into something so different that it forces me out of my regular relaxation routine into one that entirely disconnects me from my day-to-day life, and I allow myself to completely relax and renew.

Nature and wildlife provide two of the most powerful tools for relaxation that I've ever found. As an example, when I was in the Arctic, kayaking, hiking, riding a zodiac raft, seeing a blue whale and worrying about nothing more than getting too close to the business end of a large, hungry, white-furred mammal, renewed me in ways that a massage just cannot. Renewal lightens my load; my batteries get fully topped off.

4. Renew with music. Play music that energizes or relaxes you, depending upon what's called for. Choose classical for intense projects. Rock and roll for cooking, household chores or packing suitcases. At night, play slow music to unwind and relax.

5. Choose happiness. I love the comforts of my home and my cozy neighborhood. Being home is like experiencing a steaming cup of green tea—it just feels right. I also love traveling to new places and have hiked and biked all over the world.

And then there's the business travel I do for eight weeks a year. The hotels I stay in don't come close to the comforts of home, nor do they rival the remote and adventurous places I've been.

I'm not one to advocate "Barbie-dolling" it (don't you just hate that?), but one thing I've learned is that the happier I am,

the happier I am. Happiness is not only contagious to others, it's contagious to ourselves. My grandmother Pearl ("MaMa") had multiple sclerosis and spent most of her adult life in a wheelchair or confined to a bed, yet she was one of the happiest people I've known. I always wanted to be in her happy space. MaMa taught me that happiness is not a condition—happiness is a choice.

I don't always wake up happy, but wherever I am physically or emotionally, I try to focus on the part of the experience that is good. For example, I might not like the bed in my hotel room, but I am passionate about teaching and mentoring women in person. That requires sleeping in the occasional uncomfortable bed.

Life will always throw us curveballs, fastballs and, just when you think you know what's coming next, the occasional change-up. Being happy to the core helps us hit them back—no matter how fast they come or how many come our way.

People enjoy being around happy people. I recently mentored a woman who refused to move out of the drama of a negative experience. For two weeks she dwelled on something that was easily solved in three minutes. My advice to her was: "Move on and choose happiness." How many opportunities did she miss during those two weeks because she chose to grouse?

Happiness is more important to wicked success than success is to happiness. Decide every day that nothing will get in the way of choosing happiness.

6. **Monitor your intimate companions.** Your passionate vision will not live inside a negative house, and nothing drains energy faster than negative thinking. Your thoughts do control your life. They are your most intimate companions. When I notice I'm wasting energy thinking negatively about someone, the realization that I'm only attacking and harming myself with such thoughts helps me temper them.

Create an emotional house that invites the vision already inside you to reveal itself. Banish negative thoughts. This is not to say you ignore your feelings or reality. But when you learn to control your thoughts about the experience, you touch new places of feeling that are even more real.

7. Turn off the critic. Do you find your inner "critical voice" rears its head way too often? "Is it me, or was that secretary less friendly than usual?" Stop being the critic. It robs you of your success energy.

My excellent assessment skills can bring out the critic in me. I can walk into my office and, in an instant, zero in on everything that's wrong—the messy lunchroom, the missed deadline. But allowing the critic to be my dominant communication style would negatively impact my employees. Instead I intentionally notice and comment about the good things.

When that negative voice in your head gets loud, take a brisk walk or clean out a file cabinet. Let it go! Let go of the critic.

8. Be nice and watch how nice people will be in return. There is an economy of emotion with niceness. Few things will give you more energy than the rewards of being nice. Conversely, nothing will drain your emotional energy faster than not playing nice with others.

9. Dump toxic clutter. Because I have huge professional commitments, I try to eliminate toxic or emotionally draining relationships and other social clutter, just as I dump the clutter that accumulates on my desk. This gives me time for relationships that matter—husband, family and best friends.

Tame the news ticker running in your head. One morning Tom and I were sitting in our favorite Starbucks casually eavesdropping on some of the conversations around us. Soon the conversation at one table came around to the death of Michael Jackson. One of the women mentioned how upset she was, and that she'd cried about Michael's death. Another woman told the group how her mother had called the night Princess Diana died and that they'd cried together over the phone. One of the men said he'd been upset first by Heath Ledger's, then by Patrick Swayze's death; and the one who cried about Michael Jackson said she also sadly remembered when Ronald Reagan died.

News programs thrive on the "if it bleeds, it leads" mentality. Would we really want to watch Osama bin Laden being shot? We may not have control over how the media reports these issues, but we do have control over where we direct our attention.

Start your day on a negative track, and which way do you think
your emotional output will go? Avoid the negative news tickers.

I understand feeling a certain amount of sympathy for the family
of a deceased celebrity, but call me heartless, I'm not going to spend
my time crying over a celebrity's death (unless it's Richard Gere), and
I'm certainly not going to stand vigil outside the house of someone
I've never shared time with.

As a nurse, I've been there for grieving families on many
occasions, but nurses know that to pretend to feel what that family
feels will not ring true. We support; we don't collapse. When, at
age 23, I was at my mom's funeral, I was personally put off by a
hysterical woman who wasn't even that close to Mom. Some might
disagree, but I believe that mourning is a right earned, not a privilege
for the masses. Is this misplaced energy and emotion a way of not
dealing with the real-life emotions we face every day?

Each minute is a precious gift. I am often as guilty of squandering
this gift as the next guy, but I always strive to keep my energies
within my "circle of influence." We can spend our days railing about
this politician, that TV program, or some anorexic actor or we can
get to work on our own lives. I don't want to sound trite, but if
you're not part of the solution, don't rail about the problem.

10. **Detach.** When I was taking a dance class, a classmate told my friend,
    "I don't think Vickie likes me." Christine responded, "You don't
    know Vickie. She just doesn't think about you." Harsh, but true.
    I wouldn't choose to socialize with the woman, but I didn't dislike
    her. That takes emotional energy.

    Why put your own precious emotional energy into something
    or someone else that doesn't provide a positive return? Detach from
    emotional unrest that doesn't serve a purpose in your life and feel the
    increase in your own positive-energy charge.

11. **Lighten up.** Since I'm Italian, everything is intensely important to
    me. But unless I let go of some of that intensity I'm emotionally
    exhausted. When I find myself making mountains out of
    molehills, I ask myself, "In one year, will this be significant?"
    Lighten up. If you push, you get resistance. Be less serious about
    the outcome.

12. Learn a new language. As soon as you label something "bad," it limits your ability to have fun. I used to "hate" the cold, and then one day in Iceland a woman said to me, "There's no such thing as bad weather, just bad clothing." I've explored the Canadian Rockies, the Antarctic, the Arctic, trekked the Everest and Annapurna sides of Nepal, and stood among prayer flags on a 13,000-foot-high mountain pass looking across Bhutan's Haa Valley and the Himalayas into Tibet, and loved it because I brought the right gear.

When I substitute the right mental gear for the word "hate," I am amazed at how much emotional energy I gain. Take all negative words down a notch in mind and voice, and notice how different you feel.

13. Let it go. Do you suffer from dissatisfaction and frustration? Do you find yourself whining and complaining instead of acting on your passionate vision? Try letting it all go and see the difference that makes in your day. Appreciate what you have. When frustration happens, take a breath and let it go.

14. Enjoy the moment. How often do you hear or say, "Thank God it's Friday"? Do we want to enjoy only two days out of seven? Why not "Thank God it's today"? If you are living for the weekend, you aren't living. You can't repeat a day or even an hour or a minute. You'll never get that time back. Treat every moment as a precious gift.

15. Practice gratitude. For happy people, gratitude seems to outweigh desire. For unhappy people, it's about want, want, want, with little gratitude in return. There's nothing wrong with desire. Desires fire your passionate vision. But gratitude must always be greater. Otherwise, you're never satisfied, never happy. Daily, acknowledge three things you're grateful for, small or large.

Express gratitude to others. I stay in a lot of hotels and I love to express gratitude and appreciation to the housekeepers who clean my room. Their gratitude for mine is so expressive it makes me wonder if few people ever do this. Express gratitude big and small, especially to people who don't often receive it. You can transform their day.

Every Friday we turn our company phones to voice mail and share lunch together. Each week one employee expresses gratitude to someone in the company who has helped him or her in some way. Some have gotten very creative with poetry, skits and video. All share in the joy of gratitude.

16. **Accept yourself as you are.** How often do we let the comparison game rob us of joy? I'm five feet two inches tall, with sturdy ankles. I could long to be a lithe five feet seven inches, but some things we can change and others we can't. The things you can't—let them go.

17. **Find the fun.** Fun is healing and laughter keeps us sane. Laughter raises T-cell counts, relaxes blood vessels, eases muscle tension and reduces psychological stress, which enhances learning. Laughter can happen when you least expect it—if you let it.

    My sister Karen had a stroke, and one night we showed up at the hospital after visiting hours. My dad, Tom, two friends and I slipped past the nurse's station and tiptoed into my sister's room. Just as we got inside we heard the nurse coming. Tom whispered, "Quick, into the shower!" and all five of us crowded in. As soon as the nurse left, we burst out of the shower, laughing so hard we were on the floor, except for one friend who said, "How can you laugh with your sister in that condition? You're so insensitive." At that moment, Karen, who is also a nurse and was much improved, gave us a thumbs up and joined the fun by doing her impression of a gorked-out stroke victim, waving around the stuffed animal we'd brought her. That's when my "sensitive" friend got it. Fun happens even in the middle of a stroke. Laugh every day.

18. **Create your own party.** Growing up in New Orleans taught me that you can have a party anywhere—at your house, in your mind or, as my dad says while chowing down on a good muffaleta, in your mouth. Embrace life with energy and joy. Wherever you go physically, emotionally or mentally, take the party with you.

19. **Eat dessert first.** Sometimes we treat renewal like a dessert we have to earn by first eating our vegetables. Mardi Gras taught me to celebrate before the hard work. Before the sacrifice of Lent, we

would party hearty for two weeks. That's Mardi Gras, feast before fast, eat dessert first.

NURTURE AND RENEW YOUR SPIRIT

As a child I was deeply connected to my Catholic upbringing, but after college I felt I didn't need religion, that I was happy without it. Then I befriended a woman who had a spiritually enlightened peace I found fascinating. She had no successes to write about or riches that people would envy, but she had so much more. She had a completely centered way of interacting in a world that had thrust profound challenges her way, including a husband suffering from severe, debilitating depression and a series of strokes that left him requiring constant, physical care from her.

Hers was a quality I wanted. I didn't want to attain success and wake up wondering, "Is this all there is?" I wanted peace and enlightenment, too, and just going to church once a week didn't satisfy that need for me.

I noticed that my friend practiced her spiritual discipline daily; and more important, I noticed the calming effect it created within her. I began practicing a few minutes each morning and evening. I'm still on my spiritual journey, and I'm nowhere near to perfecting my spiritual discipline, but I feel closer every day.

3 Strategies for Renewing Your Spiritual Energy

1. **Quiet down.** I confess, meditation doesn't work as well as for me as it does for others. I fall asleep. My strategy is to start my day in quiet and spiritual study over a cup of steaming hot tea. A time to reflect on who I want to be, how I want to show up and what is really important.

   Whichever you choose, a quiet moment or meditation, you'll feel more balanced all day and more tuned in to your spiritual source. Refuse to rely on the oldest excuse in the book: "I don't have time." It only takes a minute.

2. **Affirm life.** I can give myself a boost just by remembering what my minister says: "Life is good—all the time!" I admit that my

prayers used to focus on asking for something, perhaps freedom from a health concern, getting paid by a client so I could pay my mortgage that month or the end of the recession. Today I focus on affirming life. Quoting a friend, "It's a good day if I wake up."

3. **Study a spiritual discipline.** Whether you choose the Bible, another religious text or a spiritually uplifting book, study that discipline a few minutes daily. Spiritual renewal can be the most empowering and renewing practice of all. Mix it up a bit too. We can all learn from other religious practices. My trips to Bhutan, Japan, Thailand and Nepal introduced me to different versions of Buddhism and taught me the best of those practices while still retaining my Christian values and practices.

RECHARGE YOUR MENTAL ENERGY

A woman can feel mentally depleted for all the same reasons she feels emotionally depleted. When I shared with a woman who owns horses that I don't watch TV, she said something I'll always remember: "You wouldn't feed a million-dollar thoroughbred potato chips all day long. So why do people do that to a million-dollar mind?" What we feed our brains influences not just our thoughts but our way of thinking, the things we concern ourselves with and where we apply our energies.

How often do we feed our brains mental garbage? We're drawn into the hypnotic effects of television, bad romance novels with bare-chested men on the cover, talk radio, or FarmVille on the Internet. None of those activities is bad in itself, but they're all negatively seductive. We turn on the television to catch a favorite show, and before we know it we've sat through hours of mind fluff. Those activities don't renew mental energy; they deplete it.

That said, we do have to take a break. For a few years, everything I read and studied related to business. I thought I was helping myself succeed. Instead I was coming up drier and drier, and my mental output was declining. I was smarter than ever, but it wasn't revealing itself in my work. Looking back, I can see that I was mentally exhausted, even though I didn't recognize it at the time.

Mental energy is needed for creativity and ingenious decisions.
I started renewing my mental energy by banning all business books from
the bedroom, then expanding my reading to include literature and good,
relaxing "trash." My business grew and I was more relaxed.

6 Strategies for Recharging Your Mental Energy

1. **Eat like a thoroughbred.** Your brain and memory depend on food to
   function. Eat well and eat regularly.

2. **Spark your intellect.** Read a thought-provoking book unrelated to
   your career. Listen to a thought-provoking audio recording.

3. **Enjoy mental junk food occasionally.** When I first met Tom I was
   reading only business books and serious literature. He brought me
   a frivolous book and said, "If you put yourself on a diet of nothing
   but turkey, rice and broccoli, you'll soon lose your enthusiasm for
   eating." Sometimes we need a book like Stephenie Meyer's *Twilight*
   or Stieg Larsson's *Dragon Tattoo* series: books that are like eating a
   bag of salty, hot, buttered (real butter) popcorn. Once you start, you
   can't put them down.

4. **Challenge your senses.** Enjoy a gallery, arboretum or museum you
   wouldn't normally visit.

5. **Create something new.** Creating anything, whether a new recipe in
   the kitchen, a new product or a sculpture, renews and improves your
   mind. Every time we link two ideas that we never before connected,
   we form a synaptic bond between two neurons and these synapses
   literally equate to brain growth.

6. **Change your mind-set.** A negative mind-set focuses mental energy
   on the wrong thing. I'm usually on time, but rarely early, so it was a
   big deal one morning when the hotel's room service was 20 minutes
   late. I was about to speak to 300 people, yet I was freaking out
   over a missing bowl of yogurt instead of mentally rehearsing my
   presentation. My focus was totally in the wrong place.

   We're all human, and we're going to lose focus at times, but
   we need to rein ourselves in. The wrong mind-set depletes mental
   energy necessary to perform at our best.

CELEBRATE TO INTENSIFY RENEWAL

People often ask me what it was like growing up in New Orleans. One word captures New Orleans perfectly: celebration. We know how to celebrate. It's in our blood.

Most visitors don't realize that the intrinsic message of Mardi Gras is "feast before fast." Outsiders see only floats, parades and colorful beads. But anyone living in that predominantly Catholic city knows that Mardi Gras prepares you to cope with the sacrifice of Lent.

To honor Lent you give up something you enjoy for 40 days. Knowing Lent is coming, we party hearty for the two weeks before Lent. Celebration, celebration, celebration, that's Mardi Gras.

What would life be without celebration? Endless to-do lists, tasks, accomplishments. Celebrating doesn't just feel good; it's the best free antidepressant on the market. The moment you experience the sweet spell of wicked success, it's time to celebrate. Even 30 seconds of celebration colors the day differently. You can give yourself a "woo-hoo!" or a moment to enjoy the view outside your window.

One evening, crammed in my tiny home office while I was packing the day's business away, my eye fell on a huge framed certificate that Tom had hung on the wall as a surprise. He was celebrating my first million-dollar year in revenue, and at the bottom of the frame was a faux million-dollar bill.

That was the moment it hit me. "I've made it! Why am I packing and unpacking my office on my kitchen table every day? I can afford office space." Then he opened a bottle of champagne. Toasting, acknowledging and celebrating my success together made that accomplishment all the tastier.

How often have you reached a goal or passed a milestone without experiencing a single moment of satisfaction? If you make a habit of celebrating your smallest victories, even those that fall short of fantastic, the big goals seem more attainable.

Celebrate before the win. Just being considered for a promotion is worthy of celebration. Even if it doesn't work out as planned, celebrate your willingness to step out into the unknown. Whatever the outcome, enjoy the possibility.

Make a celebration list. Include Big Things (a weekend vacation) and small ones (a single red rose), and celebrate every day.

RENEW YOUR ENERGY WITH THE PEOPLE YOU LOVE

Who are the people you love to be with? How often do you spend time with them? When was the last time you made a new friend? Love and life don't happen in a vacuum. Women need to make time and seek opportunity for expressing this most powerful emotion. Surrounding ourselves with people we love guarantees more positive experiences. It puts more life in our life.

5 Strategies for Renewing with the People You Love

1. **Spend time together.** Women who enjoy an intimate relationship live longer, and strong relationships generally require time. Share a hobby. Walk or bike together.

   Leigh has been married for 30 years, and every year she and her husband Tim renew their commitment to their marriage. At the hotel in San Antonio where they honeymooned, they reserve room 734. Their tradition begins on the balcony, where they exchange cards and gifts while a bubble machine fills the air with cheer. They toast each other and hang a wildly colorful wind sock off the railing. Later they look up from the pool and watch the bubbles and festivity happening on their balcony. Talk about renewal!

2. **Create traditions.** You've heard the phrase, "What do you expect, a song and dance?" Tom and I have a silly tradition. If one of us completes a task but feels unappreciated, he or she can ask for "a song and dance." The other must make up a song on the spot, along with some dance steps. It usually goes something like this: "Thomas [or Vickie] is my hero; he took out the garbage; it was really smelly. He washed out the can . . ." You get the idea. Perfection is not necessary.

3. **Create memories.** Engage your friends, coworkers and people you love in experiences you can enjoy now and remember fondly as years pass. We all love to sit around and tell stories. Things don't bring happiness, but experiences keep giving and giving.

Jan admits she's terrible at remembering dates, whereas her husband Larry is a romantic for whom dates are important. One January he called her at work and invited her to dinner at their favorite restaurant. He ordered a bottle of wine and she began to wonder what they were celebrating. What had she forgotten? Finally, he glowingly announced they'd gotten such a late start getting married they would celebrate their anniversary twice a year to catch up.

The best gift I've ever received was a big digital photo frame already loaded with photos of friends, family and vacations. Through all those photos I can relive my favorite memories.

4. Hang with your women friends. Remember to make time for your friends. We all like to be spontaneous, but let's face it, we're busy. So schedule, schedule, schedule: an early morning walk, lunch or a glass of wine after work. Even a weekend sleepover might be fun. (Your husband will love you for this one.).

When one of my best friends Missy and I traveled to Miami for a girls' weekend, we freed ourselves of work, family and responsibility. We never left the hotel grounds and did nothing but talk and talk and talk. We simply celebrated each other and totally reconnected, renewing our friendship along with our physical, emotional, mental and spiritual selves.

5. Celebrate passages and milestones. When Tom and I received our bar exam scores, we took champagne and our test score envelopes to our favorite outdoor water sculpture to read the results. When we bought a lot on which to build our house, we celebrated on the site with close friends. Susan, the master of ritual, celebrates menopause with her women friends as each one of them reaches that passage.

Even death is worthy of celebration. Coming from a world that practiced tearful, whispering wakes, Tom was shocked at his first New Orleans funeral. He sure wasn't expecting a boisterous party with lots of donuts and coffee cups of 90-proof "tea." Realizing we weren't celebrating that a person had died but rejoicing that the person had lived, Tom got into the celebration—and the "tea."

Celebrate every milestone in an inventive manner that creates lasting memories. Don't wait for the big win; start celebrating today.

RENEW BY GIVING BACK

As author Hada Bejar said, "The fragrance always stays in the hand that gives the rose." Whether you donate to favorite charities or simply make a habit of being emotionally generous to others, giving is a gratifying and renewing act. When you give, you disconnect from yourself and your own problems. Fresh perspective and renewal are the benefits.

Giving does not always mean pulling out your wallet. Time is a valuable gift. Mentoring is a valuable gift. Spiritual or emotional support is a valuable gift. Sending a person positive thoughts costs nothing and benefits you as much as the people you're thinking about. Jackie takes care of her aging father. Missy is a "big sister" to a disadvantaged young girl, Emilio coaches youth soccer and Jan takes severely learning- and mentally disabled children on rafting trips. The joy they receive exceeds the joy they give.

One of my favorite things about social media is that within seconds you can lift up a person's day, and in doing so lift yours up too. One of my best friends will often post on Facebook, text or leave me quick voice mail messages reminding me she's thinking about me. She always ends them with, "Love you." I get a big smile from each one. She makes my day.

If there's something you want more of, give it away. If you want more money, encouragement or love, give it today and you will receive it tomorrow, but not necessarily from the people you give to. It comes through other manifestations. By giving back, I have received more abundance in every aspect of my life than I ever dreamed possible.

After Katrina struck, I was lucky enough to be in a position to give financial support to my family and friends. One of my best friends who lost everything asked me to help her family instead of her. I was in awe of her generosity toward her family when she herself was in need.

Despite the loss, I never heard her complain about her situation. She moved forward, staying in the same area, rebuilding her life and keeping her "New Orleans spirit." Anytime she'd visit me in Houston, we'd go shopping as she rebuilt her home. One piece at a time, she would buy a lamp, outfit or other item. I would joke with her that her car looked like a homeless person's, packed with all the treasures she'd picked up while traveling between New Orleans, Baton Rouge, Dallas and Houston, and she'd joke back, "Vickie, I *am* homeless."

Throughout her own rebuilding, she helped and supported her family while they rebuilt their lives. Her selflessness stays with me today. She is a model to me of leaving a positive legacy even in the most difficult of situations.

The legacy my mom left me is the realization that the time to enjoy life is now. Although she never traveled past the front porch of our shotgun house, she made sure that our corner of the world was the greatest. She taught me that it is a trap to think life would be better with more money, more business or more free time. We must make the most of every moment—we'll never get back that moment, ever.

Whichever corner of the world you're on, whatever you're doing there, make it the greatest corner ever. Enjoy and appreciate the important people in your life at every possible moment. If you leave no other legacy, you will be remembered for that.

6 STRATEGIES FOR TOTAL RENEWAL

Recognize that to live a passionate life you must attend to all of your needs, not just one or two. Energy in one area (emotional) powers energy in another (physical). Here are six strategies for pulling it all together.

1. **Set renewal goals.** You are just as important as your career and family. Plan your renewal. I include everything in my renewal goals, from maintaining a daily fitness regimen to destinations I want to travel to. Regularly assess and update your renewal plan.

2. **Start small and do one thing at a time.** Enjoy 5 minutes of quiet, then 10. Add 1 vegetable a day, then eat 2. Turn off the television for 1 hour, then 2. Eliminate 1 fast-food trip a week, then eliminate 2. Eliminate 1 trip a day to the office candy bowl, then 3, and you'll lose 7 pounds a year. It takes 60 days to turn your lifestyle change into a habit.

3. **Banish all excuses.** I know a woman who works 70 hours a week, and her excuse for not getting away for a weekend is that she's too spent when the weekend comes. Yet a relaxing weekend away is

probably the perfect prescription. Renewal often takes a little time and effort, but wicked success and career are nothing without a renewed spirit.

4. **Accept wherever you are in your life now and start from there.** Know that you can always start fresh. Wherever you are in life, there was "before" and there is "now." Maybe you haven't exercised in 3 years or 30. Start now—and forget before.

5. **Take a day off from discipline.** French fries in place of one serving of broccoli won't kill you, but unrelenting discipline will make you wish you were dead. Pass the ketchup!

6. **Create a Female Fusion.** As you'll learn in Chapter 10, this is like supercharging all facets of your vitality.

What renewal strategies will you put into effect for the next 60 days?

RENEW YOUR LIFE ENERGY WITH THE
5 PROMISES

PROMISE 1
I Will Live and Work a Passionate Life

What energizes you to face the day with passion? Write down everything you can think of that renews your mental, emotional, spiritual and physical energy.

_____

_____

_____

PROMISE 2
I Will Go for It or Reject It Outright

Celebrate. What will you celebrate and with whom?

_____

_____

_____

PROMISE 3
I Will Take One Action Step a Day Toward My Passionate Vision

Schedule time off for yourself twice daily. Block it off on your calendar and write the specific times here. Commit to exercising at least three times a week. Which days and times will you schedule for exercise?

_____

_____

_____

PROMISE 4
I Commit to Being a Success Student for Life

Study yourself for one week, as if doing research. Literally journal what you do, what you're thinking, what you eat, and how you feel. Which activities and foods renew and energize you?

_____

_____

_____

PROMISE 5
I Believe as a Woman I Really Can Do Anything

In which renewal strategy do you already excel? Pick one more renewal strategy and apply that same discipline. What will it be?

_____

_____

_____

>> DOWNLOAD THE 5 PROMISES FOR RENEWAL AT **WickedSuccess.com.**

LINDSAY'S RENEWAL

THE LESSON OF A FLOWER

*I was talking to a flower yesterday while frantically running
from the rain, trying to get into my car.*

*While I was struggling, the flower asked me, "Why are you
running from the rain?"*

*I said I did not want to be late for work, and there
was going to be traffic.*

*The flower asked, "Why are you rushing?
You should be enjoying the rain.*

*"It is not going to harm you. It only gives
you a moment of refreshment.*

*"Is this how you plan to spend your life, rushing
and running from life's beautiful offerings?"*

"I don't have time for this. I have to get to work," I responded.

*"See, there you go again. You need to stop and just
look and enjoy the beautiful drops falling from the heavens.
They are tiny gifts from God."*

Before I could say anything, the flower turned
away and closed its petals.

I wanted to tell the flower it was wrong.

But at the same time I wished that I did have time to realize
and enjoy the amazing surroundings life gives us.

Lindsay, 15
STUDENT AND POET

Now that you have reclaimed your life energy through
renewal, learn how Female Fusion will unite you with
incredible women to attain the impossible.

Every day brings a chance for you to draw
in a breath, kick off your shoes and dance.
OPRAH WINFREY

A fusion of women on fire is a rush of pure energy.
VICKIE L. MILAZZO

10

FEMALE FUSION

Fuse with Incredible Women to Attain the Impossible

T he more successful you are, the less you're expected to need other women in your life and the less time you have to spend time together. Take time to spend a day with powerful, wickedly successful women and you'll come away spinning with energy and ideas. That's Female Fusion.

Fusion occurs when you merge diverse, distinct or separate elements into a unified whole. When women come together and share their passions, visions, experiences, fears and promises, an amazing bond occurs. From that bond emerge sparks of brilliance and insight that none of these women alone, or in any other combination, could have inspired. Female Fusion is the most powerful Feminine Force of all.

According to a landmark UCLA study on managing stress, the bonds we form with women also benefit our health and longevity. The hormone oxytocin, enhanced by estrogen and released as part of our stress response, encourages us to gather with other women. The bond that forms helps to fill emotional gaps and lowers the risk of early death. Men experiencing stress go into a fight-or-flight response. Women's broader response system may explain why we consistently outlive men.

Having worked almost exclusively with women throughout my career, I wasn't surprised by the results of that UCLA study. When Tom and I were in Morocco, I experienced a spontaneous example of Fusion.

Our biking group interacted as couples until one night at dinner when we split up, all the men in one room, all the women in another. My entire experience of these women I'd spent a week with changed during this one evening as we dug deep into heart-to-heart topics about fears, acts of courage, successes, failures and love. After dinner I asked Tom, "What did you talk about?" He said, "Sports, jokes, compared digital cameras, typical guy stuff. We had a great time." The women had fun, too, but while the guys were bantering and bonding superficially, the women were discussing our most profound feelings.

Yet, despite such amazing experiences with women, even I wasn't quite prepared for the incomparable results of the first Female Fusion. The Fusion that resulted from conceptualizing this book was so powerful I have to pass it along to you. The more audacious your passionate vision, the more you'll want Fusion.

THE STORY OF THE FIRST FEMALE FUSION

We gathered in a hotel, women from age 33 to 74—a learning specialist, a marketing director, a graphic design entrepreneur, a massage therapist, a writer, an interior designer, a marketing creative, my second mom and me. Many of the women had never met; I was the only person there who knew all these incredible women. Some I worked with, others were longtime friends. None of us had a clue as to what was about to happen. We sat at a large, round table and began the Circle of Fusion exercise (see page 305).

We each chose one of the Feminine Forces, the one that tugged at us most, then we broke quickly into smaller groups. In each of our small groups, one woman talked for five minutes, relating a personal experience and the feelings and memories triggered by the Feminine Force she chose. The others listened actively while writing down on small stickers positive qualities—like honor, courage, commitment, humor and joy—that the speaker's comments sparked. When the woman stopped speaking she passed her Circle of Fusion to the listeners, who then affixed their one-word labels to the Circle while verbalizing how her story had affected them. The speaker then responded to each listener's feedback.

Here's One Example

Chris: I chose endurance. Endurance is seeing a light at the end of the tunnel. A lot of women suffer hard times, and when I thought about endurance, well, gosh, by the grace of God, I've never had to endure anything terrible. Surviving cancer takes endurance, and I've never had to do that. However, as women, we all endure. I've endured giving birth four times, and every time I said I'd never do it again. The fourth time I finally got it.

I've also endured a life-altering disease. While it isn't as life-threatening as some, adult-onset asthma changes you. You have to get through it and learn what's on the other side and how your life will react to the changes. But I think sometimes we endure by choice, and that's what I'd rather talk about.

I was a graphic designer for 20 years before I became a writer. Twelve of those years I owned my business, and I loved it. I designed everything from decorated glassware to ceramic tiles, brochures, ads and magazines. I had fun doing that, but I got burned out, figuratively and literally, when my office was gutted by fire. It became an endurance test to decide what to do next.

I had to continue doing what I was doing until I found a new career. You can't just toss in the towel unless you're independently wealthy. I tested a number of ideas, including writing a first-draft novel, and I knew I was going to be a novelist. After folding my business, I needed an income while I perfected my writing skills, and I took a job at less than a quarter of what I had earned as a designer. I knew writing would take concentration, because you don't just write a draft and get it published, unless you're a lot more brilliant than I am. During the next seven years I completed five more novels, two screenplays and several short stories.

There were many days when I wanted to quit the day job. The people were terrific, but for 12 years I'd been my own boss and now I was a secretary for 22 bank auditors, so I had 22 bosses. I endured, and finally published my first novel—not the first I'd written, but the fifth. I knew what I wanted and I chose to endure to get it.

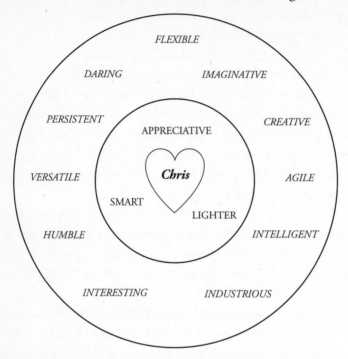

Each Listener Gave Positive Feedback for 60 to 90 Seconds

Leigh: When you were telling your story, the word that came to me was "creative." It was very creative to go into a job that was completely different from anything you were talented in and allow yourself to develop your writing craft.

We continued until all the listeners had given their feedback.

Then the Speaker Responded for 60 Seconds to the Listeners

Chris: Wow, you make me feel smart to do what I did. At the time I didn't know I was being smart or creative. I just felt this was what I needed to do. But I appreciate hearing it. It makes me feel lighter. Thank you.

As each woman took a turn, this opening exercise made it possible for relative strangers to communicate freely. One woman in the Fusion described the unexpected sense of community:

It's hard to convey how you feel when three or four women bombard you with all these positive strengths they observed in you. It was instantly empowering, a bright warmth that started inside, opening me to these women I hardly knew but who seemed to know me so well. The feeling of acceptance and community is indescribable.

When we all came back together, everyone was glowing and chattering with enthusiasm. One woman from each small group shared results, and amazingly you felt bonded to all the women there, women who an hour ago you'd never even met. It was unbelievably affirming, and it set the tone for the whole day. We shared our closest secrets with the absolute trust that we were being heard and understood, and it was okay, it was safe.

We spent the rest of the day together discussing the 10 Feminine Forces, their meanings, and how we use them. In Chapter 6, you read a portion of our free-flowing dialogue on integrity.

We made luxury an element of our Fusion. The hotel served a delicious lunch, plus champagne and strawberries with whipped cream. A gorgeous flower arrangement arrived from Maggie's husband Adrian, with the message: "Every woman is a force of nature, of spirit, of vitality. Thank you all for bringing each new day to light."

The day whizzed by, finishing with each woman telling what she'd gained from the experience, and all of us surprised by the depth of our reactions. We all went home with a glow that lasted for days, some of us lighter from unloading our secrets, others brimming with ideas and excitement for future accomplishments. Most important, we all went home changed.

3 STORIES OF WOMEN FOREVER CHANGED

I knew that a powerful force was present that day. I felt a unique release of energy charging the air, and an emotional bond that was changing our relationships forever. The other women noticed it, too. Following are three examples of the amazing results you will have with Female Fusion. You'll also find each woman's Circle of Fusion that ignited that release of energy.

Leigh: This was a beautifully planned day that didn't go as planned. I don't believe any of us expected total strangers to open up as we did.

Even those of us who knew each other were astonished to see different facets revealed. The amazing camaraderie came not from talking about work or recipes but from being women. I discovered that people I work with every day didn't know what I do outside my job. I devote a big part of my life to family and organizations that focus on women's advancement.

Usually, I'm reticent to talk about myself. I concentrate on the task at hand, do it and take on the next task. As I described my commitment to my marriage, I recognized how much strength I draw from that relationship. Then as I talked about my community involvement, and these women responded with awe, I realized how much I actually do and how important it is. I left that day with a better sense of myself than I've ever felt.

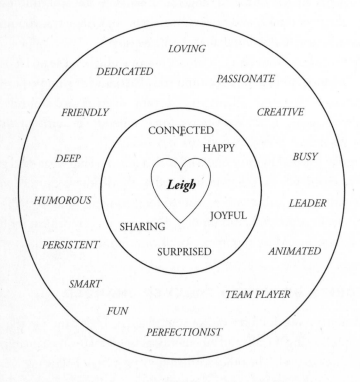

Maggie: I was hesitant, knowing I was one of the youngest women in the group. I wasn't sure I had any lessons to pass on or experiences worth sharing, or whether I was ready to open up around strangers. It was also the first time I had listened to myself speak out loud, and that alone had a substantial impact on me. I heard a voice that had been muted for so long.

My family has always carried a great deal of pain for my brother, who wasn't born with the same level of abilities that most of us have. People never realize what effect this has on a family. My mom is a strong, selfless and stoic woman who always put on her best face in spite of everything. We all did. And every day, that pain was like a lead weight I dragged around, even as I centered my life around my husband and beautiful daughter.

On that day of the Fusion, one of the things I came to realize was that I had lived a more intense life than most people my age. My beliefs are very strong and central to my character. There, among strangers, listening to women share their personal stories, my heart spoke. I was able to unload some of the emotional burden I had carried in silence for so long. These exceptional women immediately understood, and my heart opened. They helped me to liberate my soul and to better understand the spirit inside me. In the process, the emotional burden lifted and I felt a freedom to

drive my life forward. From that point on, I decided not to live in sadness, but in grandness.

Evie: When I found myself in that room filled with such amazing women, women I respected, I knew I was there to listen and learn, but I had no idea I would leave so totally changed. During the Circle of Fusion exercise, when we all opened up to one another, these women responded to me by stating the qualities I secretly hoped they would see in me. Women I would like to model my life after saw me as one of them, and I felt instantly validated. In their eyes, I shared many of the strengths I admired in them. I remember leaving with a clearer sense of who I was and what I needed to do to get where I wanted to go.

I knew it was up to me to take the ball and run with it, so run with it I did. Although we have some amazing people at the company I work for, I started questioning why I was taking a backseat to these other professionals. I tended to go along, letting others make the decisions. Female Fusion gave me the backbone to be more vocal and openly express my opinions. That was a risky move, and I did rock a few boats.

Surprisingly, as I expressed my opinions more, people seemed to value them and me more. Since the Fusion I've received two significant pay increases, far beyond the average raise for my position, and I feel as if I can run with the top people in my company, my ideas equal to anyone's. That's a big shift for me. Personally, I feel like the luckiest person in the company.

I am truly living my dream, doing what I set out to do. During that day of Female Fusion I noticed that every woman present seemed to be living her dream, but at the same time striving for an even bigger dream. That's where I see myself now.

The process of collaborating, mentoring, masterminding ideas together and encouraging our individual passions and visions enabled each of us to better withstand elements that might otherwise erode our lives and careers. We received wisdom and protection at the same time that we provided wisdom and protection for one another. We are now stronger because of our alliance.

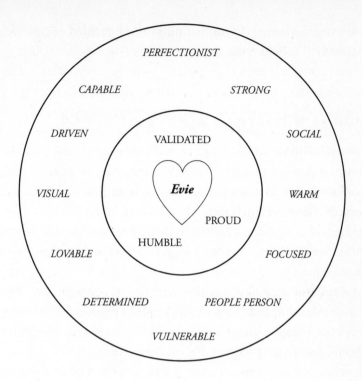

FEMALE FUSION IS A PROTECTIVE CAPROCK

Our Fusion reminded me of the hoodoos I saw while hiking through Utah's Bryce Canyon National Park. A hoodoo is a pinnacle or odd-shaped rock pillar left standing under a cementlike cover of protective caprock.

Hoodoos are often found clustered together, an echo of the ridge they once were, and their proximity as a group protects them all from the full intensity of the elements, guaranteeing a longer life span than those left standing alone. Like hoodoos, women engaged in Female Fusion enjoy the protective caprock of the entire group. They are stronger together than individually.

As a result, when you must stand alone, you are strengthened by your Fusion with other incredible women. You are at once challenged by and nurtured within the safety of Fusion. You are empowered to rely on your inner guidance and to creatively adapt the results of your Fusion to your own radically distinctive career and life. We are women, and singly, women can do anything; but we are more magnificent together.

Every woman in our Female Fusion gained a protective caprock, and left empowered to withstand the elements. We all wanted to hold the vision for as long as possible, knowing that we had been changed forever.

FUSION IS MORE THAN A WOMEN'S GROUP

I collaborate with women, brainstorm with women and work side-by-side with women daily, but Female Fusion is deeper. Fusion happens not only from brain to brain as we exchange ideas, or from flesh to flesh as we embrace, but from soul to soul.

In science, many situations exist where the sum of the parts attains different characteristics—and is stronger than—the parts themselves. For example, the metal alloy chrome-nickel steel, which results from combining chromium, nickel and iron, is far stronger than the sum of its individual elements, and is used in jet engines, where other metals would melt. Female Fusion is that type of synergy, but is deeper than what is commonly known as synergy in the business world.

Most of us have felt fusion with at least one other woman—our best friend, sister, mother, favorite aunt or grandmother. To feel fusion with several women at the same time is indescribable. To say you won't know what it's like until you've been there sounds like puffery, but trust me, it's true.

FUSION NEEDS HEAT

Just as you would not lay chromium, nickel and iron alongside one another and expect them to magically fuse, neither can you put several women in a room and expect Female Fusion to happen. Although it often occurs spontaneously, usually when friends share their deepest fears and wildest desires, a planned Fusion requires a coordinator and a dedicated measure of time.

Fusion needs both planned and spontaneous heat. Choose women you admire and trust, women who will pull together for everyone's purpose. Plan for a diversity of age, profession and talent. Choose women who are alike in some ways and different in others. The commonalities to look for are integrity and commitment. Female Fusion is not a "come and go as you please" event, especially if you are all progressing through the 5 Promises that accompany each chapter of *Wicked Success Is Inside Every Woman.* Every woman must commit to attending, participating fully and working through goals.

Expect to share stories of triumph and terror, brilliance and bafflement, honor and humiliation, as you bond and explore your passions. Just because we know one thing about a woman doesn't mean we know everything she is. You'll learn more about every woman in your group as the gathering heats up and you laugh and cry together. Expect to occasionally feel anger, and certainly to feel joy. At this deepest level, fusion happens.

You can keep your discussions purely intellectual and have an interesting conversation, but that's not Fusion. It's from a place of mutual soul-stripping heat that unbridled power and the potential of amazing reward can occur. In Fusion, you're going to strip bare and let it all hang out. It may not be pretty, but it's real. I've belonged to associations, networking groups and CEO organizations, but none of these come close to the off-the-chart phenomenal success that Female Fusion will accomplish for you.

Expect to have fun. Female Fusion isn't serious and solemn. At our all-day gathering we shared a fabulous meal, celebrated, received gifts of praise and encouragement, strategized and laughed a lot. We all walked out of that room feeling lighter and wiser and connected.

To heat up your first Female Fusion, use the sample invitation on the next page.

YOUR EXCLUSIVE INVITATION TO A
FEMALE FUSION

•

You have inspired me, instructed me, accepted, honored and encouraged me. I want to share you with my friends, and them with you, in an unforgettable experience.

You are invited to a phenomenal gathering of exceptional women. We will make history together as we harness our 10 Feminine Forces:

Fire, Intuitive Vision, Engagement, Agility, Genius,
Integrity, Endurance, Enterprise, Renewal and Female Fusion

We'll talk about how we can excel with these 10 Feminine Forces, and encourage each other to live the passionate life we envision for ourselves.

_____

Hosted by:

_____

Time:

_____

Place:

_____

RSVP to: _____ By: _____
          (name)   *(date)*

_____

(phone number or email address or both)

▸▸ DOWNLOAD THIS FUSION INVITATION AT **WickedSuccess.com.**

FEMALE FUSION REQUIRES PURPOSE

While you can use Fusion in many ways, it's not a social or networking group. Everyone in the Fusion needs to have a desire to improve her life.

If you choose to work through the 10 Feminine Forces and 5 Promises together, you'll develop powerful goals, objectives and strategies. It will take time, but collaboration will move you toward your passionate vision more swiftly than working through them on your own. Specifically, you will engage all 10 Feminine Forces at a higher level as you:

- Explore your passions together, ignite your inner fires and connect.

- Intuitively envision your individual futures and collectively validate one another's visions, no matter how audacious.

- Engage in, and hold one another accountable for, achieving Big Things.

- Flex your agility by diving deep into your passions and stretching further than ever before.

- Accelerate success through ingenious collaboration.

- Inspire the highest integrity for attracting authentic success.

- Collectively fuel individual endurance.

- Apply enterprising strategies to excel at being CEOs of life.

- Reclaim your life energy through renewal.

- Unite in Fusion to attain the impossible.

After you complete all the chapters, I encourage you to start over again from your new altitude of growth and attainment. Then begin another book together.

THE BASIC FUSION FORMAT IS SIMPLE

Any time a group of people meets regularly there's a tendency to create rules, dues, dos and don'ts. That will stop Fusion cold. Yes, you need a format and someone to get the Fusion started, but you won't need officers, and you won't be inviting outside speakers.

Keep it simple. This is all you will need:

o   Three or more women (10 maximum).

o   An intimate location.

o   Two to four hours of uninterrupted time for the first Female Fusion.

o   A goal for the Fusion (e.g., complete the 10 Feminine Forces using *Wicked Success Is Inside Every Woman*).

o   A copy of *Wicked Success Is Inside Every Woman* for each woman present. (Read the Contents and the introductory chapter on the 5 Promises before the first Fusion.)

Create a safe environment where members can expose their most closely held secrets. At our first Fusion, women exchanged stories they'd never told anyone, not even their closest family members. Two things that can help to foster a safe environment are:

1. **An agreement on how to offer advice.** Only when asked for? Or openly and freely? Sometimes we need to vent our feelings without anyone trying to "fix" us. Other times we truly need and want suggestions.

2. **A confidentiality agreement.** It might be as informal as a handshake commitment that "whatever is shared in Fusion stays in Fusion," or a simple document that every woman signs.

To facilitate Fusion the first time you come together and any time a new woman is brought into the group, engage in one of the bonding exercises in the next section.

ACTIVATE YOUR FIRST FUSION

Complete one of these three exercises together before you start working through the book. For all exercises, you'll need a timekeeper to tactfully move things along and a recorder to communicate results. Whichever exercise you choose will take 45 minutes to an hour. If you have more than five members, break into smaller groups for the exercise. When you come back together, each recorder will share her group's experience.

This is not critique time. It's an informal, impromptu outpouring of ideas and information. Keep all feedback positive.

Exercise 1: Your Most Audacious Desire

In this exercise, it's a good idea for the woman who brought all the others together to go first, because she will probably feel most comfortable.

Disclose a secret wish, something very few people know. Start with the word that most defines your wish, selected from the following list:

○ **LOVE**	○ **FUN**	○ **RESPECT**
○ **HEALTH**	○ **POWER**	○ **KNOWLEDGE**
○ **PEACE**	○ **ECSTASY**	○ **EXCITEMENT**
○ **WEALTH**	○ **JUSTICE**	○ **FAME**

The woman speaking describes her wish and a personal experience that stimulated her wish. She takes a full five minutes, using vivid detail. Speaking for five minutes is critical for the woman to go deep. While she's talking, everyone else jots down one of the 10 Strengths that can help her attain that wish.

When she's finished, everyone in turn affirms her audacious desire.

After each woman has presented her positive comments to the speaker, she takes an additional minute to respond to what she has heard.

Exercise 2: Your Personal Promises

Take turns describing in detail one promise you made to yourself that you kept, and one promise you broke. Take a full five minutes to describe the experiences that surrounded these promises. While the speaker describes her promises, everyone jots down one of the 10 Strengths exhibited in keeping the promise and a strength needed to recommit to the broken promise.

When she's finished, give her the positive feedback you jotted down. Spend no more than one minute each.

When everyone has presented positive comments to the speaker, she takes an additional minute to respond.

A sequel to the Personal Promises exercise can include discussing what the 5 Promises mean to each woman.

Exercise 3: The Circle of Fusion

This is the exercise most recommended for activating Fusion. Each woman chooses a Feminine Force—fire, intuitive vision, engagement, agility, genius, integrity, endurance, enterprise, or renewal. Each woman will describe how this strength has impacted her life.

It is important to choose the strength that tugs at you. Don't be analytical, just go with the one your intuition chooses. Use specific, detailed examples to illustrate that strength and how you've used it.

While one woman talks about everything the strength means to her, the others jot down positive feedback on small stickers. You are not trying to think of something clever; you're saying, "This is what I noticed about you as you related that situation." Give only affirming comments about the positive qualities you noticed as her story unfolded, such as optimism, endurance, humor, compassion or commitment. Use as many stickers as you need.

The speaker talks for a full five minutes, then gives her Circle of Fusion (see the next page) to the woman on her left. Every listener in turn expresses positive feedback for one minute, while attaching the stickers to the outer ring of the Circle of Fusion as she speaks. She then passes the Circle of Fusion to the next listener. When the Circle of Fusion returns to the speaker, she takes a moment to respond to the powerful insights she's just received, writing key words only in the inner ring of the Circle of Fusion. She responds for one minute, relating with her open heart how their feedback made her feel.

Continue this process until everyone has spoken, received feedback and responded. One by one you'll witness the effects of the positive transformation.

Revisit these three Fusion exercises any time your Female Fusion needs to rekindle its fire.

CIRCLE OF FUSION

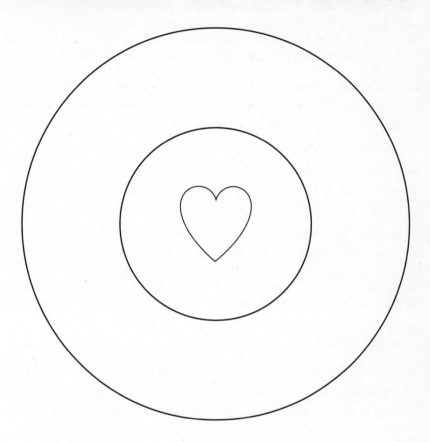

INSTRUCTIONS

1. Write your name in the heart.

2. Ask the listeners to your story to place their positive comments (key words only) on small stickers or labels as you talk, then paste them in the outer ring as they respond verbally.

3. Write your response to them (key words only) in the inner ring as you verbally acknowledge their positive comments.

>> DOWNLOAD THIS CIRCLE OF FUSION AT **WickedSuccess.com**.

SPARK FUSION THROUGHOUT THE ENTIRE GROUP

Like an alloy, Fusion is stronger when every woman is engaged. Here are seven strategies that will help facilitate engagement.

1. No individual should be placed in authority over the others.

2. All decisions should be agreed on by discussion and, if possible, unanimity. When a consensus cannot be reached, consider tabling the decision until more information can be collected and members have had a chance to sleep on the idea.

3. Commit to growth, for yourself and every woman in the group. It's natural that some women will progress more in one area or at a specific time than others. It's also natural that one woman will be on a fast track to external successes, while another may be exploring internal advancement. Overall, Female Fusion should result as every woman makes extraordinary leaps to astonishing successes.

4. Hold your Fusion as a sleepover retreat. Book a condo in a nearby resort area, or stay at someone's weekend house. Divvy up the responsibilities.

5. Hold Fusions in "neutral" territory so that no member misses out on the Fusion energy by playing hostess. If a home environment is the only place available, consider rotating locales, keeping snacks simple and banning spouses or children for the day. Send them to the zoo, a park or the beach. Some neutral meeting locales:

   o Hotels, where you can often book a conference room free when you pay for breakfast, lunch or dinner. Everyone pays for her own meal.

   o Restaurants that have private meeting rooms.

   o A room at a church or a local club.

6. Refuse to tame your ambitions. So often we are taught as women that we should tame anything within us that is bold and affirming. In Female Fusion, encourage one another to be audacious, to project their vision way out there, and go for it.

7. Ask for a volunteer to keep track of time. It's normal for some members to be more talkative and for others to listen without

speaking up, but listeners need to be drawn out, and chatterboxes need to be tactfully quieted. Encourage every member to participate in every discussion so that Fusion will happen consistently.

UNLEASH BOUNDLESS FUSION ENERGY

Invigorate your Female Fusions with energy and mutual benefit.

1. Leave time at the end of the first Fusion to decide where and when you will meet again and the frequency of future Fusions. Attempting to do this or to make other routine decisions at the beginning will inhibit Fusion. Consider gathering:

   - Weekly, to complete the 5 Promises in all 10 chapters quickly.

   - Monthly or semimonthly, if a weekly schedule is too intense.

   - Every other month or quarterly, if members intend to complete the chapters on their own, coming together for Fusion reinforcement and feedback.

   - Once or twice a year, after you've completed *Wicked Success Is Inside Every Woman* and want to maintain Fusion but not move on to other purposes.

   - Spontaneously, for special needs, announcements or celebrations. Special Fusions can be called to brainstorm ideas for one individual's current and pressing goal.

2. For additional fun, design rituals to start and end your Fusions. You might:

   - Play uplifting music before the Fusion and during breaks.

   - Start by sharing results of action steps taken since the last Fusion.

   - Start with a provocative question or statement, such as:

     · When you realize your passionate vision, what changes will your friends and family notice about you?

     · Choose an imaginary mentor, either real or fictional. From your mentor's perspective, what sage advice would you give yourself?

     · What will be the epitaph on your tombstone?

- End by having everyone commit to an action step to accomplish by the next Fusion.

- End with a devotional, a moment of meditation or a theme song.

- End by reciting together a meaningful or humorous Fusion statement (e.g., We are women and we can do anything!).

3. Differentiate between critique time and non-critique time.

- Nonjudgmental sharing of important triumphs and letdowns, fears and frustrations, expectations, desires and humorous or moving encounters can facilitate Fusion at any time. Keep the account moving, allowing two or three minutes to each speaker and keep responses brief, positive and supportive.

- Reserve critique time for strategizing goals, objectives and action steps.

4. Discuss each chapter thoroughly. Focus on each Feminine Force in turn, and engage the 5 Promises before moving to the next chapter. Your discussion might include:

- What this strength means to each member.

- How she has relied on or developed this strength in the past.

- How this strength can activate her passionate vision.

5. Turn off cell phones and discourage any other interruptions. It's important to be emotionally focused as well as physically present.

6. Sit at a round table, where no one is at the "head," or pull your chairs into a circle. Or get into your pajamas and sit on couches or cushions.

7. Take a five-minute stretch break every hour.

8. Celebrate frequently. Especially celebrate one another for what you each bring to the Fusion.

9. Share your successes with other women at our website: WickedSuccess.com.

FUSE WITH PROFESSIONAL COLLEAGUES

Since that first Female Fusion I have created Fusions for professionals (both men and women) with amazing results. I've had Fusions with small entrepreneur groups (of 10), and large entrepreneur groups (of 150), the latter divided into smaller Fusion groups. Using all of the principles discussed in this chapter, but with a very focused business objective in mind. I've also used Fusion in my office to get the staff heated up for a tough business brainstorm.

Corporate professionals can fuse with a group of like-minded professionals who want to expand career goals.

Entrepreneurs can fuse with other entrepreneurs. You can also fuse with your employees. The deepest, most effective Fusion will happen when you connect with entrepreneurs who are not your direct competitors, so fuse with entrepreneurs from different businesses or, if in the same business, from a geographical location that doesn't compete with yours.

Fusing with entrepreneurs at a distance will take some planning, but it's worth it. Don't expect to have monthly meetings. Instead, plan for getting together quarterly or twice a year. To keep the Fusion going between get-togethers, use Skype or other videoconferencing technologies, a Facebook group and monthly chats or emails.

Whoever comprises your Fusion group, set accountable and measurable business objectives. This is your private brain trust, exclusive board of directors and personal planning committee.

HAVE FUN WITH FUSION AS YOU ATTAIN THE IMPOSSIBLE

The bottom line of that UCLA study seems to be that having close female friends is beneficial in many ways. Yet when women get overly busy with work and family, often the first thing they set aside is the time they spend with other women.

Female Fusion is an opportunity to engage the 10 Feminine Forces in your life at levels you might never reach alone. Each Fusion will take you further and will cement your group socially, emotionally, spiritually, intellectually and physically. Expect to be together for a very long time after completing the 10 Feminine Forces in *Wicked Success Is Inside Every*

Woman. You will look back and be amazed at how far you've come, and without the stress that might otherwise have accompanied such strides.

Female Fusion is such an amazing Feminine Force that I'm willing to guarantee it will change your life if you let it. In Leigh's thank-you note following the event, she eloquently captured the power of this life force:

Dear Vickie,

Your vision took awesome form today. Female Fusions are now set in motion. Word of how we united through you this day will spread and grow even before your book achieves its final form.

Thank you for gathering me into an elegant place set with sparkling cool women. I am honored to be a part of this process.

ACTIVATE FEMALE FUSION WITH THE
5 PROMISES

PROMISE 1
I Will Live and Work a Passionate Life

Who are the women you trust, admire and respect enough to invite to join you in Female Fusion? Write down at least three names.

_____
_____
_____

PROMISE 2
I Will Go for It or Reject It Outright

Schedule the date of your first Fusion and send out the invitations. Visit the Female Fusion website at **WickedSuccess.com** to download the invitation and other Fusion tools. What's the date?

_____
_____
_____

Where will you hold your first Fusion?

_____
_____
_____

PROMISE 3
I Will Take One Action Step a Day Toward My Passionate Vision

Which exercise will you use to activate fusion at your first gathering?

_____
_____
_____

PROMISE 4
I Commit to Being a Success Student for Life

Write down one thing you plan to learn from this collection of incredible women.

_____

_____

_____

PROMISE 5
I Believe as a Woman I Really Can Do Anything

What is your most audacious desire? How will you engage Female Fusion to make that desire come true?

_____

_____

_____

>> DOWNLOAD THE 5 PROMISES FOR FUSION AT WickedSuccess.com.

VICKIE'S FUSION

My whole life has been about fusing with women, formally and informally. The rush of pure energy that comes from fusion has helped me reach levels of success I didn't know were possible. At the office, we'll stop in the hall, chat for a moment, an idea will spark and we'll move into the conference room for a crash brainstorm, or just heat up the hallway with the fire of our visions. I also fuse with my personal women friends, often spontaneously when one of us calls the other and we have a good long chat.

But the fusion that occurred from bringing together a group of phenomenal women gave me a wake-up call to what I'd been missing in my life. It jolted me back to high school, hanging out with my best girlfriends, confiding our desires and boohooing over the tragedy du jour. I realized how much I missed that intimacy.

It also brought home to me how much I miss my mom. After the age of 23, I missed out on her wonderful guidance and encouragement. And she missed my important adult milestones—getting married, starting my business, being featured in the New York Times, *breaking $16 million and creating this book. I wish she could have known Tom and all the other cool people in my life. My legacy to her is seeing the world she always yearned to see. I know she's happy that I'm living every moment and using the tools she gave me to help other women live their every moment.*

I still have intimacy with my friends individually, but experiencing that collective jolt of Fusion energy was pure, soul-felt elation. My brain was sparking on all levels. Female Fusion brought me back to my mom's greatest corner of the world. I was totally emotionally and spiritually engaged, laughing, crying—caring—and the same thing was happening all around me. Attaining the impossible didn't seem so impossible at all.

I thought I had everything. But this collective force is a piece of my life that was missing, and I want it. I want more of it. And I want you to have it, too.

Vickie l. Milazzo, 51
WRITER, SPEAKER AND ENTREPRENEUR

•

Activate your own Female Fusion with the sparkling cool women in your life to more deeply release the 10 Feminine Forces inside you, and you will attain the impossible.

We are women and we can do anything!
VICKIE L. MILAZZO

SAVOR YOUR
WICKED SUCCESS

IN THE BEGINNING of this book I suggested that we live in exaggerated times, which call for an exaggerated, wicked mind-set. I promised you a buck-up book with a buck-up plan to realize your boldest visions for your life and career.

By now you've made my 5 Promises your 5 Promises and are undoubtedly already amplifying your 10 Feminine Forces—fire, intuitive vision, engagement, agility, genius, integrity, endurance, enterprise, renewal and fusion—with wicked focus. Summoning these strengths, there is no limit to where you can go.

It's been my honor and privilege to share this time together with you. Remember the promises you've made to yourself, and remember to promise big.

I invite you to sit down often with me and a cup of healthy green tea or a glass of healthy red wine. As a good woman friend, I'll continue to inspire, encourage and push you to think in a more exaggerated, uncommon and wicked way. I can't wait to hear your wicked success story.

Wicked Success Is Inside!

Vickie

>> FOR MORE RESOURCES, HELPFUL GUIDES AND SUCCESS STORIES VISIT WickedSuccess.com.

ACKNOWLEDGMENTS

—

I FIRST MET Matthew Holt, a patient, straight-talking publisher at John Wiley & Sons, Inc. at a speakers' conference in Cancun, Mexico. Somehow, in that crowded convention hall, my husband Tom found me refilling my cup with healthy green tea. He took my hand and led me away, telling me, "Skip your next session; there's someone you must meet." That someone turned out to be Matt. With Matt, who published my first book with Wiley, and editor Lauren Murphy, I am blessed to be in expert hands.

Of course, *Wicked Success Is Inside Every Woman* started well before that sunny winter day I met Matt. Everything in this book, everything I know and everything I love about being a woman comes from the amazing women and men in my life—starting with my mom and dad, Marise and Sal, my grandmother MaMa Pearl, and my sister Karen. My best women friends continue to teach me the power of fusion. My great teachers and mentors, especially my second mom, Blanche, all gave me models that I can only aspire to emulate.

Thanks to the Female Fusion women—Blanche, Chris, Evie, Jan, Leigh, Maggie, Martha and Susan—who inspired the Fusion, and inspire me to attain the impossible.

I'd also like to thank the entire team at Vickie Milazzo Institute, for their passion and for helping me create a business and story to write about, and the thousands of Certified Legal Nurse Consultants, who have inspired me to live my 5 Promises as I help them to live theirs.

The following people helped me bring this book to life: Leigh Owen and Chris Rogers—you gave time, patience and massive amounts of red ink in teaching me everything you know about bringing words to paper. You are not only terrific mentors but awesome friends. I thank you both from the bottom of my heart. Jennifer Tyson, thank you for creating a design for the book that matched my vision exactly. Megan McCready, thank you for all of your marketing expertise and spreading the word to women everywhere.

Most important is Tom Ziemba, who gives me daily inspiration, is always there when my computer isn't, and constantly helps me rediscover some of the stories I'd almost forgotten.

BOOK CLUB GUIDE

·

THE QUESTIONS in this guide are intended to enhance your reading group's discussions and help you discover and harness your own 10 Feminine Forces.

1. Which Feminine Force did you identify as most important in your life? Where do you see potential for increasing that strength? What will you do to make it happen?

2. Which Feminine Force surprised you? How might you more fully incorporate that strength to enhance your life and career?

3. Being on fire about something can drive you to make great strides. When have you been fired up about something that resulted in positive change? How can you apply what you learned about passion to future changes?

4. Your strongest guiding influence may be your Feminine Force of intuitive vision. How has intuitive vision guided you in the past? How would encouraging your intuitive vision benefit you in the future?

5. When opportunity arises, your Feminine Force of engagement enables you to take action. What positive impact could a specific, focused engagement make on your life and career?

6. Agility is the Feminine Force that opens your life and career to a wider range of choices. Do you stretch in all the areas of your life, or do you find yourself following rigid patterns? How would increasing your success agility improve your prospects?

7. The Feminine Force of genius can be expanded. In what areas would you like to amplify your intelligence?

8. Personal integrity is the one Feminine Force that must not be compromised if you expect to achieve the highest levels of success. How has your integrity been tested in the past? How might you strengthen your integrity?

9. Women are masters of endurance. How can you make endurance a positive factor on your path to having the career and life you really want?

10. Enterprise is a Feminine Force you can apply to any undertaking, and improve the results. Where have you applied enterprise and what was the payoff?

11. The mind, body and spirit are wonderfully elastic in their ability to renew. What renewal practices are you willing to engage to reclaim your mental, physical, emotional and spiritual energy?

12. Female Fusion can amplify or multiply all of your other Feminine Forces. How do you engage Female Fusion in your life?

ABOUT THE AUTHOR

FROM A SHOTGUN HOUSE in New Orleans to owner of a $16-million business, *Wall Street Journal* bestselling author Vickie L. Milazzo, RN, MSN, JD, shares the innovative success strategies that earned her a place on the *Inc.* list of Top 10 Entrepreneurs and *Inc.* Top 5,000 Fastest-Growing Companies in America.

Vickie is the owner of Vickie Milazzo Institute, an education company she founded in 1982. Featured in the *New York Times* as the pioneer of a new profession, she built a professional association of 5,000 members.

Vickie has been featured or profiled in numerous publications, including the *New York Times, Entrepreneur, Houston Chronicle, Ladies Home Journal, Texas Bar Journal, Los Angeles Times, Philadelphia Inquirer* and in more than 220 newspapers.

Vickie has appeared on national radio and TV, including the National Public Radio program, "This I Believe" and more than 200 national and local radio stations.

She is the author of the *Wall Street Journal* bestseller *Inside Every Woman: Using the 10 Strengths You Didn't Know You Had to Get the Career and Life You Want Now.*

Vickie is recognized as a trusted mentor and dynamic role model by tens of thousands of women, a distinction that led to her national recognition as the Stevie Awards' Mentor of the Year.

Vickie was recognized as the Most Innovative Small Business by Pitney Bowes's *Priority* magazine, and received Susan G. Komen's *Hope Award for Ambassadorship.*

Author, educator and nationally acclaimed speaker, this multimillionaire entrepreneur shares her vast experience and the experiences of thousands of women **(thisibelieve.org/essay/22873)**.

INDEX

A

Acceptance, 274
Achievements, 244-245
Action(s)
  vs. caution, 79
  daily steps, 10
  vs. fear, 77
  and observation, 154
  selection of, 27
Addictions, 52, 83.
    See also Feel-Good Addiction
Advancement, 221
Advice, reactions to, 140-142
Agility
  about, 107-109
  investing in, 122-123
  in management, 124-125
  and odd couples, 127-128
  stretching to achieve, 116,
    130-131
  tools for, 120-122
Agility breaks, 118-119
Alcott, Louisa May, 18, 71

All Things Considered, 60
Alonso, Alice, 23, 32, 62
Analysis paralysis, 55
Angkor Wat, 123-124
Attention to detail, 98-99
Automation of processes and
  systems, 252-253
Avatar, 145

B

Bad habits, 156
Bad ideas, 90-91
Balance, 31
Baldwin, Faith, 167
Bannister, Roger, 15
Barriers, as gate to new
  perspectives, 110
Bed tea, 267
Beethoven, 62-63
Behavior, change of, 157
Bejar, Hada, 281
Belief in self, 14, 16
Big Things, 12, 80, 84-85, 87, 90,
  103-104, 226, 301

bin Laden, Osama, 271

Blanche's agility, 132-133

Borg, Anita, 19

Brain clutter, 53-54

Brainstorming, 11, 62-63, 145, 156

Breaking rules, 118

Breathing meditation, 92

Brevity, 160

Brown, Christy, 195

Budgets, 11, 230

Burdens, 295

Butcher, Susan, 194, 200

Butler, Frank, 194

Butterflies, 205-206

C

Cameron, James, 145

Camp Buck-Up, 97-98

"Can do" vs. "should do," 74

Career change, 79

Career transformation, 2

Caution vs. action, 79

Celebrations, 280-281

Certainty vs. mystery, 57-58

Certified Legal Nurse
    Consultants, 117, 179

Challenges
    of change, 111
    from differences, 119-120

Change, 16, 277
    challenge of, 111
    courage for, 110

Chaos
    dancing through, 57-58
    trust through, 56-57

Chödrön, Pema, 95

Choice(s), 220
    and engagement, 74
    menu of, 47-49

Chris's genius, 165-166

Circle of fusion, 290, 293-297,
    304, 305

Cirque du Soleil, 99-100

Client relationships, 239

Clinton, Hillary, 175

Clutter
    mental, 53-54
    physical, 51-52
    social media, 51
    toxic, 271

Collaboration, 13, 136-137

Colvin, Geoffrey, 151

Commitment
    to dreams, 7
    and passion, 9
    to passionate level, 73
    to self, 170

Commitment queens, 100-101

Commodity companies, 245-246

Complainers and complaining,
    183-185

Complaining, 184, 219

Complexities, elimination of, 158

Confidence, 15

Confidence, loss of, 75

Connections, 249-250

Consensus, 142

Consultants, 231

Conventional wisdom, 145

Corporate formula, 220-221

Courage for change, 110

Credit collapse, 8

Criticism, 270

Curiosity vs. fear, 111-113

Current interests, 25-26

Customer service

  airline industry, 242-243

  Apple, 243-244

  excellent, 41, 241-242

  unsatisfactory, 241

Cyberspace, 85, 162

D

da Vinci, Leonardo, 45, 47

Dancing through chaos, 57-58

Death, 9

Delany, Sarah, 259

Desire expression, 303

Detachment, 272

Details, 98-99

DeVito, Danny, 141

Diana, Princess, 271

Dieting, 148-150

Differences, challenges from, 119-120

Digital footprint, 186

Dirty laundry, 186

Discomforts, 204-205

Dissenting viewpoints, 142-143

Distractions, 83

Diversity, 125

Douglas, Emily Taft, 258

Downsizing, 11

Dreams, commitment to, 7

Dune (Herbert), 75

Dynamic vs. static existence, 123-124

E

Early interests, 24

Early work experience, 4-5

Eating habits, 263, 264

Ederle, Gertrude, 194, 200

Edison, Thomas, 150, 190

Einstein, Albert, 16, 45, 46, 47, 62, 145, 154-155

Emotional energy, 268-275

Emotional intelligence, 193-195

Emotional needs, 235

Endurance

  about, 191-192

  building, 209-211

  energy for, 208-209

  examples of, 193-194

  and fire, 206-208

  and persistence, 195-197

  strategies for building, 209-211

Endurance dance, 192-193

Engagement, 306-307

  and choice, 74

  of fears, 75-77

Enjoying the moment, 273

Enterprise

  about, 217-218

  financial control for, 228-230

  foundation of, 223-228

  shaping, 226

  stability, 225-226

  strategic life plan for, 223-227

  vision for, 224

Entertaining, 27

Entrepreneurial formula,
222-223

Everyday responsibilities, 27

Evie's fire, 41-42

Exercise habits, 264

Exhaustion, 73-74

Expectations, 203

Experience and failure, 139-140

Experts, reliance on, 144-146

F

Facebook, 32, 51, 53, 83, 89, 90,
108, 126, 156-157, 178, 186,
222, 244, 281

Failure
and experience, 139-140
and success, 66

Faith, 15

Fear, 17
acknowledgment of, 76
vs. action, 77
vs. curiosity, 111-113
engagement of, 75-77
and lack of enterprise, 218-219
and worry, 11

Feel-good addiction, 82-84, 86

Female fusion. *See* Fusion

Feminine forces, 17-18

Finishing, 201

Fire. *See* Passion

Firing employee, 96-97, 180

5 promises
agility, 130-131
on endurance, 212-213

engaging to achieve big things,
103-104
of enterprise, 255-256
fire, 39-40
fusion activation, 311-312
on genius intensification,
163-164
on integrity, 187-188
of intuitive vision, 68-69
of life energy renewal, 284-285
passion, 39-40
of vision, 68-69

Fixed viewpoints, 113-114, 115

Flexibility, 108

Flying high, 78-80

Focus, 91-96, 199-202

Foolishness, challenges
from, 120

Frankl, Viktor, 168

Free products, 238

Froman, Jane, 200

Fuller, Margaret, 135

Fun, 4, 203-205, 230, 262,
274, 303

Fusion. *See also* Circle of fusion
about, 289-290
activation of, 302-304
and endurance, 291-292
energy unleashed, 307-308
first female, 290-293
format for, 301-302
fun with, 309-310
invitation for, 300
with professional
colleagues, 309

as protective caprock, 297-298
purpose, 301
requirements for, 298-299
sparking, 306-307
value of, 298

G

Gatekeepers, 231-232
Gaudio, Bob, 118
Genius and hard work, 150-151
Gere, Richard, 61
Gift with purchase (GWP),
    136, 238
Going all in, 49-50
Gossip, 182-183
Gossip buddy, 183
Graham, Stedman, 57, 110
Gratitude, 273
Gray matter, 13, 135
Group therapy, 148-150
Groupthink, 147
Growth, 116-117
Guarantees, 49-50, 245-246

H

Habits, 264-265
Happiness, 24, 269-270
Hard work and genius, 150-151
Herbert, Frank, 75
Herd mentality, 147
Heroin, 114
Himalayas, 20, 203, 273
Ho Chi Minh City, 56-57
Holocaust victims, 168
Hoodoos, 297

Housework, 101
Hypnagogic imagery, 63-64

I

Icebergs, 228
Imagination
    vs. knowledge, 45-47
    and silence, 51-54
Imperfection, 80-82
Incremental payoffs, 198-199
Independence, 146
Individual passion, 31-32
Inner fire, 24, 262
Inner teacher, 147
Integrity
    about, 167-168
    accountability to, 177
    at all levels, 169-170
    breach of, 168-169
    consensus about, 172-176
    and corporate culture, 179
    economic value of, 169
    public view of, 186
    standing up for, 170-171
    when alone, 177-179
Integrity victims, 180-181
Intelligence, kinds of, 135
Intensity, 272
Interruptions, 88-89
Interruptions policy, 88
Intimate companions, 270
Intuition, 43
    as cognition on steroids, 45
    trusting, 44
Intuitive vision, defined, 44

J

Jackson, Michael, 271
Jan's integrity, 189-190
Jersey contract, 118
Job dissatisfaction, 1-2
Just say no, 101-102, 263

K

Kagan, Daryn, 30-31
Kennedy, Rose, 191
Kirungi, Rosebell, 194, 200
Knight, Margaret, 46, 47
Knowledge vs. imagination,
   45-47

L

Larsen, Miriam Viola, 43
Leadership, 232
Learning from others, 13-14
Learning styles, 13
Legal nurse consulting, 144, 147
Ledger, Heath, 271
Leigh's engagement, 104-105
Less is more, 159-160
Leveraging successful people,
   138-139
Lindsay's renewal, 286-287
Listening, 161
Listening to opposing viewpoints,
   142-143
Living passionately, 24-29,
   32-38
Loans, 229
Lombardi, Vince, 152

Longevity, 191
Loser culture, 148-150
Lost passion, 27

M

Maggie's vision, 70-71
Management theories, 125
Mandalas, 109
Manipulation, 181-182
Market, understanding of,
   236-237
Marketing
  about, 233-239
  to existing clients, 238-239
  foundation for, 237
  needs fulfillment, 234-235
Marketing strategies, 237
Martha's enterprise, 257-258
Meditation, 91-95
Memories, 239-244, 279
Memory, improvement
  of, 161-162
Mental junk food, 277
Mental practice, 61-62
Mental repetition, 201-202
Mentoring, 140-141, 281-282
Mentors, 14, 17, 153
Mindfulness, 64
Mind-success connection,
   56-57, 62
Mistakes, 80-81, 140, 236
Molchanova, Natalia, 116
Momentum, safeguarding, 91
Momentum engagement, 85-91
Momentum time, 87-89

Moses, Phoebe Ann, 193

Moving with stillness,
154-155

Music, 269

My Left Foot (Brown), 195

Mystery vs. certainty, 57-58

N

National Alliance of Certified
Legal Nurse Consultants, 45

National Public Radio, 58-60

Natural state, 111

Nature and wildlife, 269

Needs, methods to fill, 235-236

Needs fulfillment, 234-235

Negative attitude, 114-115

Negotiating, 246-248
asking in, 247
bullying in, 248
detached appearance while,
247-248
with the person, not company,
248

Networking, 237
selectivity when, 250
vs. socializing, 251

New Orleans, 2, 4, 9, 20, 127, 133,
160-161, 172, 274, 278, 280,
281, 282

New perspectives, 110

New York Times, 5, 98, 313

No pain, no gain experience, 205

Note-taking, 161-162

Nurturing and renewal
of your spirit, 275-276

O

Oakley, Annie, 193, 200

Observation, 154

Obstacles, 157

Off the record speech, 248

O'Keefe, Georgia, 289

Old comforts, 128-129

One big thing at a time,
84-91

One step at a time approach, 10

Optimists, 99

Orchids, 125-126

Overcommitment, 74, 176

Overpromising, 176-177

P

Pace, 197-198

Pain, 191, 206

Pain vs. suffering, 94-95

Passion
about, 19-20
and commitment, 9
commitment to, 30, 34
defined, 34
individual, 31-32
maintaining, 36-37
practice of, 33
and purpose, 24
reality about, 28-29
relationships and, 36
self definition, 31
and success, 21-22
and talent, 23
time and opportunity for, 36

Passionate drive, 22-24
Passionate faith, difficulties
    of, 29-31
Passionate life
    living and working, 4-7
    and skydiving, 79
Patterns, breaking, 155-156
Pay cuts, 11
Payoffs, 23, 218, 220
Perfectionism, 54-55
    escape from, 82
    and perfectionists, 80
Performance, 233
Perpetual lists, 253
Persistence, 195-197
Personal promises, 303-304
Personnel framework, 230-233
Perspective, 9
Pessimism, 99
Practice with form, 152
Preparation, 207
Problem analysis, 157-158
Problem solving steps,
    253, 254
Processes and systems,
    automation of, 252-253
Procrastination, 54
Profit, 228
Promises, 176-177
Public vs. private discussions, 186
Purpose and passion, 24

Q

Queen Latifah, 133

R

Rationalism, 55
Reagan, Ronald, 271
Recession, 6, 8, 9, 11, 17, 222
Recharging, 208-209, 261, 276
Referral letters, 249-250
Referrals while connecting,
    249-250
Relationships, 221, 239, 249
    maintenance of, 125-127
    passion and, 36
    with vendors, 171
Relaxed manner
    All Things Considered
        interview, 60-61
    NPR interview, 58-60
    Sydell interview, 58-60
Renewal
    about, 259-260
    celebration to intensify,
        278-279
    of emotional energy, 267-275
    of energy with people you love,
        279-281
    formula for, 262
    by giving back, 281-282
    goals and strategies,
        261, 282
    of mental energy, 276-277
    of physical energy, 263-266
    planning for, 261-263
    strategies for total, 282-283
    of yourself, 260-263

Repetition, mental, 201-202

Responsibility, owning up to, 179-180

Restrictions, 99-100

Risk taking, 296

Roosevelt, Eleanor, 106, 183

Routines, 118

Rowling, J. K., 46, 47

Rozen, S. J., 190

Rudolph, Wilma Glodean, 193, 200

Running on empty, 197-198

S

Saigon, 56-57

Self discipline, 142

Self-analysis, 151, 152, 153

Selflessness, 281-282

Self-perception, 61-62

Self-promotion, 244-245

Self-reliance, 146

Shaking things up, 109-114

Sheehy, Gail, 83

Shelley, Mary Wollstonecraft, 215

Silence and imagination, 51-54

Simplicity, 158-159

Skydiving, 76-78, 79

Sleep habits, 264

Slumdog Millionaire, 63

Soccer moms, 231

Social media, 51, 73, 86-87, 156-157, 281

Spark, 35, 38, 39

Speaking voice, 160-161

Speech Management, 160

Speed, 253

Speed of activity, 64-65

Spiritual discipline, 276

Spiritual energy renewal, 275-276

Stamina, 191

Starbucks, 156, 183, 197, 239, 244, 271

Stepping out, 8, 76-78, 79

Stories of women changed forever, 293-297

Strategic life plan
    for enterprise, 223-227
    form for, 227

Strategic plan, 224

Streeter, Tanya, 116

Subcontractors, 231

Success
    and behavior, 231-232
    defined, 50
    elements of, 12-14
    encore to, 65-66
    and failure, 66
    learning from, 66
    of next vision, 66-67
    and passion, 21-22
    and showing up, 33, 105

Success apartheid, 139

Success percentage, 81

Sucking up, 143-144

Support teams, 78

Susan's endurance, 214-215

Swayze, Patrick, 271

Swoopes, Sheryl, 81

Sydell, Laura, 58-60

Systems, 252-253

T

Talent

   and passion, 23

   value of, 151-153

Talent Is Overrated (Colvin), 151

Teaching, 5

Technology, 90, 108, 110

Television, 85-86

Thatcher, Margaret, 73

Theresa, Mother, 218

Thompson, Dorothy, 166

Thu, Thi, 31-32

Timidity, 50-51

Titanic, 59, 228

Toxic clutter, 271

Traditions, 279

Traffic lights, 56

Transformation, 205

Transgressions, forgiving, 178-179

Travel, 9, 20, 29, 206-207

Trust through chaos, 56-57

U

Uncertainty, 50, 77

Underpricing, 245-246

V

Vacations, 7, 20, 268, 269

Validation, 296

Valli, Frankie, 118

Vélib, 115

Venture capital, 229

Vickie's fusion, 313-314

Virtual vacation, 269

Vision

   and passion, 65-66

   success of next, 66-67

Visions, 63-64

Visualization, 61-62

W

War of the Roses, 141

Weed pulling, 89-90

Whacking, 91-96

What's right vs. what's easy,
      96-97

Whitchorn, Katherine, 217

White matter, 13, 135

Wicked success, personal nature
      of, 34

Wildebeest, 218-220

Wine tasting memories, 240

Winfrey, Oprah, 287

Women changed by circle
      of fusion, 293-297

Women's intuition, 43

Work ethics, 177-179

Writing, 62-63

Written goals, 35

Z

Zazen session, 93

Zipcar, 115

Zuckerberg, Mark, 156-157